# THE JURISPRUDENCE OF POLICE

# THE JURISPRUDENCE OF POLICE

## Toward a General Unified Theory of Law

*Thomas Vincent Svogun*

palgrave
macmillan

First published in 2013 by
PALGRAVE MACMILLAN®
in the United States—a division of St. Martin's Press LLC,
175 Fifth Avenue, New York, NY 10010.

Where this book is distributed in the UK, Europe and the rest of the world,
this is by Palgrave Macmillan, a division of Macmillan Publishers Limited,
registered in England, company number 785998, of Houndmills,
Basingstoke, Hampshire RG21 6XS.

Palgrave Macmillan is the global academic imprint of the above companies
and has companies and representatives throughout the world.

Palgrave® and Macmillan® are registered trademarks in the United States,
the United Kingdom, Europe and other countries.

ISBN: 978–1–137–36623–8

Library of Congress Cataloging-in-Publication Data

Svogun, Thomas Vincent.
    The jurisprudence of police : toward a general unified theory of law /
    Thomas Vincent Svogun.
        pages cm
        ISBN 978–1–137–36623–8
        1. Police. 2. Jurisprudence. 3. Justice, Administration of. I. Title.

HV7921.S86 2013
344.05′201—dc23                                                    2013017360

A catalogue record of the book is available from the British Library.

Design by Newgen Knowledge Works (P) Ltd., Chennai, India.

First edition: October 2013

*To my wonderful wife, Margaret, and our splendid sons,*
*Daniel and Nathaniel*

# Contents

# PREFACE

Daniel Bell observed that wisdom is "the bridge of experience and imagination over time."[1] In the two decades or more that I have been engaged in the higher education of police, I have found that while police are intelligent and experienced, they often lack the kind of imagination on which wisdom must draw to reach insights needed by municipal administrators, lawyers, judges, legislators, social scientists, and most importantly the communities they serve. Without the cultivation and refinement of that imaginative faculty, disciplined by the habits of mind and heart in which law abides, the judgment the police profession brings to bear on its experience is compromised.

The kind of imagination to which I refer enlarges vision and mind. When these are coupled with heart and conviction, they fire vocation. Focused as they are on the narrow details, however, police often miss the forest for the trees. Having expended considerable resources in the development of professional technique, they have, for the most part, neglected the subject of police philosophy. Bereft of a larger vision addressed to ultimate ends (which would inform the work of police as a whole and help unify it under a common professional vision), the police remain mired in a highly fragmented practice that fails to fulfill the promise of vocation.

As a profession (and there has been debate over whether police rise to the level of a profession), the police are not alone in this. The nineteenth century, which saw the creation of formal police departments, first in metropolitan London, witnessed as well the emergence of modern professions and the establishment of a professional ethos that bracketed questions of ultimate ends, or *teloi*, and focused instead on means. The new professions came to be evaluated by criteria developed by the new positivist social sciences, focused as well on means. Law itself, largely through the influence of legal positivism, was reduced to a set of techniques for enforcing the sovereign's will, contributing to what the late Harold Berman called "a crisis in our legal tradition" and contributing as well to the declining standards of the legal profession.[2]

As for the police in America, what emerged by the mid-twentieth century was a "professional law enforcement" based on a mobile yet rootless "professionalism" that centered on technique and specialized skills acquired through a system of training, as distinguished from education. Police focused on present concerns or incidents, not on how things should be,nor did they see law enforcement as part of an enterprise that tied practice to a larger social and historical whole. Police lacked a vision that took in the past and the future.

These deficiencies were accompanied by a deficiency of aspiration, indicated by the profession's limited response to the call of higher education. While in various states police have been provided inducements such as tuition remission and/or incentive pay to pursue college degrees, surprisingly many have not enrolled, preferring instead to accumulate overtime pay and/or additional income derived from detail work at road construction sites, etc. In some instances, officers were discouraged by their departments from entering college. While the former American Police Association and its successor the Police Association for College Education have worked diligently to realize the goal of a four-year college degree as an entry-level requirement for policing, relatively few police agencies have adopted it. While the number of college-educated officers has risen in recent years, as a whole in this area and others, police have set their sights too low.

During World War II, Robert Wherring of Nebraska rose in the Senate of the United States to declare that after the war America should aid China, so that "Shanghai can be raised up and up until it is just like Kansas City" (qtd. in Brinkley xii). Apparently, no one laughed. What would the Chinese even then have thought of Kansas City as the aspiration for a rebuilt Shanghai? There are police who suffer from limits of imagination not unlike those afflicting the Nebraska senator, limits that stem from their parochialism and the poverty of their education. How many could articulate a vision of law's *telos* in a justly ordered city governed by a historically rooted law—a vision that inspired their professional work?

This book is in part an invitation to the police to raise their sights and enlarge their vision. To do this, they must undertake the necessary humane education in law and its enforcement that will supplement their training. The liberally educated police will then be equipped for the expanded role required of them in the twenty-first century. An enlarged vision, informed by an enhanced experience coupled with wisdom and expertise, would be the source of distinctive contributions that police can and need to make to the legal enterprise—an enterprise whose end commits practitioners not merely to the enforcement of rules but to the establishment and preservation of a just order. I do not know how many will respond to this invitation. Yet, there clearly are in policing individuals of large vision and heart who would be prepared to take up these broader ends of vocation. I have had the honor to meet many of them in my classes over the years. They and those like them are the hope of the profession. This book is addressed to these talented visionaries and to those aspiring to be like them.

This book is also an invitation to the legal profession and in particular the legal academy to broaden the scope of jurisprudence (beyond the principal focus that has been on what judges do) to include the study of what the police do and how it informs our understanding of what law is. The recent success of problem-oriented/community policing and the often compelling nature of "Broken Windows"[3] analysis suggest the limits of legal positivism as a lens through which to study law and the potential rewards of focusing on the implications of social context for law's historicity specifically and for law generally. Overall, the success of the new policing signals the promise of an integrative jurisprudence. It also suggests the limits of much contemporary "natural law" theorizing, where the natural law is misconceived as a set of metaphysical principles from which to draw criticism of the positive law, but abstracted from facts on the ground. Indeed, the conflict between positive law and the moral principles of a natural law (the conflict that jurisprudence has almost exclusively focused on in recent years) cannot be properly analyzed and resolved without consideration of the customs, conventions, and traditions of the community—the substratum of a historically rooted law. It is through the medium of shared experiences and shared norms that form the basis of a customary law that the limits of both the positive law and the natural law are to be found. A jurisprudence of police provides an integration of this local organic law with the positive and natural law.

While legal philosophy over the past decades has been quite active, this book is a general call now for more systematic examination of the implications of theorizing about law for law enforcement, as well as a general call for the examination of the implications of police philosophy and practice for theorizing about the legal enterprise in general. Indeed, jurisprudence as a science cannot be considered complete—nor for that matter can a unified general theory of law be produced—until legal science has grasped and assimilated into its account of law's general nature, the account of the nature of law's material enforcement in particular circumstances, and this requires integration of the perspective of policing.[4] It is the intention of this book to elaborate the theoretical framework underlying an integrative jurisprudence of police that provides the basis for a new philosophy of police, which integrates professional law enforcement and community policing in a broader analysis. An integrative jurisprudence provides the theoretical and practical basis for a learned profession of police as it illuminates the path to that elusive general unified theory of law that transcends the binary positivist and natural law jurisprudence dominating current thinking.

This broadening of perspective has sociological implications beyond drawing police and their communities into a close partnership. It requires the integration of scholarly and professional communities, bringing police into closer professional association with lawyers, legislators, and judges, and their allied academic communities. An educated police profession deserves a seat at the table of the legal profession. The legal profession (not to mention academe) very much needs its insight and point of view.

Finally, this book is addressed to the general reader who is prepared to do some philosophical digging into how law is better understood and better enforced in our times, troubled as they are by the threat of crime and other disorders. Each one of us, after all, has a responsibility to partner with justice professionals to realize the promise of our law.

# Acknowledgments

A considerable debt is acknowledged to the late Patrick V. Murphy, distinguished commissioner of the New York City Police Department and president of the Police Foundation, and the late Louis Mayo, executive director of the Police Association for College Education (PACE), and member of the founding staff at the National Institute of Justice. Both men were national leaders in the promotion of best practices in policing. I have had the opportunity to learn much from them about the police profession and have enjoyed formal association with both on the Board of the American Police Association and with Dr. Mayo on the Board of PACE. In the summer of 2002, Patrick Murphy joined me in teaching a graduate course where we explored the philosophy of police in a preliminary way with a small but talented group of police graduate students. The course further inspired me to write this book.

I owe much to the countless police officers and justice professionals, many of them now leaders of their departments, whom I have had the privilege to teach as graduate students in administration of justice over two decades. I have learned a great deal from them about the practice of policing, both its rewards and its frustrations. I am also very grateful for the encouragement and stimulation of academic colleagues, especially Lubomir Gleiman.

By far the greatest debt I owe is to Margaret, Daniel, and Nathaniel—my wife and our sons—whose love and support sustain me. A special thanks to Margaret for expert assistance with editing and to Daniel, our in-house computer wizard, who solved technical problems during the course of this project.

# Introduction

*"And to make an end is to make a beginning. The end is where we start from."*[1]

                                                                T. S. Eliot

In the spring of 2009, a man rushed to the hospital but arrived at his mother-in-law's bedside a few minutes too late; she had just passed away. A most unfortunate scenario, but what brought it to national attention was that the son-in-law's lateness was due to his being detained in the hospital parking lot by a Dallas police officer, who had stopped him for speeding. Even though he explained the urgency of his situation, the officer held him. The media pounced on the case as it turned out that the son-in-law was an NBA basketball player. The Dallas police chief said he was appalled by what happened and the officer was suspended with pay pending review of the incident. The motorist happened to be an African American and suspicion circulated—was the white officer's handling of the case affected by race? The officer, who had been on the force for several years, said he was "just doing his job."

An incident such as this calls into question what police conceive their proper work to be. This book pursues the pressing inquiry through examination of the nature of the polic function and various theories that have been offered to explain it. A survey of the literature reveals that considerable work needs to be done.

Much theorizing about the police today is stuck on a number of persistent problems. There is difficulty defining the police function. On the one hand, there are those who adhere to a simplistic view that policing in its essence is making arrests for violations of the criminal and traffic codes, and that may have been the Dallas police officer's view. After an extensive multiyear American Bar Foundation Survey of the criminal justice system,[2] however, this view is untenable as a description of what they do, although it has been offered alternatively as a prescription about what they should be doing. Some police regard the investigation and apprehension of criminals as the "meat" of the profession and other tasks, such as maintenance of order and the provision of various "social services," as "garbage work," better avoided. One can provide a philosophical rationale for the former job description. Certain libertarian theorists have argued for the narrower description of the law enforcement function as a way to limit police power and to preserve individual liberty. The Professional Law Enforcement Model that embraces this more limited conception of the police function arose partly because of the influence of this liberal individualist philosophy. Communitarians, on the other hand, who adhere to a philosophy that places increased value on social goods such as community, allocate to government increased responsibility for the welfare of citizens. From this a conception of the police function is derived that commits police to fostering social goods and "enhancing quality of life." This expanded role presupposes far broader police discretion. The trend toward community policing is in part stimulated by this philosophy. The description of the role, then, is highly contested as it bears on issues of political philosophy and public policy. The prevalent view today acknowledges that police perform a myriad of tasks, although there is no consensus about how these may be best explained, let alone justified.

Can these tasks be organized around a unifying end or set of ends? John Kleinig has argued that the end of "social keeping" (as opposed to law enforcement) is broad enough to do the necessary organizing (*The Ethics of Policing*). On the other hand, Egon Bittner and those who adopted the lens of social science positivism had rejected teleology on grounds that police can be described as pursuing almost any end and that police practice is not coherent but incongruous. Police shoot people and they administer CPR; they are nurses packing heat, walking oxymorons. Bittner, who rejected normative-based analysis could only find a "thematic unity" in the distinctive means of police— their use of coercive force (Bittner, *Aspects* 127).

Related to this debate over what police do or should do is the controversy concerning the nature, scope, and limits of police discretion. One issue that has received attention is whether the discretion exercised by police in enforcing law is consistent with their duty to "fully enforce the laws." Do police have discretion whether or not to make an arrest when they have probable cause to believe that a crime has been committed? Is police discretion consistent with the rule of law? Is it consistent with our constitutional order?

There is also debate over "models of policing" and talk about shifts in paradigms in the course of police history. Is police history in the

United States "incoherent," a comment made by Kelling and Moore in "The Evolving Strategy of Policing" (2), or in some sense coherent? Does the periodization of American police history in terms of a "political era," a "professional era," and a "community policing era" make any developmental sense or can it be said to reflect phenomena natural to the police function? It is said in some quarters that "professional reform era policing" is today being supplanted by a "community policing/problem solving era." With respect to the latter, however, there seems to be no definitive account of what it is. Usage reveals a diffuse or at least highly plastic concept. Norman Inkster, a commissioner of the Royal Canadian Mounted Police, remarked: "I think the essence of community-based policing still eludes some of us and many of our efforts do not yield results because we have not properly understood the concept we are trying to apply" (28).

Is community policing an "organizational strategy," a "professional ethos," or a "philosophy?" A considerable literature refers to it as a "philosophy." Mark Harrison Moore has referred to community policing using as all these expressions and there is considerable imprecision here.[3] Moore's main focus is on the concept "organizational strategy"; however, he does not clarify how a "philosophy" or an "ethos" is different from a strategy, or how a philosophy may require an analytical framework different from his managerial one.

Recently, it has been suggested that police theorizing would benefit from a closer study of jurisprudence. Nigel Fielding, for example, has written that in the philosophy of the common law and its promise of "a system of enforcement finely tuned to the prevailing local standards" (210), one may find a solution to the "imprecise specification" (207), of community policing today. Some police writers have crossed over to the field of legal philosophy and the literature pertaining to judicial discretion to address the issue of police discretion—an example is John Kleinig (*Handled with Discretion*). Some have raised important questions with jurisprudential implications. In "Police, Discretion, and Professions," Michael Davis asks: "How much the problem of [police] discretion...is derived from legal positivism?" (34). Joan MacGregor in "From Mayberry to the State of Nature" queries whether in the police function "there is no unified theory of discretion at work...whether there is not some meta-principle that makes sense of the police function" (55). While these questions point in the right general direction, satisfactory answers have not been provided.

George Kelling and other advocates of community policing might have observed that the critique of "Professional Law Enforcement" is by itself an implicit critique of positivist jurisprudence necessitating a new jurisprudence. Is it Ronald Dworkin's? Dworkin's "Model of Rules" is usually the reference made when making an attack on positivism's account of discretion and searching for an account of police discretion. (Both Kleinig and MacGregor cite to it.) While Dworkin's work is worthwhile, it is of limited value. It does not develop the empirical/historical jurisprudence that addresses what may be referred to as the living law that police enforce on the streets. (Dworkin's account of judicial discretion emerged from the jurisprudential debates between natural law and legal positivism and is somewhat narrowed by the parameters of that debate. It is also narrowed by its political morality, which de-emphasizes the requirements of the common good when compared to the individual's autonomy.) It is the overlooked sociological/historical perspective that has the potential to supplement the other perspectives and thereby illuminate the field of problem-solving/community policing, not to mention "Fixing Broken Windows" analysis. Lon Fuller's work on the interaction of law and social context merits particular attention, as well as literature in sociological and historical jurisprudence.

Heuristic parallels may be drawn among the accounts of the law offered by natural law, legal positivism, historical and sociological jurisprudence, and the movements in police theory and practice—parallels between positivist jurisprudence and professional law enforcement, parallels between historical jurisprudence and community policing, and parallels between natural law jurisprudence and literature focusing on normative policing and police ethics.

While there is no model of policing that is explicitly naturalist, Kleinig's theory of police ethics is in part naturalist, though it is also in part historical. Kleinig organizes the police role around the normative end of "social peacekeeping." His emphasis on the value of human flourishing may be further illuminated by John Finnis's natural law theory in *Natural Law and Natural Rights*. Finnis's work, as well as Robert George's work on the development of a theory of pluralistic perfectionism (sketched in *Making Men Moral*), deserves attention on the issue of law's *telos*. Kleinig's discussion of authority as in part derived from tradition rather than formally from consent alone is an implicit critique of liberal positivism. His use of the metaphor of Theseus's ship to account for how law over time evolves and yet remains the same recalls to mind that Sir Edward Coke, one of the great theorists of the English common law and one of the originators of historical jurisprudence, used this very metaphor to describe law.[4] The common law theorists characterized law as both a constant and a dynamic phenomenon, as "changing changelessness." Meriting attention in historical jurisprudence is the work of the three great theorists of the common law in England: Coke, John Selden, and Sir Matthew Hale, as well as the work of Edmund Burke, and on the continent, Karl Freidrich von Savigny. In sociological jurisprudence, there is the work of Emile Durkheim and Eugen Ehrlich and other more recent authors who have stressed the importance of social context to law. Integrating these jurisprudential perspectives assists in the effort to develop a unified theory of the police function. Harold Berman's work in integrative jurisprudence is of great value here.[5]

## I

This book is divided into two parts. In Part I, I engage the literature and tradition of thinking about police. Chapter 1 defines the jurisprudence of police and argues that jurisprudence is not only germane to the study of police but also that police officials require a jurisprudence if they are to fulfill those duties entailed by the police function.

In chapter 2, I provide a critique of positivist police science, which until recently constituted the most dominant approach to the study of police. I focus principally on the work of Egon Bittner, one of the most influential social scientists to direct his attention to the subject. By rejecting teleology, prescinding discussion of police from the goods sought by policing, and focusing instead on their use of coercive force, his theory and positivist theory generally distort our conception of police and undermine the moral analysis that must form an integral part of any study of the police profession.

Chapter 3 addresses normative police theory, an alternative to positivism. I center on John Kleinig's work and provide a critique of it. While an improvement on positivist police theory, Kleinig's teleological theory defines police in terms of the end of social peacekeeping rather than law enforcement. I conclude that his theory, by failing to shed a positivist conception of law, falls short in capturing the breadth and depth of the legal enterprise and, derivatively, the law enforcement function. By failing to subsume police discretion under legal authorization, he also fails to provide a theory that limits police authority by the rule of law.

Chapter 4 examines the rise and the limits of formal positive police, focusing on the establishment of the London Metropolitan Police. I examine the social conditions that gave rise to formal bureaucratic policing and argue that modern society still contains within it social conditions analogous to those that required the more informal police that had been the prevailing method of policing before the "Met". Furthermore, today, the restoration of the public order requires the rehabilitation of social conditions linked to informal policing. Contemporary solutions, therefore, must fuse modern and classical methods of policing.

Chapter 5 addresses the American police experience, providing an overview of the widely adopted periodization of police history into three eras: a political era, a reform era, and a community policing era. The chapter is principally concerned with evaluating the management-oriented model that dominates the discussion. While acknowledging the major contributions to the field made by George Kelling and Mark Moore, I argue that their analytical framework may be improved when modified and subordinated to a framework derived from integrative jurisprudence rather than management analysis.

Part II follows the general critique of the discipline undertaken in part I. Using the current paradigm shift from professional law enforcement to problem-oriented community policing as the point of departure, part II elaborates the theoretical framework that accounts for the integrative nature of law, law enforcement, and the new police. The analysis exposes the implications of the new policing for our conception of law, law enforcement, and the values underlying our law. By drawing from the perspective of the police, generally overlooked in the jurisprudential literature, the analysis affords one step in the direction of a general unified theory of law that reconciles what the legislatures and courts do, with what the police do.

Part II addresses the following subjects. Chapter 6 focuses on the implications of the new police for the conception of law, arguing that the former requires an expanded conception of law that accommodates law's teleological and prescriptive character. Chapter 7 defines integrative jurisprudence and examines law's three dimensions, describing their axial structure and normative architecture. I identify and describe the different species of law's formality and the variety of reasons employed in legal argument. Chapter 8 traces the relativity of justice, law, and police to variations in the social bond and considers the implications of that analysis for contemporary social reality, accounting for why policing today must be protean in form. One salient point to emerge is that if police are to adequately enforce law in the various contexts to which they are called, they must have access to a variety of ordering mechanisms, not adequately accounted for by current theory. Chapter 9 provides a summation and closing reflections.

## II

In this book, I introduce a fundamentally new perspective on the police role, one that is derived from an integrative jurisprudence. It is intended to replace the positivist methodology that dominates discussion with a normative analysis that is integrative. It introduces to police and legal theory a new vocabulary giving centrality to terms such as "prudence," "integrity," "justice," "prescription," "*telos*," "formality," and "historicity." It redefines familiar terms such as law, law enforcement, and police. In particular, the theory isolates various kinds of formality generated by the legal enterprise and traces the interaction of law's axial principles with variations in social contexts.

Integrative jurisprudence asserts that law is best understood when seen from the combined (as opposed to the individual) perspectives of the traditional schools of legal theory: natural law, legal positivism, and historical/sociological jurisprudence. The dominance of legal positivism over the others in the last two centuries has impoverished accounts of law and correspondingly narrowed our conception of what it means "to enforce law." To enforce law from the perspective advanced in this book means to animate law, seen not as an externally imposed structure of "posited" norms but as an enterprise for establishing a just order having distinct formal, social/historical, and teleological dimensions. To enforce law is not necessarily to make a formal arrest for violation of some "enacted" legal norm (giving rise to the celebrated ceremonies of due process such as the criminal trial), although that is a common conception implicit in most accounts. In fact, in the instance of an unjust positive law, the formal arrest sought by the civilly disobedient is one step toward what is hoped will be the rejection of the positive law, and the reaffirmation of justice in law, by the courts, as well as the broader court of public conscience. Rather, to enforce law is to make it an active internal principle of volition determining the actions of private citizens and public officials including the police. To enforce law is to make it an enduring material principle regulating the order of society over time—either or both of which may demand more informal or discretionary acts (in lieu of arrest) by officials who seek to do justice according to law.

The benefits of such an expanded jurisprudential perspective for police theory are multiple. The perspective provides a solution to the problems of disjunction and subsumption in present accounts of the police function. It is said, for example, that police are either "peace officers" or "law officers"; rather they are both. Or it has been said that police authority may be legitimated on the basis of appeal to some overarching concept external to law, under which all police work (including law work) is unified. An example is Kleinig's "social peacekeeping," but that concept is plagued by problems—vagueness in the concept, the problem of determining whose "peace" is to be enforced, and the problem of reconciling the "peace" kept to the rule of law. Availing itself of the Aristotelian concept of the pros hen (the idea that a phenomenon should be defined not in terms of those factors it has in common with other phenomena sharing its name, but in terms of its central case or core normative meaning), an integrative jurisprudence of police finds coherence in the conception of police as "social peacekeepers," "law enforcers," "maintainers of order," and "enhancers of community." They are or rather should be all of these and more. The theory derives the authority of police practice, however, from law itself (applying a triune theory of authority grounded on law's formal, teleological, and social/historical axes), resolving the problems of legitimating police actions beyond the sphere of formal law enforcement in the restricted positivist sense, while at the same time upholding the tradition of the rule of law. In exercising discretion, in taking affirmative steps to advance the peace (as suggested by the conception of the "king's peace," rich in tradition and history) in enhancing "community" or in "solving problems," police remain subject to law's normative structure. The "order" they invigorate, the "peace" they keep, and the "community" they enhance is an "order," a "peace," and a "community" achieved through law. The theory reconciles the expanded conception of the police function, as well as the expanded role of the community in police practice, with the vital tradition of the rule of law. The police in their official action remain subject to law and the requirements of respecting the rights of individuals. The theory supports the view strongly held by police that they are law enforcement officials, while reconciling professional law enforcement with community policing in a new synthesis. To be competent agents of law requires that the police develop a jurisprudence that informs their conception of the role. This book provides an elaboration of the theoretical framework of that jurisprudence applied to the police function.

In chapter 1, I make the case for an integrative jurisprudence of police arguing that the substantial discretion necessitated by the police role requires that police cultivate a practical wisdom about law. Jurisprudence should not be the exclusive province of judges or legislators. I maintain that current police theory suffers from disintegrative jurisprudence, the limitations imposed by our fragmented understanding of what law is. In particular, it has suffered from the long-standing dominance of legal positivism, which has led many of the theorists to read the law enforcement function along a single dimension of law's form (the fact of its valid enactment as opposed to its history and rational purpose). The result is a monolithic conception of the police function that is left with the problem of failing to relate much of what police do to law (as we shall see with Kleinig) or is committed to the description of the function in disjunctive terms (as with Bittner). While John Kleinig, in particular, has advanced normative police theory, further progress can be made by explicit connection of the theoretical conceptions to parallel discussions in jurisprudential perspectives that are not positivist. An integrative jurisprudence will help illuminate the path toward reconciling the conflicting accounts of the police function.

# PART I

# The Need for an Integrative Jurisprudence of Police

CHAPTER 1

# The Jurisprudence of Police Defined

*"Only those who know the law shall be appointed justiciars, constables, sheriffs, or bailiffs"*

*Magna Carta (1215)*[1]

The term "jurisprudence" combines two words, the Latin *juris* meaning law and prudence (from the Latin *prudentia*) meaning practical wisdom. Jurisprudence is practical wisdom—a virtue—applied to law. The great thirteenth-century summa on English law, Bracton's *Treatise on the Laws and Customs of England*, defines jurisprudence as a science concerned with "knowledge of things divine and human, the science of the just and unjust."[2] As science, we might say that it is concerned with acquiring knowledge of law, discovering its nature, and the "laws" of law. Bracton also refers to jurisprudence as a "medium" that is "a way to a good end" (Kmiec 32). As a means, or applied science and art, it is directed toward the establishment and preservation of a just order. Bracton, however, does not define jurisprudence itself as a virtue.

On the relation of virtue to art and prudence, Aristotle in his *Nicomachean Ethics* observes, while there is a virtue of art, there is none of prudence (Ostwald tr. 154). That is because prudence is itself a virtue and, therefore, needs no virtue in addition to make it virtuous. Art, on the other hand, is not itself a virtue and therefore requires virtue if it is to achieve some good.[3] Virtue is for the same reason distinct from science and technology—either may be put to vicious ends. So, having some art, science, or technology, man yet requires virtue in addition to make good use of them.

Jurisprudence as science requires intellectual virtues (perception, understanding, and the capacity to reason and correctly draw conclusions from premises) that produce theoretical wisdom. As art, it requires prudence, the practical wisdom to discern the good sought by the art and to identify the efficient means to its production. It also requires moral virtues (particularly justice, integrity, courage, and moderation), the characteristics necessary to conforming the will and actions to the requirements of practical wisdom. These are called for in a world where temptation to wrongdoing, conflicting interests, moral dilemmas, and tragedy put considerable demands on human character. It is especially required in professions, such as law enforcement, where the power conferred on officials may itself pervert judgment. Prudence and moral virtue are both necessary for the exercise of the jurisprudential art, if it is to procure the comprehensive good of justice that Aristotle states "produce[s] and preserve[s] happiness for the social and political community" (*Nicomachean Ethics*, Ostwald tr. 113). I shall use the term "jurisprudence," which contains the root "prudence," to denote not just art and science, but virtue as well. Jurisprudence is intellectual and practical wisdom applied to law as science and art.

One may undertake legal science in order to understand legal phenomena for the sake of understanding. The knowledge itself is the good sought; it is the end of theoretical science. The science of law concerns not only what holds universally (Aristotle thought that there is but one constitution according to nature) but also what holds only in particular circumstances and what is changeable since law pertains to human affairs, and human affairs are, as Aristotle said, "irregular." Constitutions and laws vary, partly according to customs and conventions, and each may be said to vary with time.[4] Some contemporary legal scholars, albeit not without controversy, refer to our "evolving constitution." That the law evolves, however, is not a view exclusive to modern liberals; Edmund Burke himself held to such a view.[5]

Harold Berman identifies several characteristics necessary for the legal scientist if he or she is to be well suited to pursuing knowledge of law. These include the capacities of objectivity and integrity in conducting research, the evaluation of that research according to universal standards of scientific merit, openness to the possibility of error and "organized skepticism" about theories and theses, tolerance of new ideas until disproved, and an assumption that science is an "open system" based on "increasingly close approximations to truth rather than final answers" (*Law and Revolution* 155). Because law often entails the balancing of conflicting interests, the student of law must be prepared to avoid ideological and other biases, be open to admitting error, and be tolerant of new ideas. These virtues will also be of value to those involved in law's application, the practitioners of the art of jurisprudence, as their work requires, inter alia, the resolution of conflicts that arise among individuals pursuing diverse interests. Law is often studied not with a view to knowledge alone but with a view to legislation, judicial decision, or the faithful execution of laws. Here, the ends require applied science or art. The study informs and is a critical predicate to intervention by officials in the world of human affairs. The wisdom involved requires more than mere knowledge of the universal, the particular, and the variable. It requires not only practical wisdom, which includes intelligence, understanding, good sense, experience, and maturity of judgment, it also requires, as noted above, moral character. Practical wisdom determines the means that are conducive to certain ends, Aristotle asserts, but moral character determines that the end chosen is good. If legal officials are to achieve the complex end that Aristotle sees in the nature of law, that is, to make the citizens virtuous and to promote the common good so as to procure happiness for the social and political community, they must themselves be morally good and practically wise. In fact, Aristotle held that to be practically wise in the precise sense, one must be virtuous as well. Wisdom in the service of vice is not true wisdom but shrewdness or cunning. Today liberal philosophers define law's ends in terms more narrow than Aristotle's, often rejecting legal moralism (the use of law to enforce morals as such) and legal paternalism in the instance of mentally competent adults (the use of law to benefit individuals preempting their will to act to their own detriment). They typically define the end of law to be the establishment of ordered liberty—a composite end with the two goods, order and liberty, standing in a dialectical relationship. This end, however, remains sufficiently complex to preclude a mechanical jurisprudence.[6] Practical wisdom, as it bridges the intellectual and moral virtues, remains a necessary virtue for legal officials.

Sir Edward Coke understood that jurisprudence required long study. The knowledge, skills, and moral character implied by the term "jurisprudence" presuppose then a learned and ethical profession, responsible for cultivating the knowledge, capacities, skills, and characteristics necessary to procure the complex good that is the form, the substance, and the end of law. Such a profession requires professional schools. The first law school in the West was established at the University of Bologna in the eleventh century. Law schools provide not only for the education of lawyers and jurists, but also for the development of legal science. They produce a meta-law, a body of critical legal scholarship, that then informs practice.

Jurisprudence is generally thought to be the virtue of judges.[7] It is consistent with conventional usage to refer to the jurisprudence of John Marshall, to speak of his characteristic approach to the resolution of legal issues. Marshall's jurisprudence includes his considered judgments about the nature of the constitutional order and the separation of judicial, legislative, and executive powers. It is evident in his reasoning in *Marbury v. Madison* where he derives and justifies the Supreme Court's power to declare legislative or executive acts unconstitutional. That power, however, may become the predicate to law making itself and improperly encroach on the legislative authority. Some have argued that in recent years the Supreme Court in various areas, but particularly in its "substantive due process" decisions, has usurped legislative authority and acted like a super legislature. Similarly, in declaring executive or police acts unconstitutional, the Court may err and undermine proper executive authority. In either case, the judges may be criticised for judicial juris-imprudence.

Jurisprudence is applied with less frequency when referring to legislators. Perhaps this is because the term presupposes a specialized profession incongruous with an image of populist lawmaking by people very much like the average person on the street—lawmaking that is reflective rather than refractive of the popular will. To conjure with such a conception of profession is to engage a tension between a democratic and a republican vision of our constitutional order that involves different interpretations of representation. In the former view, the legislator mirrors his or her constituents' will, whereas in the latter view, the legislator is elected for his judgment (enjoying not only authority based on election but also epistemocratic authority based on assumed expertise) and leads his constituency, but is periodically held accountable to them through the process of elections. (The latter view is espoused by Edmund Burke when he states: "Your representative owes you, not his industry only, but his judgment; and he betrays, instead of serving you, if he sacrifices it to your opinion.")[8] Constituents in democracies, however, may find such views less than fully palatable. Burke we might note was defeated in the next election. Our constitutional order seems in various ways to accommodate both views. The United States House of Representatives was designed to be more democratic. The representatives hold office for short terms and are accountable to smaller constituencies, conditions tying them more closely to popular will. The Senate was designed to be more aristocratic. Senators hold longer terms of office and are responsible to larger and more diffuse constituencies, conditions providing for more separation from their constituents' immediate will.

(Originally, senators were not even elected by the people but by the state legislatures. This persisted until 1913 when it was changed by the Seventeenth Amendment.) The division of power among executive, judiciary, and legislature (with a Court that it appointed and not subject to electoral accountability) suggests a democratic/republican constitution that resolves the tensions between democratic and republican principles through checks and balances of various sorts.

It is difficult to defend the view that deliberation about the substance and form of legislation to enact is not a matter requiring specialized judgment and skill, nor of expertise informed by knowledge of the nature of law, its forms and ends, with sensitivity to its historicity— that is, how the law is shaped over time by the particular facts and circumstances of the society the legislator serves. Aristotle's view suggests that the legislative art demands the highest, most sophisticated sort of judgment and practical wisdom, as it is concerned with achieving the highest most comprehensive good of human action—the happiness of the body politic ( *Nicomachean Ethics* Book X). Indeed, one of the most significant problems confronting the police (that August Vollmer, the father of modern American law enforcement, identifies in his seminal text, *The Police and Modern Society*), is the enactment of unenforceable laws (or laws whose enforcement comes at too high a price) and the failure to repeal laws that have become unenforceable—what may be called acts or omissions constituting legislative juris-imprudence.

Jurisprudence is, however, rarely if ever explicitly associated with the police. There has been no comprehensive treatise on the jurisprudence of police, that is, no systematic study that integrates the philosophy of law with the philosophy of police. The phrase "jurisprudence of police" occurs with the utmost rarity in the literature. (I have seen it used once by Kenneth C. Davis and once by Lawrence Sherman.[9]) As mentioned earlier, certain connections have been recently suggested between the contemporary discussion of judicial discretion in legal philosophy (particularly, Ronald Dworkin's treatment of discretion) and the discretion exercised by police, but these references do not amount to anything like a full dress review of the matter.

Our underdeveloped jurisprudence (or in the area of policing, our nonexistent jurisprudence) is partly due to persistence of the view that police work does not require a jurisprudence. Police according to this view are low-level officials who are handed a book of laws that they are told to enforce. In this scenario, police are ministerial agents of law. They do not exercise significant discretion either in interpreting law or applying it. Parratt, for example, states: "The police in our legal tradition, are essentially ministerial officers. To them have been delegated relatively few grants of discretionary power."[10]

The American Bar Foundation (the former research arm of the American Bar Association) in the mid-1950s conducted an extensive field observation study, however, that should have dispelled the empirical assumption that the police do not exercise substantial discretion. Kenneth Culp Davis, a participant in the study and one of the leading authorities to emerge on the subject, concludes: "The police are among the most important policy makers in the society. And they make far more discretionary determinations in individual cases than any other class of administrators; I know of no close second" (*Discretionary Justice* 222). He observes that police decide what laws to enforce, when they shall be enforced, in what circumstances, and in what manner. The laws that police are charged with enforcing particularly in the area of public order (ordinances prohibiting "disorderly conduct" come to mind readily) are neither narrowly nor clearly defined and invite discretionary interpretation. The late Chief Justice Warren Burger commented: "The policeman on the beat or in the patrol car makes more decisions and exercises greater discretion affecting the daily lives of people every day and to a greater extent, in many respects, than a judge will ordinarily exercise in a week."[11] Burger also said: "No law book, no lawyer, no judge can really tell the policeman on the beat how to exercise this discretion perfectly in every one of the thousands of different situations that can arise in the hour-to-hour work of the policeman."[12] Yet, the police have exercised that broad discretion often beneath the radar of enfranchised public scrutiny and with insufficient guidance and education on its use. It is necessary to take up discussion of the nature and limits of that discretion and to consider how that discretion may be groomed by education and training. The very high price of police misjudgment and corruption for the public safety, for order, and for the rights of individuals demands the subordination of that discretion to a jurisprudence. Yet, while legal philosophers have devoted considerable time to discussion of judicial discretion, they have devoted virtually no attention to police.

Kenneth Culp Davis in *Discretionary Justice* asserts,

> We need not only empirical studies but also, I think, more philosophical digging. Our jurisprudence of statutes and judge-made law is overdeveloped; our jurisprudence of administrative justice, of police justice, of prosecutor justice—of discretionary justice—is underdeveloped. We need a new jurisprudence that will encompass all of justice, not just the easy half of it. (233)

This book is a response to that call with respect to law enforcement justice. The wise exercise of police discretion, whether in the enforcement of the criminal law, the maintenance of order, or keeping of the peace requires development of professional judgment specific to the police. The substantial discretion entailed, which arises from the complexity of enforcing law in light of an infinite variety of social facts, requires a rationale if it is to be supported—a justificatory theory about the police function that relates it to the nature, function, and limits of law in society. The jurisprudence specific to police also demands the development of a police profession, which produces the requisite knowledge and skills, and provides conditions for cultivation and preservation of the moral character necessary to police if they are to fulfill their proper role in the society. Such a profession would be a great resource to, among other persons, legislators and judges as they labor to fulfill their respective roles in the enterprise of establishing a just order through law. The jurisprudence of police is a necessary complement to the jurisprudence of judges and legislatures.

The phrase jurisprudence of police may be read in a number of ways. It may refer to the practical wisdom proper to police officers as professionals having the primary duty, as Charles Reith the British historian of police puts it, of "securing observance of law" ( *The Blind Eye of History* 11). Observance means at a minimum external conformity to law; but in the fullest sense, it means law abidingness, the internalization of legal principle. Although police must embody law-abidingness in this full sense themselves, they can only encourage or facilitate this internalization of legal principle in the citizenry. Yet, their vocation commits them to this end. Efforts directed toward the end of internalizing law abidingness in the citizens (which will include being models of it themselves and being good educators of it) are surely more vital than making arrests only to secure external compliance.

In another sense, the jurisprudence of police entails a state of affairs—the rational organization of society through a general system of laws and institutions for administering them, that promotes the human flourishing entailed by law's *telos*—as suggested by Patrick Colquhoun's usage. In the first modern *Treatise on the Police of the Metropolis* (a book published in 1795 which influenced Sir Robert Peel in his formation of the first modern police force, the London Metropolitan police), Colquhoun wrote of police as an improved state of society: "Next to the blessings which a nation derives from an excellent constitution and system of general laws, are those advantages which result from a well-regulated and energetic plan of police, conducted and enforced with purity, activity, vigilance, and discretion" (1).

The right use of the technical competences of police and the instrumentality of law (including its system of administration) depend on both the law's virtue (and this will be discussed in terms of four cardinal legal virtues: justice, integrity, prescriptiveness, and prudence) and the virtues of the law enforcer (prudence, specifically jurisprudence, justice, integrity, courage, and moderation). The jurisprudence of police, in a third sense (its pros hen or core normative meaning), is the activity of these virtues in the exercise of the police power for the purposes of establishing and preserving a just order through the enforcement of law.

Jerome Hall, who apparently coined the term "integrative jurisprudence" and who took a large view of law, provided some of the initial inspiration for my current project in legal and police philosophy. His work sought to integrate the perspectives associated with natural law, legal positivism, and sociological jurisprudence in an effort to interpret law as a coherent whole:

> Rules of law are certain standards and commands, expressed in thousands of statues, decisions, regulations, and in constitutions. It is important to note the interconnectedness of the entire body of legal rules. They are arrangeable in a harmonious order extending from the very general propositions of constitutional law through the middle range of statutes and decisions, down to the very specific concrete applications of them by police officers. (144)[13]

Hall couples that perspective on law with a correspondingly large view of the police function, seeing police as agents of this integrated law:

> The policeman who conforms to law is the living embodiment of the law, he is its microcosm on the level of its most specific incidence. He is literally law in action, for in action law must be specific. He is the concrete distillation of the entire mighty, historic corpus juris, representing all of it, including the constitution itself. Thus the law-enforcing activity of the policeman takes on its significance not only because it is the law in the concrete form in which it is experienced by individual persons, but also because the meaning and value of the entire legal order are expressed in the policeman's specific acts or omissions—so long as he conforms to its law. (144)[14]

The policeman in a democratic society ruled by law when enforcing or animating that law may well become what Hall thought, "the most important person in the entire hierarchy, able to facilitate the progressively greater realization of democratic values" (145). In fulfilling that end, police paint on law's broad canvas:

> Our enlightened police Captain, like an artist having many brushes and colors or like an engineer with a large assortment of tools and instruments, has access to many legal controls which, if he employs them skillfully and persistently, can effect enormous change in conduct in the direction of achieving democratic values. Certainly we must believe that a thorough understanding of the police functions in a democratic society, combined with a knowledge of law and of the facts comprising serious social problems, necessarily operates to improve the quality of police service. What is suggested in effect, is abandonment of the notion that the police function is purely negative, and the substitution of a creative role designed to increase and expand democratic values. It is precisely in areas of racial conflict and aggression that the challenge to implement this perspective is greatest. By like token, here, too, is the best opportunity for imaginative, disciplined police to make a major contribution by strengthening the democratic way of life. (161)

What is needed today is an imaginative yet disciplined artisanal police. As for the object of their productive (creative) capacity, consider Daniel Webster's eloquent declamation:

> Justice is the great interest of man on earth. It is the ligament which holds civilized beings and civilized nations together. Wherever her temple stands, and for so long as it is duly honored, there is a foundation for social security, general happiness, and the improvement and progress of our race. And, whoever labors on this edifice with usefulness and distinction, whoever clears its foundations, strengthens its pillars, adorns its entablatures, or contributes to raise its august dome still higher in the skies, connects with name and fame and character, with that which is and must be as durable as the frame of human society.[15]

A just order will be built up with the help of the wisdom, experience, imagination, and vocation of morally based officials working toward the building of this dome. The police, however, remain the most conspicuously neglected corps of artisans. This neglect has been partly due to public attitudes, which Jerome Hall contends have included a damaging condescension toward police: "The supercilious condescension of respected classes toward policemen reaps its inevitable crop—low self-esteem, little insight into basic functions, and no appreciation of potential contributions to enrichment of the democratic way of life by superior police service, especially in relation to the weaker members of the community" (145).

Hall states that the following is incumbent on the public (and I would stress especially incumbent on the academic profession dedicated to professional education of police, which has at times also betrayed a condescending attitude):

> Intelligent Americans therefore have a major job to do—first, to understand the meanings of police service in a democratic society; then, by their support and cooperation, they must create a police force that is capable of discharging its duties in a manner that strengthens the democratic way of life. The most important step in this reorientation of a public institution is a change in attitude toward police functions. (145)
>
> We must come to regard the police not as our substitutes for police service, releasing us from any obligation, but as our trained specialized helpers in a type of law enforcement that is compatible with democratic values. (146)

It is not only the police but also the public that requires an education in what police means. For Hall, the challenge for police and laymen alike goes beyond seeing the function of police as tied to "biological survival" or "controlling antisocial conduct." He challenges us to conceive that function as tied to the service of democratic values:

> It includes the positive conception of maintaining order in ways that preserve and extend the precious values of a democratic society. For while democratic societies, need order, they need a distinctive kind of order, one that is not imposed by an uncontrolled force, but one that is achieved by police methods that reflect democratic values. (146)

The requisite conception of police, I contend, necessitates cultivation of a teleological perspective on law. By such a perspective, I should make clear that I am referring to one that discerns the end(s) immanent in the legal enterprise. What is presupposed is a conception of law that contains within it a principle that drives it toward a fuller realization of its ends. Aristotle had explained teleology observing that in the acorn one may find that principle that directs it toward its completion in the fully mature oak tree. Law likewise has within it a principle (or set of principles) that directs it toward completion. (Different from the tree of course is that this principle(s) of law entails conscious human intervention in the form of practical reason applied to the development of law.) This "growth" or maturation of law may be accomplished in various ways, such as by legislation, interpretation of legal texts by judges, or the application of law by police and prosecutors. Sometimes the text of law makes explicit what the end(s) of law are. An example is in the US Constitution's Preamble, where it is stated that the Constitution is ordained to "form a more perfect order, establish justice, insure the domestic tranquility, provide for the common defense, promote the general welfare, and secure the blessings of liberty for ourselves and our posterity." However, ends are also presupposed in the document as the whole, given its structure, division of legal labor, etc. The ends are also revealed in law's historical development. (Hall's integrative jurisprudence, therefore, should have also included the historical school of law.)

I think, however, the *telos* of our law is both broader and more complex than Hall's "democratic" vision. One might note that the US Constitution does not once use the term "democratic" in referring to the order established but instead guarantees to the States a "republican government" (Article IV). How is that to be construed? One approach is to see the Constitution as organically rooted in historical developments. From that perspective, our written Constitution, a product of the debate between federalists and antifederalists, is a synthesis of those democratic/republican principles that, on the one hand, are solicitous of the civic virtues necessary to the moral order of community and, on the other, embrace the dynamic liberal principles that fire a commercial state and are centered on the liberty of individuals. The disorders of recent times have made clearer the continuing importance of the former. Our police are a vocation directed toward a balance of these principles. They are animators of a morally ordered liberty.

"Police," then, refers to more than uniformed persons engaged in directing traffic or investigating crimes. It is more than any group of persons. It is a principle, a system of justice, a state of affairs. A jurisprudence is vital to police if the police, as professionals, are to fulfill the promise of securing observance to law.

Harold Berman holds: "an integrative jurisprudence would emphasize that law has to be believed in or it will not work; it involves not only reason and will but also emotion, intuition, and faith. It involves a total social commitment" (*Law and Revolution* vii). Respect for law is not mere mechanical obedience but faith in and fidelity to law. It engages not merely external practice but heart and mind as well. If police are to fully serve their communities that service must be inspired by a sense of vocation (a piety appropriate to the work) complemented by a philosophy, applied science, art, and technique all of which would be informed by an integrative jurisprudence of police.

## CHAPTER 2

# A Critique of Positivist
# Police Science

It has been said that the police exercise the most extraordinary discretion of any official in the justice system. This considerable discretion is accompanied by the formidable powers of arrest, detention, and the explicit authority to use physical force in the execution of their duties. The modern liberal state governing by and under the rule of law (in German, the *rechtsstaat*) depends on police. However, it is well worth remembering that a dictatorship depends on them as the chief instruments of oppression. Police are the sine qua non of either society.

Notwithstanding their critical importance, of all professions the police may be the most neglected, the most maligned, and the most misunderstood. In the 1960s, in our urban centers and on the college campuses, epithets were hurled at them. They were called "pigs" and were seen as embodying the worst aspects of authoritarianism. They were considered to be neither society's brightest nor its best. Yet at about the time when these condemnations were being made, we find that the average IQ of a New York City police officer was an impressive "125" (Morris 21). Moreover, far from being a menial profession, the police were required to enforce an increasingly complex legal system and expected to meet the public's increasingly high demands.

High expectations, however, are not of recent vintage. August Vollmer famously observed more than seventy years ago that citizens had come to demand that their police have: "the wisdom of Solomon, the courage of David, the strength of Samson, the patience of Job, the leadership of Moses, the kindness of the Good Samaritan, the strategic training of Alexander, the faith of Daniel, the diplomacy of Lincoln, the tolerance of the Carpenter of Nazareth, and finally, an intimate knowledge of every branch of the natural, the biological, and the social sciences. If he had all of these, he might be a good policeman" (222).

Vollmer's ironic tone calls to mind the ironies of this profession—
a profession that, on the one hand, is expected to meet the public's
high demands but that, on the other, lacks professional education and
licensure and occupies an inferior and in the eyes of some a stigmatiz-
ing social status. A profession that, according to James Q. Wilson,
places the greatest discretion not in the hands of the highest ranking
most experienced police officer but in the lowest and most inexperi-
enced, the patrol officer ( *Varieties of Police Behavior* 8). The police we
might aver are the ironic profession; our expectations of them do not
match the realities, nor do our stereotypes do justice to their talents.

Vollmer's characterization of the police officer as a factotum of the
virtues is somewhat typical of the hyperbole found in the police literature and reflects the defensiveness of a profession not fully understood nor fully appreciated by the public: a public that expects the
police officer to behave like Superman, but treats him like Clark Kent.
The American attitude toward police has been one of deep ambivalence that ranges from trust to fear, love to hate. To some extent as
Americans we prefer what Patrick V. Murphy has called our "absurd,
fragmented, non-system of more than 17,000 local departments" to
a more organized force, because we fear the more centralized police
may be a threat to our liberties (Forward, in Delattre xv).

In the 1970s and 1980s, people did not walk freely through Central
Park in New York City, because it had become an urban jungle over-
run by gangs and muggers. However, Central Park today is no longer
a Hobbesian state of nature. The Park has been wrested from the
criminals and, one could persuasively argue, the civil peace that has
been established and currently invites mothers, children, and senior
citizens in large numbers into the Park has been achieved in large
measure because of the work and continued presence of the NYPD.
While police may bear down too heavily and threaten our liberties,
their presence, given contemporary social reality, has become a pre-
condition of our liberties.

Herman Goldstein characterizes police as "an anomaly in a free
society" ( *Problem Oriented Policing* xii). The police power, Goldstein
writes,

> is awesome in the degree to which it can be disruptive of freedom, inva-
> sive of privacy, and sudden and direct in its impact upon the individ-
> ual...Yet a democracy is heavily dependent upon its police...It looks
> to its police to prevent people from preying on one another; to provide
> a sense of security; to facilitate movement; to resolve conflicts; and to
> protect the very processes and rights—such as free elections, freedom

of speech, and freedom of assembly—on which continuation of a free society depends. The strength of a democracy and the quality of life of its citizens are determined in large measure by the ability of the police to discharge their duties. (xii–xiii)

Rather than anomalous in liberal society, then, the formal police are its natural product, a critical medium through which (if they do their work well) the tension between liberty and order, inherent in the legal enterprise, may be relieved and the ends of that enterprise advanced.

The police are crucial to the preservation of the modern liberal democratic republic and it is important how the public sees them and how they see themselves. In this chapter, I shall argue that the dominance of social science and legal positivism has contributed to a distortion in our conception of police. From that perspective, the police are typically seen as the enforcers of the sovereign's will, as its efficient machines. The danger is that they become "Robocops" without a conscience—an image suggested by a cover of *Police Magazine* where a SWAT team clad in military fatigues and donning gas masks that completely conceal the face, is shown charging into a dwelling. What is needed is a new science of police that yields a conception of a humane police officer who in addition to being a master of technique is a guardian of civil order, an animator of law, and an agent of justice, rather than the fearsome instrument of those in power. The highly trained police must acquire the qualities of character evocatively depicted in Norman Rockwell's famous painting of the officer who treats the boy running away from home to an ice cream soda at the local diner.[1] While there is no chance that we can turn the clock back to Rockwell's mid-twentieth century Stockbridge, Massachusetts, or pretend that Stockbridge is a metaphor for contemporary social reality, the virtues portrayed by Rockwell's depiction (which includes the officer's solicitude for the boy who represents the future) transcend that time and place.

# I

High crime, increased tension between police and citizens, and police corruption in the 1960s and 1970s focused increased attention on police behavior—particularly from academic social scientists. Studies undertaken during this period found that police did more than had been commonly assumed. They provided an array of services that went beyond criminal law enforcement and included: dealing with the mentally deranged, domestic crisis intervention, mediating neighborhood disputes, directing traffic, escorting vehicles, and responding to emergencies—to name a few. Carl Klockers concluded that police perform so many different functions that any definition of police in terms of their ends would be impossible (*The Idea of Police*). Egon Bittner, a prominent sociologist, wrote in a similar vein that police perform "an almost infinite range of repairs on the flow of modern society" acting as nurses, rescuers, and social workers depending on the occasion (*Aspects* 233). This led him to characterize the police officer as "Florence Nightingale in Pursuit of Willie Sutton"—a nurse packing heat, a walking oxymoron (233). Goldstein, Bittner, and others wrote of conflict and incongruity built into the police function. Sometimes the tension in function is put in terms of an alleged basic tension between the law enforcement function of the police, where their "coercive role is paramount," and their peacekeeping function, where their "public servant" or social service role is paramount (Potts 8–9).

Bittner's incongruity thesis, that police perform a diverse set of functions that cannot be rationalized in terms of law's norms or any coherent set of ends, was the basis for his rejection of efforts to find a rational concept that explains the nature of the police function. While Bittner thought police could not be defined through any coherence of function or unifying ends, he was able to find a "thematic unity" in their means (*Aspects* 127).

Police deal, Bittner thought, with all problems that may require the use of force for their solution and so in his work, he gives centrality of focus to the use of force. In this respect, Bittner carries into police science a basic tenet of modern social science, which defines social phenomena, given the alleged indeterminacy of ends, in terms of means. Max Weber, the father of modern social science, in his famous essay "Politics as a Vocation" contends: "the state cannot be defined in terms of its ends. There is scarcely any task that some political association has not taken in hand...Ultimately, one can define the modern state sociologically only in terms of the specific means peculiar to it. Namely, the use of force" (77–8).

For the most part, police science has followed the lead of positivist social science generally and has defined the police phenomenon in terms of factors that can be found in all things that officials called the police do. This has produced a nonteleological and nonnormative conception that centers discussion on the least common denominator in police work, the use of coercive force. This parallels classic positivist legal science that had, as in John Austin's jurisprudence, centered the definition of law on the sovereign's power to inflict evil. A good example of this positivist approach in the police literature is Carl Klockars' work. In his book *The Idea of Police*, he defines police as: "Institutions or individuals given the general right to use coercive force by the state within the state's domestic territory" (12), a definition that faithfully parallels Max Weber's definition of the state. Klockars in his book explicitly drew from William Muir's influential *Police: Streetcorner Politicians*. As essentially agents of coercive force, police activity Muir contends takes the form of the "extortionate transaction" (4ff). In speaking this way, however, both authors treat the legally authorized activities of police officers on the same level as the activities of kidnappers, spouse beaters, blackmailers, and other miscreants. The failure to distinguish these offenders from police officers is a by-product of the underlying positivistic focus on means and the rejection of normative-based analysis.

Bittner defends his focus on the use of force this way: "as the capacity to cure lends unity to medical practice, the capacity to use force lends thematic unity to all police activity" (127). Bittner's analogy, however, misses the mark and exposes a characteristic deficiency not only in Bittner's approach but in the approach of positivism generally. The capacity to cure involves *technē* as applied to *telos*. To cure is to restore the good of health. The pursuit of that good may be said to be the end that defines the medical profession. The physician who applies his skill to kill (by administering a poison for example) directly acts in violation of that good. As such, he or she no longer acts as a physician but as a murderer. This essential discrimination, however, is blocked when one adopts an exclusively means-oriented definition of the profession that precludes stipulation of the end and then organizes practice around what Kant called "imperatives of skill."[2] When the medical profession is defined in terms of these imperatives, the murderer and the physician can be one and the same. The teleological definition of the medical profession, on the other hand, precludes that. This normative-based definition of profession, moreover, requires that the physician maintain an ethical character and an ethical practice. The physician must possess qualities of ethical character in order to make the right choices, choices that cure rather than kill, and so that the capacity to cure is activated not just incidentally but deliberately and consistently, thereby constituting a professional practice. Such a physician appropriately swears to a Hippocratic Oath and binds himself or herself to a medical code of ethics. The Code constitutes an integral part of the concept of a profession that tethers practice and practitioner to the good. The Code is not merely an optional appendage. The capacity to use force in contrast to the capacity to cure, then, is *technē* detached from ends and the virtues of character that commit one to pursue only ethical ends. Unlike health, force is not itself an end or a good. It is means only. It may, as Bittner understood, be used for good or bad, and as technique "the better it is perfected, the more neutral it becomes and the more readily it is available for both good and evil" (207). The unity that the capacity to use force imposes, if it can be called a unity, is that of competency and efficiency applied to technique alone. It is of a different *genus*, from the unity of purpose achieved by the capacity to cure.

The work of police cannot be understood without distortion prescinded from the discussion of ends. In the following set of facts, where do you find police? One day after teaching a class on Plato's *Republic* (to a group of graduate students—mostly police officers), I returned to my car only to find that I had locked the keys inside. I could not reach my wife Margaret, who was not at home, and I needed to get to an appointment. One of the officers in the class suggested that I call the local police department, which I did. In a very short time a policeman arrived, pulled a device out of the trunk of his cruiser, applied it between the front door and window of my car, and with a jiggle or two, the door was open. I was most grateful, but where was the police work? In the efficiency with which he got into my car? If that, what is the difference between a police officer and the best thief? A competent thief should be able to break into cars as rapidly as possible. Imagine a police department recruiting from the prisons looking for those who were best at the craft of crime, thinking that in order to enforce law you must have demonstrated the capacity to commit crime? We recognize that the know-how and skill to commit crime are not the essence of police work.[3] The police in the facts is not in the competence, skill, or mechanical efficiency employed by the officer, although these capacities are necessary for police work, but rather the essence of police is in the character of the action and the character of the agent and these can be understood only in light of the purpose of the action; the end to which the skills were put. The officer acted in accordance with lawful purpose to restore to the citizen the exercise of his legal right to use the car, by enabling him to enter. If while I were still in class, he got into my car and stole my copy of Aristotle's *Nicomachean Ethics*, then he would have acted like a thief, not a police officer.

Rather than focusing on the lowest common denominator of characteristics found in a phenomenon (which is the approach of positivism), natural law in defining something focuses on what John Finnis has called "the central case" of the phenomenon, that example where the phenomenon is exhibited in its completeness, its flourishing. In

Aristotle, the central case conveys the focal meaning or pros hen of the phenomenon.[4] For Aristotle, a thing is to be defined in terms of its proper functioning and it functions properly when it acts best in accomplishing its end. Accordingly, Aristotle defines a profession according to the end natural to it. This end, Aristotle contends, is constant—whereas means may vary, particularly when concerned with human affairs that admit of much irregularity or contingency. In Book III of the *Nicomachean Ethics*, Aristotle states: "no physician deliberates whether he should cure, no orator whether he should be convincing, nor does any expert deliberate about the end of his profession. We take the end for granted, and then consider in what manner and by what means it can be achieved" (Ostwald tr. 61). The police profession takes as its given the enforcement of law and this end (which entails the *telos* of law itself) when understood in its completeness, makes sense out of the myriad day-to-day activities police perform, and anchors police discretion to a set of ethical ends.

Jerome Hall in "The Police in Democratic Society" argues that police work must be understood as determined decisively by the duty to uphold the law and that every police action should be interpreted in relation to this objective. Of course, what we take law to be becomes critical—as what we take law's end to be. Much of the police literature, however, is at odds with Hall's contention that the duty to enforce law is capable of performing such a unifying regulatory function. Egon Bittner, for example, writes that police work: "appears to consist of rushing to the scene of any crisis whatsoever, judging its needs in accordance with common sense, and imposing solutions upon it. In all this they act largely as individual practitioners of a craft" (*Aspects* 255). When police exercise discretion (which Bittner felt they do far more often than is generally appreciated) their judgment is not based on formal legal inference, but on informal considerations and practical common sense. Bittner writes:

> I am not aware of any description of police work on the streets that supports the view that patrolmen walk around, respond to service demands, or intervene in situations, with the provision of the penal code in mind, matching what they see with some title or another, and deciding whether any particular apparent infraction is serious enough to warrant being referred for further process. (*Functions* 129)

Bittner holds that what actually occurs in police work where the law has some connection to the case (which apparently in his view it often has not) is the inversion of the normative derivative account of what should happen. Drawing on James Q. Wilson's *Varieties of Police Behavior*, Bittner contends: "In the typical case the formal charge justifies the arrest the patrolman makes but is not a reason for it" (129). The reasons for it fall within the domain of considerations Wilson vaguely characterizes as the need "to handle the situation" (129). "Even when the law is invoked in some case," Bittner claims, "the decision to invoke it is not based on considerations of legality" (129).

The law-based normative derivative approach, therefore, would appear to be at odds with the facts of police behavior, as Bittner reads them. Bittner may be correct about the motivation and behavior of some police. However, that motivation and behavior may be changed unless there is something in the nature of law and its connection (or disconnection) with social reality and police, which dictates it. But I fail to see how this is so. One might reason, if police behavior is not determined by legal norms to a significant degree or if the nature of police work gives rise to special opportunities to deviate from them, that legal norms, then, be defined with greater specificity to ensure the applicability of law to the facts. This may be accompanied by firm directives to police to enforce these legal norms and strict sanctions when they do not. Bittner's rejoinder would appear to be that no matter how specific legal norms can be framed, they are defeasible in the concrete situations to which they are applied. He states: "no matter how far we descend on the hierarchy of more and more detailed formal instruction, there will always remain a step further down to go, and no measure of effort will ever succeed in eliminating, or even in meaningfully curtailing, the area of discretionary freedom of the agent whose duty it is to fit rules to cases" (4). Rules remain "essentially open ended and uncertain" (4). That discretion may be narrowed asymptotically, however, is quite a different claim from saying that it cannot be "meaningfully curtailed." One may in narrowing discretion meaningfully curtail it. Be that as it may, we might consider how rules in particular cases may fail to dictate a certain police response. A legal rule may be interpreted out of a case, perhaps because the situation has some unique features that make it distinguishable from the class of cases to which the legal rule seems to apply. A rule may fail to control the judgment on which a police action is taken because there is a feature of the case that justifies an exception to the rule's application in light of some broader legal principle or policy. Ambiguity in the rule may require a legal judgment as to the best interpretation or application to this case and reasonable officers may disagree as to the best interpretation or application. Or the rule simply, in bad faith is ignored. Only the last case necessarily involves defeasement of legal norms. All the others involve police discretion (or judgment), but that exercise of discretion is not an act that of itself defeases law.[5]

Bittner's position is based on a conception of law that sees it as a formally posited phenomenon (as in the Penal Code whose titles are then matched to the situations at hand). While posited law is law, however, it does not rule out what Fuller refers to as "implicit law." One needs to see implicit in law's positive formalities, among other things, a larger vision of law's aspirations. Bittner's positivist conception of law is accompanied as well by a characteristically positivist interpretation of discretion influenced by Kenneth Culp Davis's *Discretionary Justice: A Preliminary Inquiry,* a work widely relied on in the police literature and explicitly cited by such diverse authors as James Q. Wilson and Egon Bittner. In this book Davis asserts that "Where law ends discretion begins" (3) and that a public official has discretion "whenever the effective limits on his power leave him free to make a choice among possible courses of action or inaction" (4). If one puts these two premises together, one may infer that law is presumed to be a body of norms that determine an official's action, so that the official acts ministerially when applying law to some case. This could be possible in that case of highly specific rules applied to particular cases by a deductive logic. However, such a rule-based definition of law, as H.L.A. Hart recognized, leaves gaps in the law. In these situations where the rules do not quite fit the facts, Hart believed that officials do what they think is best. They exercise a discretion not bound to law. This positivist conception of law seems to be at the basis of Bittner's claim that when police exercise discretion, which in his view they do in the vast majority of situations they confront, they are not engaged in enforcing law, but instead in a myriad of other functions. But Hart's view is highly problematic. Officials, as Ronald Dworkin appreciates, apply law in cases even where rules are indeterminate because law contains standards such as principles and policies that justify the rules and bind officials (not by a deductive logic but in terms of their weight and importance) to a certain decision ("Model of Rules"). In fact, even when the rules are specific and clear, officials may be legally bound to depart from their literal or positivist meaning because the weight of these norms requires it. In Part II, I shall develop a conception of law as an enterprise whose norms vary in the kind and degree of formality they generate. I argue that law's norms authorize discretionary judgments of varying kinds and degrees. The rule of law must be understood in light of the limited discretionary authority that officials legitimately possess.

The most likely explanation for police action that is not self-consciously a matter of some legal rule's application is that the officer has failed to understand how law is relevant to his or her situation. Law involves more than just the formal rules on the books (or the penal code that Bittner refers to) and law enforcement is not by its nature exclusively a matter of deductions from posited rules. Both law and law enforcement involve norms other than rules, which operate differently from rules. These norms generate different degrees and kinds of formality and involve discretion and reasoning that differs in degree and kind. Law and law enforcement may engage customary norms practiced by the community as well as norms reflecting the rational purposes behind the rules. When the officer acts to advance a rational purpose attributable to law (perhaps self-understood as acting in accordance with its spirit) or enforces a customary practice that can be considered legally binding, even though in both instances the action seems counter to law's letter, the officer gives effect to rather than defeases (or nullifies) law.

While Bittner is aware that his theory would raise concerns about the rule of law, his rejoinder is disturbingly dismissive:

> All I intended to argue is that their [the police] mandate cannot be interpreted as resting on the substantive authorizations contained in the penal codes or other codes. I realize that putting things this way must raise all sorts of questions in the minds of people beholden to the ideal of the Rule of Law. And I realize that the Rule of Law has always drawn part of its strength from pretense; but I don't think that pretense is entitled to immunity. (*Functions* 143–144)

If the police are to be responsive to the moral aspirations of our democratic republic, as Bittner wanted them to be, it will have to be based on an account of their discretion that ties it to a satisfactory conception of law, rather than an essentially formless discretion. This is necessary if we are to have government by law and under law. The fact that law's norms may be defeased in police practice—through ignorance, arrogance, good but misguided intentions, and bad faith—makes all the more necessary that in elaborating the police function emphasis be put on the binding nature of legal norms and these include not just rules but principles, policies, doctrines, binding customs, the weight of legal arguments, et cetera. William Pitt's admonition that "Where law ends, tyranny begins" bears repeating here. Law, however, does not end where positivism thinks it ends. Positivism reads law too narrowly and by doing so reads police discretion too broadly. The result is a conception of the law enforcer, developed largely by sociologists and related social scientists, that practically takes the law out of law enforcement.

I shall next elaborate on two effects of positivism on thinking about police, before turning in chapter 3 to a possible alternative in current normative-based police theory. Legal positivism tends to see law as a set of techniques for carrying out the will of the sovereign. When applied to the police profession, policing becomes a set of techniques for getting police things done. To professionalize police is in effect to mechanize them. A professional police force is one that is "programmed for precision." But technique, the more it is perfected, as observed earlier, the more it is serviceable for good or for bad. To reduce the police to the limited sense of the professional produced by positivism (limited in part because it does not read moral principle or the human good as at the basis of professionalism) is to risk that the police produced will become faceless Robocops unconstrained by conscience and the discipline of the natural law.

In the absence of a deeper understanding of the law's commitment to justice; in the absence of a conception of a higher law within the law; in the absence of a code of professional ethics that is written in the souls of the police that binds them to using the knowledge, skills, and methods of the profession in accordance with its rules and principles; and in the absence of a practice committed to giving effect to the political morality presupposed, for example, by the American Constitution, the police become merely the instruments of the sovereign's will. The profession collapses into the ministerial profession. Police become masters of efficient technique, machines trained to inflict physical violence. Something like this happened in Nazi Germany before the Second World War. The dominance of legal positivism contributed to the subservience with which German officials responded to Nazi policies, contributing to their tendency to simply follow orders (the excuse offered at Nuremburg) and to their failure to see their duty to do justice. We must therefore be on guard against seeing law as merely a set of techniques for getting things done and against seeing policing as merely a set of techniques for controlling crime.

We, therefore, need a conception of professionalization different from the one offered by positivism. Jerome Skolnick put it this way: "What must occur is a significant alteration in the ideology of police, so that police professionalization rests upon the values of a democratic legal polity, rather than merely on the notion of technical proficiency" (233). To accomplish the appropriate professionalization, I contend that police science must embrace a jurisprudence grounded in the political morality that underlies and justifies our law and from which may be derived a morally based conception of the police function. When police exercise a discretion that is governed by such a jurisprudence, they animate rather than defease legal norms.

The second specific effect of positivism I shall discuss is the broader distortion that it produces in the way we speak and think. Positivism alienates our normative vocabulary of its traditional meaning, substituting a meaning that is purportedly value-free, but one that is based on a separation of means from ends (objective human goods) and prepares for the deconstruction of meaning. A possible outcome is the inversion of meaning. This is evident in the earliest manifestations of positivism. In Book I of Plato's *Republic*, the Sophist Thrasymachus transposes the meanings of justice and injustice, calling "justice" the advantage of the stronger. For Thrasymachus, who is perhaps the first in the literature to articulate a position that is recognizably that of legal positivism, law is the expression of the will of the most powerful (sovereign) element in the regime. He equates "justice" to this "law." Socrates is perplexed when Thrasymachus later inverts conventional usage and refers to justice as vice and injustice as virtue. For Thrasymachus, might makes right.

John Austin's analysis of the term "duty" is also characteristic of the inversion. One of the principal legal positivists in the history of English jurisprudence, Austin holds: "Being liable to evil from you if I comply not with…your command…I lie under a duty to obey it" (Feinberg and Coleman 57). Few people, however, would say that when robbed at gunpoint the victim is "under a duty" to hand over his wallet. Rather, having no duty to do so, he is coerced by the threat to do so. However, in Austin's vocabulary, threat corresponds to a formerly moral term. Likewise, for Austin the term "superior" (as in, law is commanded from "superiors" to "inferiors") means not excellence or virtue or moral authority but power over. A "superior" is one who can inflict some evil upon you (61). The robber then is the "superior" of his victim to whom the victim is "duty" bound.

Given such usage, positivism stands customary meaning on its head. It produces definitions that invert the normative meaning imbedded in traditional language. Law itself would not be as Aquinas defined it, "an ordinance of reason for the common good by one who has the care of the community"[6]; instead as in Austin's conception, it is the sovereign's general commands where the sovereign is an individual or a group in power and its commands may be perfectly immoral.

Muir's account of police activity as a form of the "extortionate transaction" is a contemporary example in police theory of this alienation of customary meaning that initiates the uninformed into the positivist's "realistic" approach to things, but is also one that prepares for Thrasymachus's inversion of meaning. By disabling our moral vocabulary and neutering our moral concepts, positivism removes an important inhibition to the co-option of police by a Machiavellian tyrant.

A glance at linguistic history reveals that the term "police" has undergone positivization in the modern period. One can detect a significant denotative shift over the last one hundred and fifty years. This is revealed in *The Oxford English Dictionary*, a geological survey of words displaying strata of meaning over time—like layers of rock exposed on a cliff side. The first definition of police as a body of men having power to enforce (or coerce compliance with) regulations in a political organization occurs, not surprisingly, in the mid-nineteenth century with the emergence of modern departments. This modern definition makes no reference to the purposes of a legal system or the purposes of its enforcing officials. Go back a century before this, however, and Edmund Burke could write: "A barbarous nation [the Turks], with a barbarous neglect of police, fatal to the human race"(qtd. in *Compact OED*, 2227). Burke is not referring to a group of officials but to a state of society, or more precisely, to a condition of social civility. Burke is not saying that the Turks lacked domestic officials who enforced Turkish positive law, he is saying that they lacked civilization. In Burke's day, the word "police" was synonymous with civilization.

"Police" has its origins in the ancient Greek word *polis* and in Aristotle's political philosophy the *polis* is the locus of the active civic life and of human flourishing. The late historian Sir John Hale noted that Cicero translated the word *politikos* into Latin as *civilitas*, a term that meant "living usefully and enjoyably" in accordance with moral virtue within "a large community" (358). These earlier meanings were carried forward into the Renaissance where civility came to mean living rationally in a community according to moral and legal rules (Hale, see generally the chapter on "Civility," 355–419). This etymology reveals that the police, as in the officials who police, are guardians of civilization and agents of civic virtue.

When I bring this earlier denotation to the attention of contemporary police, however, I find that they have no knowledge of it. Yet, Colquhoun in *The Treatise on the Police of the Metropolis*, was still using "police" at least to some degree in this normative sense. (Colquhoun's book, first published in 1795, however, seems to be forgotten even by the police theorists.) More recent police codes of ethics bear the imprint of this earlier meaning. Some of the codes, for example, Orlando Wilson's very influential "Square Deal Code" of

Wichita Kansas, 1928, which served as a model for the IACP Code of 1957, specifically enjoined officers to have the manners of gentlemen.[7] Outward civility, the demeanor of the good citizen, is the "external wardrobe" (to borrow a metaphor from Burke) of an inner sociability, the qualities of character of the just man who is law-abiding, who knows right from wrong, and who has acquired the civic virtues. To be animators of law in the fullest sense, its pros hen form, police officers must be such persons.

Traditionally, the police power is defined as that comprehensive power exercised, e.g., when the sovereign makes law "to promote order, safety, health, morals, and the general welfare of society, within constitutional limits" (16A *Corpus Juris Secundum* 432). It used to be said that laws were enacted with a view to establishing police, which William Blackstone described as a form of domestic order: "Whereby the individuals of the state, like members of a well governed family, are bound to conform their general behavior to the rules of propriety, good neighborhood, and good manners and to be decent, industrious, and inoffensive in their respective stations" (*Commentaries*, Book IV 162).

The Preamble to the United States Constitution of 1787 indicates that the Framer's intended to bring about a "state of police" as they sought to "establish justice," "promote the general welfare," etc. Article 29 of the Universal Declaration of Human Rights of the United Nations suggests another articulation of this state, wherein the "free and full development of [the human] personality" is achieved through a community respectful of the equal rights of individuals, where individuals in turn fulfill duties owed to their communities and individual rights are subject to "the just requirements of morality, public order and the general welfare in a democratic society" (brackets mine).[8] Both documents indicate the *telos* that underlies and drives the legal order forward. Today, however, the words "police" and "state" are apt to be arranged in reverse order as in the expression "the police state," which clearly is an inversion of Blackstone's meaning and is the antithesis of the *rechtsstaat*, the law state.

Positivist police science has focused not on the police power that comprehensive morally based power that generates and preserves Blackstone's constitutional order, but on police powers, the plural— the multiple individual powers of police, such as that of detention, arrest, the use of deadly force—that can, when detached from the *telos* of law, be so destructive of the citizen's liberties. It is no wonder that the term "police" is capable of stirring up the intense ambivalence that it does given the contradictory double states the term can connote.

The incongruity thesis of modern police science—which disjoins the law enforcement function from the social service function of police and which in its acute form exposes the antinomy between the state of police and the police state—seems to correspond to a theory of law as the will of the sovereign that is inconsistent with the traditional understanding of law as rooted in a commitment to a just society. Law is not the externally imposed coercive force of the sovereign (although it often must express itself through the sovereign's commands); law rather is the enterprise through which a just order is established and preserved. Law serves the community by maintaining order and keeping the peace—preconditions to the exercise of rights and the pursuit of happiness. This complex function requires imagination and creativity on the part of police, who make use of a variety of formal and informal means, ranging from persuasion, example, and education to coercion and the use of physical power to "enforce" (give force to or animate) law. The incongruity thesis is inconsistent with the police profession's own understanding that its role of upholding law commits police officers to a coherent rather than a conflicting set of functions. The adoption of the positivist's methodology has meant that what governs the discussion of the police in the literature is the rule of the lowest common denominator. The emphasis on means (as in Klockars) has meant that the profession has not focused on the rational ends that police as law's agents serve.

By taking law out of law enforcement, police science makes unintelligible what police do. It is a failure to see law as the *logos* of police, a failure of jurisprudence, that is the stumbling block in these theories to a unified account of police practices. This failure is understandable because these theorists labor under a conception of law that is itself too narrow, too formalistic, and one that is devoid of moral and social/historical content (i.e., the conception of legal positivism) and thereby fails to provide the unifying principle that orders and makes sense of the many activities police perform.

Not only does this modern form of police science remove law from the law enforcer, but it also removes "police" from the police officer. The end-product is an official who performs a potpourri of incongruous tasks that make little sense when put together and are better performed by other vocations. The sole constant is that this official is armed, waiting for the occasion to put his arsenal to use. However, a persistent worry remains: to what purpose will he put his formidable skills? Unlike positivist police science, an integrative jurisprudence of police affords us the possibility of an adequate answer. To redraft the police officer in the mold of social worker, however, as police theory in the hands of some current social scientists tends to do, is not to solve the problem. Absent the law as authorizing norm, the police mandate is boundless. Society should beware of a police force exercising "discretionary justice" under such a mandate, taking orders from social engineers dressed as social scientists.[9]

## CHAPTER 3

# A Critique of Normative Police Theory

Theories of the police function can be sorted into two broad categories: nonnormative and normative. Egon Bittner's work, which I examined in the previous chapter, is a good example of the former. John Kleinig's work, particularly his *Ethics of Policing*, is a fine example of the latter. Each sort has been concerned with resolving a characteristic difficulty. Bittner, focusing on what police actually do, concludes that police perform a multiplicity of incongruous tasks, preventing any unified account of their ends. Foregoing a teleological account of the function, Bittner contributes an account centering on the instrumentality of coercive force. Bittner's solution to the problem of incongruity, as we have seen, is a nonnormative theory centered on means, a solution characteristic of social science positivism. Coupled with a positivist legal theory, this positivist police theory, however, blocks from view how law regulates much of the discretion police exercise and distorts contemporary conceptions of police.

John Kleinig, on the other hand, argues that a unified account of police ends can be found. His teleology is organized around the normative conception of police as "social peacekeepers." While Bittner's rejection of normative teleology follows from an incongruity thesis, Kleinig's embrace of normative teleology implies a thesis of its own. I shall call it the thesis of subsumption.[1] The claim is that the tasks of police are subsumable under the norm of social peacekeeping, which legitimates them. Kleinig selects social peacekeeping over law enforcement partly because he believes the latter to be too narrow to subsume the others and partly because it is too "hard edged."

Kleinig's account and teleological theories of policing, such as community policing, however, give rise to a central problem. The end that Kleinig in particular chooses, social peacekeeping, must not only provide authorization for the actions of police generally, but also be capable of subsuming the law enforcement function of police. This means that the various activities are not authorized by law as such, but the broader social peacekeeping. This approach, however, raises a series of questions. Can social peacekeeping *simpliciter* authorize law enforcement? Are not the activities of the police, given the rule of law, supposed to be under law? Isn't the authority of police circumscribed by law? How then can social peacekeeping stand above law? How can a theory that provides an extra-legal license for police activity be squared with the ideal of the rule of law?

In this section, I focus on John Kleinig's normative theory of the police function as elaborated chiefly in his *Ethics of Policing* and the attendant problem of subsumption. The solution to the problem of subsumption, I argue, can be found in an integrative jurisprudence of the police function, which organizes police tasks, especially those connected to the maintenance of order, around the unifying legitimating duty to faithfully enforce law.

The fundamental difficulty in Kleinig's normative police theory is generated by an implicit conception of law that is positivist, from which the overly narrow conception of law enforcement is derived. Kleinig's critique of positivist nonnormative police theory then is deficient (it is critique *manqué*) because of its failure to reject and provide a substitute for an underlying conception of law, and derivatively law enforcement, that is positivist. What is needed is a jurisprudence that is integrative, one that gives positivism its due, but by the same token incorporates a normative teleology and a normative historicity. Such a jurisprudence provides a satisfactory substitute for the positivist conception of law and police that it replaces. The details of that jurisprudence will be elaborated in part II.

## I

John Kleinig's *The Ethics of Policing* develops a philosophy of policing that is normative derivative. In response to Bittner's focus on the use of coercive force, Kleinig concentrates on the authority that legitimates it. The authority to use coercive force, he rightly observes, is "subject to normative constraints." We should not, he admonishes, "confuse their role with means that are available to them in fulfillment of that role" (18). Kleinig finds in the police role the normative authority for police activities, including the use of coercive force. He commences his analysis with a brief account of governmental authority generally, before examining the nature of police authority, and the police role specifically.

We are accustomed to thinking of governmental authority as resting on the consent of the governed and are familiar with the liberal tradition that theorizes the legitimacy of government rests on a kind of social contract in which certain rights in a state of nature are given up in exchange for a certain security—secured are rights to protection of life, liberty, and property. One has only to consult John Locke's political philosophy for a systematic elaboration. Since the eighteenth century, the idea of contract has come to occupy a central place in our political and legal culture. It is, for example, central in John Rawls' influential, *A Theory of Justice*, where the principles of justice themselves are the product of a hypothetical contract. Contract is normatively attractive because it is predicated on the paradigm of free and equal parties reaching an agreement as to the bases of their interaction. It gives rights to liberty and equality (rights Locke found to be extant in the state of nature—natural rights) a key role in the generation of principles of justice and the limitation of governmental authority (*Two Treatises*). The contract presupposes the priority of the rights of the individual whose willing cooperation must be sought before basic governmental powers are justified.

Proceeding on such assumptions, Locke imagines a system of laws enacted by a representative legislature duly enforced by an executive and applied by the judiciary in accordance with the legislated will. This liberal scheme, notwithstanding the account of natural rights, seems to yield a largely positivist account of law as applied to the executive authority, reading such authority, and derivatively police authority, as formally bound to the rule of law, with police exercising little discretion. It is readily adapted to what has been referred to as the Professional Law Enforcement Model.

In challenging the Lockean account of authority outlined above, Kleinig points out that institutions, procedures, etc. are legitimated not on the basis of formal agreement alone—such as contract—but also on the basis of inherited traditions that constitute a stratum of shared expectations and meanings. "Our social existence is governed as much by inherited traditions – linguistic, cultural, moral, political— as it is by structures and institutions for which our consent may or should be sought" (15). Contractual meanings and expectations, Kleinig asserts, are more based on "voluntaristic, deliberative accords" (17). They are more grounded in the explicit formal act of contracting. Traditional meanings and expectations, on the other hand, are "rooted in affective bonds and communal ties" (17). These meanings and expectations are more implicit in relationships and interactions that have taken place over time. Kleinig observes, "If police are not to lapse into private decisions about how they are to act, they must be attuned to the cultural traditions and mores that inform the world they serve" (17). Police authority to act, therefore, may be derived in part from these inherited traditions that prescribe meanings and produce bonds that regulate human interaction. These ordering traditions used to be referred to as constituting part of the customary law, although Kleinig does refer to them in these terms. (I shall dilate on their relevance to law enforcement in part II.)

Kleinig explicitly examines police authority in terms of two sources: contract and tradition (or we might say custom). We may observe that these correspond to positive authority (a particular action or interpretation is validated by positive norms) and empirical/traditional authority (where official action is legitimated by customary practice that effectively orders human interaction). However, there is a third source of authority that oddly Kleinig does not make explicit but is implied by his teleology. This is to be found in the practice's goodness, whether intrinsic (in itself) or instrumental (as a means to some good). For police action, ultimately it is in the action's conduciveness to what Kleinig asserts is the overarching end of police: social peacekeeping. The social peace is a good. This good organizes Kleinig's normative account of the police role from which the authority of police is derived.

In "speaking of a role" Kleinig holds "we are referring to more or less determinate social relations that are governed by certain norms. Roles are not constituted simply by habits or patterns of conduct. They are structured by obligations and responsibilities, rights and privileges. We may occupy various roles—familial, occupational, and associational—and our roles may change over time" (23). Roles are normatively binding. They are defined over time by patterns of conduct that give rise to relationships and corresponding expectations. The expectations may when reasonable give rise to duties and rights. While it is unclear what Kleinig intends by the last phrase that our roles "may change over time," he may simply mean that in the course of our lives we change roles; for example, from child to spouse, to parent, from worker perhaps to employer. He might also mean that the roles themselves may change over time. Being a mother in the 1950s is different from being a mother in the twenty-first century. Being a police officer in the 1950s is different from being a police officer today. This requires that in elaborating a conception of a role we should account for the historicity of roles. Can one, for example, explain why the police role in America today appears to be shifting from professional law enforcement to problem-oriented community policing? (In chapter 5, I shall examine why. In part II, I shall argue that the police role is in part relative to social context and that given the heterogeneity and dynamism of social contexts confronted by contemporary police, their role is protean.)

While Kleinig admits that the police "tend to be perceived, and indeed tend to perceive themselves, as law enforcers first and foremost," he would like to change that (68). He contends that redefining the role of police as "social peacekeepers" offers "the best potential for accommodating in a practical and normatively satisfactory way the varied tasks that police are called upon to perform" (27). The "role of social peacekeeping" he argues provides the basis of police authority. "The police are vested with authority in respect of a role that I have broadly characterized as social peacekeeping" (210). That this is "normatively satisfactory," however, is questionable. It is not clear, for example, why *telos* as such provides the basis of authority rather than *telos* in combination with the normative force of contract and tradition. While Kleinig may be assumed to mean that social peacekeeping implies a contractual and customary component (they are after all components of authority under his analysis), it is necessary to explain how it does and how these distinct sources of normative authority interact. It would still remain unclear why "social peacekeeping" itself constitutes law's *telos* as that *telos* would also include securing individual rights.

Another difficulty with Kleinig's normative theory lies in his overly narrow conception of law enforcement, which may be exposed in his critique of the various models of the police role. He takes up the crime fighter model, the emergency operator model, the social enforcer model, and offers his model of the social peacekeeper as superior to all of them. Remarkably, he does not identify a law enforcer model as such (although that is the basis of professional law enforcement), nor does he identify the community policing/problem-solving model (although his model has much affinity with that one). We shall see that when Kleinig refers to law enforcement his conception of the function shares the positivism that dominates current thinking.

The crime fighter model is the one that comes closest to what Kleinig apparently means by law enforcement. He states, for example, "my purpose in emphasizing 'peacekeeping' is not to downplay the importance of 'crime fighting'. Law enforcement is indeed the 'hard edge' of police work" (29). He characterizes the Lockean conception of "effecting the rule of law" as "crimefighting" (23). Even a positivist jurisprudence of police, however, must recognize that the law police enforce includes various municipal ordinances and traffic laws that are regulatory rather than criminal. And so crime fighting is underinclusive even as a positivist category. When contrasting law enforcement with "communal peacekeeping," Kleinig presupposes a positivist conception of law when he states: "Communal peace as I understand it here is not simply a matter of some externally imposed structure (law enforcement), but of a perceived security, of ordered liberty" (28). What he does not explicitly acknowledge is how the phrase "ordered liberty" presupposes a constitutional order, that an integrative jurisprudence is necessary to illuminate it, and that the law enforced is based on it. Law enforcement is not necessarily a matter of imposing an external structure, as law does emerge (in the instance of customary law) from the ground up and as a moral order (in the instance of the natural law) partly from the inside out. To enforce law means to realize the good of community, as well as other goods, such as liberty and justice, that form law's *telos*.

Kleinig rejects the conception of the police role as "effecting the rule of law" on grounds that the majority of what police do cannot be characterized in terms of "strict law enforcement" (23). Here, he echoes Bittner and the positivists. (His modifier "strict" is curious. It allows that law enforcement may be pursued by less than strict means and hence be a broader category than his account suggests. However, he does not take up what such a broader law enforcement might cover.) Kleinig enumerates various "social service functions" police perform that he supposes are not matters of law enforcement: "intervention in family crises, searching for lost children, rescuing animals, directing traffic, supervising crowds, assisting the elderly, and so on" and various administrative tasks. (23) However, it is not clear how social peacekeeping, Kleinig's overarching subsuming norm, itself consists in rescuing animals, searching for lost children, assisting the elderly, or traffic regulation. At the very least, police regulate traffic in part by enforcing traffic laws. Police "social service tasks" to some extent reflect the expansion of the scope of government from the Lockean liberal state (in which the police power is principally directed toward the protection of life, liberty, and property) to the welfare state. This entails a correspondingly expanded conception of the police power, a normative theory that goes beyond Locke's limited state to embrace duties to contribute to the social good, and laws enacted to secure this broader good. In consequence, the law enforced will include substantive laws directed to securing social welfare.

While Kleinig's account suggests the incongruity of the functions, Kleinig nonetheless asserts that law enforcement and social services are not necessarily disjunctive activities: "So-called domestic disputes, for example, are not either exclusively law enforcement or exclusively social work matters. They may be both." (24). In a similar vein, he states: "Crowd and traffic control, too, may involve a convergence of functions" (24). With respect to domestic disputes, some commentators have observed that arrests alone will not solve the problem, requiring that police adopt a more informal mechanism, perhaps mediation. When mediation is successful, although police action here might resemble social work, it may prevent future disputes that produce violations of the criminal law. A deeper conjunction of the two functions is to be discerned here. Domestic mediation, for example, can help restore and strengthen the familial order, thereby strengthening the larger legal order, as the family is an intermediary association upon which the larger more formal legal order (and the goods it is directed to securing) depends. Good solid families tend to produce law abiding citizens. Broken families, conversely, have been connected to juvenile crime and other disorders.[2] I shall argue that the conjunction of tasks is not foreclosed by a view of police as enforcers of law; rather, these tasks are best pursued via the duty to make law effective. However, I shall interpret the law enforcement function without the restrictions imposed by positivism or Locke's conception of the liberal state.

In contrast to the law enforcer, however, Kleinig asserts that the role of "the peacekeeper is broad enough to encompass most of the work police do, whether it is crime fighting, traffic control, intervention in crisis situations" (28–9). He claims that it has the additional benefit of giving an "irenic" cast to police work (29). Coercive means become appropriate only when necessitated by the end of social peacekeeping. "If police are seen as possessors of authority and not simply as wielders of coercive power, and if that authority is vested in their perceived ability to preserve and restore a peaceable social order, then their use of coercion becomes a last (albeit sometimes necessary) resort rather than their dominant modus operandi" (29). Kleinig argues that social peacekeeping "refocuses" attention from coercion to authority (29). Yet, it is unclear how it does this. Police authority is not "vested in their perceived ability" to achieve the end of social peacekeeping but rather in their legal authorization to fulfill their duty to enforce law. The authorizing law, in turn, derives its authority from its directedness to realizing human flourishing in community (which includes not only the social peace but also a host of individual goods entailed by law's *telos*), from its limiting formalities (which function, inter alia, to prevent officials from abusing their discretion and violating the rights of individuals), and from its material efficacy in solving coordination problems that arise in human interaction. While material authority presupposes the sufficient power to coordinate human action to the securing of multiple goods, in liberal society that power is circumscribed by formal limits that officials and official bodies (charged with a duty to administer a legally defined peace) must respect. Police normative theory must be able to account for this duty in light of the teleological goods advanced by the legal enterprise.

The law itself restricts use of force to where reasonable and police policies in furtherance of that law articulate a continuum in which physical force is a last resort. Law is committed to the social peace. The enforcement of law prefers irenic to violent means. Yet, while peacemakers, police nevertheless must harness their spiritedness and courage in the service of authorized force. Plato recognizes this requires that police be not only gentle but also fierce; not only liberally educated and philosophic but also physically strong and spirited (*The Republic*, Books II–IV). These dialectical principles, imbedded in a peaceful yet spirited police, need to be explicitly synthesized and the concept of social peacekeeping does not do so.

In support of his thesis that the police role be defined as social peacekeeping Kleinig stated: "Having regard to the values we associate with police, a climate of trust in which our human selves may flourish in community with others, I suggest that, if taken seriously, this conception could provide the basis for a profoundly renovating and conciliatory style of policing through which both police and community might be brought together in a joint and mutually supportive enterprise" (29). This means that the end is not just peace, but community. Peace is not merely the absence of conflict, but also, as in the Jewish sense of "Shalom", it is a state of fulfillment. For human beings such fulfillment is found in community—a common good in the sense that all human beings rationally desire it. Aquinas defines the common good in terms of life in the perfectly just community.[3] Where peace as the avoidance of conflict is a detriment to that end, it involves injustice. (Consider Neville Chamberlain's "peace" with Nazi Germany.) Hence, community police are dedicated to enforcing a law whose *telos* entails human flourishing in community where peace is sought sometimes through violent means. The term "social peacekeeping" does not quite capture that commitment or make explicit the commitment to the good of community.

Kleinig does acknowledge that there is "a certain vagueness to the idea that police are social peacekeepers" (*Ethics* 30). Vagueness, however, is quite problematic when it occurs in the basic normative concept that must, among other things, confine the police power.

Vagueness may well provide a cover for police overreaching and abuse of authority, especially when these acts are committed in the benign name of "peacekeeping." Vagueness in law is a substantial infirmity and we should recall that some laws regulating the public order, laws that police enforced on a daily basis, have been successfully challenged as unconstitutional on vagueness grounds (ordinances prohibiting vagrancy are an example).[4] Vagueness in these matters, then, entails costs in terms of those goods secured by formality in law and summed up in the expressions due process of law and the rule of law. Citizens are entitled to clear notice of the limits of police authority and the nature of the acts which run afoul of that authority. What is needed, then, is a fundamental conception of the police role that grants police the discretion necessary if they are to maintain, restore, or build community (i.e., act in ways that fulfill law's *telos*), but at the same time confines that discretion to the rule of law and, thereby, secures those goods associated with formality in law. That I argue may be found in an integrative jurisprudential conception of policing as law enforcement, one that subjects police authority to law.

Kleinig does insist, nevertheless, that he is not advocating "downplaying the importance of crime fighting" (and hence in his view law enforcement) in part because of its historical roots in the notion of the king's peace: "The King, as the protector of the realm, was concerned primarily with a public rather than a private order and peace" (29). (I shall dilate on the "king's peace" and its connection to law in the next section.) Kleinig rightly observes, however, that what is public and private is a difficult distinction to make, in theory and in practice. As an example, he notes: "Domestic disputes are now seen as falling within the domain of public concern, but school demonstrations generally do not. What happens in such cases is that police must judge whether a particular form of disorder has reached a point at which wider social order is implicated" (29). However, it is unclear how they may do this on the basis of the charge of social peacekeeping. How does that concept tell us what order is to be enforced and whether a wider order may yet have to accommodate a more local order? Will the applied conception of the peace turn out to be the officer's preferred conception or that conception dominant within the officer's department or community? Or may the officer be held to some conception of the peace that the law understood integratively can be said to presuppose? This issue of discerning the boundaries between public and private underscores my main point, which is that a jurisprudence is necessary for resolving the problem, in theory and practice, because it is law that determines what the relevant orders are and where the boundary lines are. Police, in the United States, for example, need to conjure with what order the Constitution establishes, with what it leaves private (and is protected by negative liberty) and what it leaves public (and within the domain of the police power). What police need to be aware of is that the legal axes, implicating the public/private distinction, may shift over time affecting, for example, the Fourth Amendment validity of searches and seizures. In the instance of schools, the Supreme Court has prescribed a "totality of the circumstances" test for searches. Social problems such as the rise in juvenile drug use and the threat of Columbine-type terrorism lead courts to construe law so as to shift the legal axes to favor more intrusion by public authorities into the lives of students. One example of judicial sensitivity to context in the instance of a student's First Amendment right to speech is the Supreme Court decision in *Morse v. Fredericks*, 1275 Sup.Ct. 2618 (2007). There a juvenile's free speech right was curtailed to accommodate the legitimate interests of a high school to enforce discipline and combat juvenile drug use. So, what happens at school is a matter of public concern. Analysis and evaluation of such shifts demands a jurisprudence that, among other things, addresses the political morality of rights and duties that underlie the constitutional order and helps justify the balances struck in the legal axes as law and police respond to the requirements of the social order as these change over time.

If the constitutional order is libertarian, then the law may be said to endorse only the night watchman state. The public realm, and the law that the police enforce, is restricted to defense of life, liberty, and property. However, if the constitutional order involves commitment to the common good defined as human flourishing, the public realm is expanded and likewise the law that police are called to enforce. Here the police assume affirmative duties to promote the common good. However, there must be limits to this expansion, if liberty and a measure of the private is to be secured. By the same token, the degree of liberty itself will depend on underlying social conditions being favorable—that is sufficiently orderly so as to secure those social goods that support the individual right to liberty. And that will depend in part on the history, traditions, and customs, that contribute to the order of the society in question. How does social peacekeeping address these complications? With Kleinig, law becomes the instrument of a particular good—social peacekeeping. The law instead must be seen as the pathway or as Bracton puts it the "medium," which provides formal boundaries within which this good, among others, may be achieved.

Let me turn to some of Kleinig's specific points regarding the subsumption of law enforcement by social peacekeeping. In his response to an essay by Joan MacGregor, Kleinig argues that the International Association of Chiefs of Police (IACP) "Police Code of Conduct" includes among the fundamental duties of the police officer: "serving the community, safeguarding lives and property, protecting the innocent, keeping the peace; and ensuring the rights of all to liberty, equality, and justice," but does not explicitly include the enforcement of law. He adds that the Code explicitly endorses what he calls "selective enforcement" when the Code admonishes the police officer that "it is important to remember that a timely word of advice rather than arrest...can be a more effective means of achieving a desired end" (*Handled With Discretion* 68). Kleinig infers from the Code's failure in paragraph one to explicitly mention law enforcement in the list of fundamental duties, together with the passage urging sometimes a warning rather than arrest, that the Code subsumes "the specific task of law enforcement under the more general social ends. And by not requiring full enforcement it acknowledges that discretionary authority may attach (albeit in limited ways) to every dimension of police work" (68).

This inference, however, is not justified. Inspection of the IACP Code reveals that the end "keeping of the peace" is listed as one among five—it is a particular end standing on the same level as the other particular ends listed with it. How does it then subsume them? There is nothing in the text of the Code that indicates the drafters considered it as summing up the other four. While it is true that law enforcement is not mentioned in the list of specific duties, the better view is to see law enforcement as the general end subsuming all the listed items—which can explain why it is not listed along with the others. That it is an overarching end that transcends and subsumes them is supported by the fact that the Code is officially designated a "Law Enforcement Code of Ethics"—not a "Police Code" as Kleinig put its—and that the Code closes with the officer reciting the phrase, "My chosen career law enforcement." It should not pass notice that Kleinig himself titles his anthology of police codes, which includes the IACP's, *Professional Law Enforcement Codes*. Moreover, we should not dismiss the fact that police overwhelmingly define their role as law enforcement. Kleinig's reference in this context to the "Police Code of Conduct" rather than the "Law Enforcement Code" then is a departure from the more conventional (not to mention his own) usage. That conventional usage militates against substituting the term "social peacekeeping codes" for "law enforcement codes."

Certainly law commits officers to fulfilling the stated fundamental duties, such as protecting lives and property. The rights to liberty, equality, and justice are secured by the Constitution—rights that limit the conception of the peace to be achieved, rights limiting the way the police, for example, control crime, and maintain order. The concept of the social peace itself, on the other hand, does not perform these functions and should not be seen as a substitute for law enforcement.

On the question of "selective enforcement," to use reasoned persuasion rather than force (as with an arrest) more fully enforces law, as law is more a force in the person who gives it his assent. When law is obeyed only from fear, it is disobeyed when fear, that is, external police, is not present. Thus, the admonition to sometimes advise rather than arrest does not abrogate the duty to fully enforce law; instead, it illuminates the means to it. "Selective enforcement" is a misnomer, here. Instead a police officer exercises discretion in determining when arrest or use of more informal means will better effect the enforcement or animation of law.

That law enforcement is not the same as making an arrest is illustrated in the tradition of civil disobedience. To make an arrest may serve to undermine positive law, which is a reason for the civilly disobedient to seek arrest. The arrest is a means for the disobedient to bring to the court of law and public opinion the issue of the positive law's injustice—which is why in some cases officials try to avoid arresting protestors. The disobedient hope that the positive law will be changed in the direction of its justice—reconciling positive law with natural law. As an arrest may weaken positive law, or set in motion events that bring it down altogether, nonarrest may serve to strengthen positive law where other means better serve to produce willing consent to it—as the IACP Code recognizes a warning or lecture can sometimes prove more effective. Law is more vigorous when rationally consented to and when embodied in habit, than when imposed from without through threat of punishment. Yet, for some that threat is necessary.

The American Bar Foundation finding in the 1950s that the police do not arrest in all cases of disobedience, does not by itself indicate violation of the duty to enforce law; one must delve further into the reasons for not arresting. It may well be that in certain circumstances informal means such as persuasion, lecture, or warning serve to enforce positive law, while an arrest does the opposite. Even if one were to endorse Kleinig's view, however, one would have to ask by what authority may a code enacted by the IACP amend a statutory duty to fully enforce law or a constitutional duty to faithfully execute the law? If it did purport to do that, it would be void. Thankfully, it does not do that.

There is a better way to approach the problem of subsuming police activities in a teleological account of the police role. In the law state, the *rechtsstaat*, where the rule of law and by law obtains, authorization is through law. Where law, however, is only understood as what is formally enacted by legislative bodies and law enforcement is the formal enforcing of what is enacted, one is left with the problem that much of what police do does not readily fit into the category of formal arrests for violation of the law code—police maintenance of order and problem-solving/community-policing activities being prime examples. The positivist conception of law and the mechanical (ministerial) description of police practice fails to account for let alone legitimate the extraordinary discretion that the police in fact exercise—discretion, which when properly limited, is necessary for community policing and would be endorsed by Kleinig's philosophy. If, on the other hand, law is understood as an enterprise authorizing varying degrees of discretion and if law's legitimacy and derivatively police authority is found in three sources: in law's teleology, its formality and its historicity—through its normative ends (summed up in the idea of justice), through goods associated with its formalities (summed up in the expression "integrity in law"), and in its historical rationality (as derived from its history and traditions as summed up in the term "prescription")—then one has a normative account that enlarges the role to include the discretionary practices but which by the same token subjects them to law. This enlarged conception of law enforcement (giving full force to such an encompassing enterprise) subsumes law enforcement in the restricted sense of arrests, as well as the more discretionary and informal practices referred to as maintenance of order and social peacekeeping. An integrative jurisprudence gives access to such a larger conception.

This is the general solution to the problem of subsumption. Certain police activities will be clearly subsumable, others more at the periphery of the law enforcement function, and still some things police happen to do may well not be subsumable in any convincing way (the proverbial rescuing cats from trees is perhaps an example). My main concern will be with what is nearer to the core function of police, particularly what is referred to as their maintenance of order activities. Police action here is central to "broken windows" theory, the new problem solving/community policing, and current efforts to reduce crime and improve the citizens' quality of life. These activities are subsumable by an integrative conception of law enforcement.

The role of the police is to secure not just any order, or any conception of the peace, but the *ordo juris*. The *ordo juris* as a living order (at the basis of a living constitution) is reflected in the interaction of law's teleology, historicity, and formality over time. We should be wary of theory that detaches order from law even in the name of a particular human good (such as social peace) where the result is the exercise of a "discretionary justice" that may run roughshod over the rights of the individual.

# II

As Kleinig is aware, the norms that bind police are not simply "read off" of the community but instead are derived from "historically legitimated traditions and ideals," from "liberal democratic values" as much as from "the immanent demands and expectations of those who are being policed." One such tradition that Kleinig himself raises is that of the "king's peace" and he discusses it in connection with redefining the police role as "social peacekeeping." I shall demonstrate that the significance of the "king's peace" lies not in its connection to "social peacekeeping" as such but in its connection to the rule of law.

The king's peace was in its conception and development a legally ordered peace, inextricably tied to the development of the rule by and of law. Historically, the king's peace was a legal peace. In England, the king's peace was enacted in the royal law with the king asserting the principal authority to legislate for the whole realm. It was from this royal law that the English common law emerged. The king's peace in the German principalities was also a legal peace promulgated in peace statutes enacted by the emperors. The European cities and towns that began to be founded in the eleventh and twelfth centuries had their own versions of the peace enacted in the city charters, which were the first modern written constitutions in the west.[5] Today's social peace, as a descendant of the king's peace, is to be construed a legal peace. Derivatively, the social peacekeeping function of the police is none other than a species of their law enforcement function—although seen more from the perspective of that function's teleology.

For the historical roots of the conception of the king's peace, it is important to return to the emergence in the twelfth century of certain vigorous kings who "were all builders of centralizing territorial states" (*Law and Revolution* 488). In the German territories Frederick Barbarossa was elected "King of the Romans" by an assembly of bishops and princes in 1152. Professor Berman observes:

> Frederick's purpose was not merely conquest, although without conquest none of his other purposes could have been accomplished. It was

primarily the construction of a well-ordered state based on law. That purpose was not unconnected with conquest, of course, since it was much more efficient to rule by law than by force: where one's judges were obeyed it was not necessary to be present with one's armies. Law was also closely connected with revenue: litigants paid high fees into the coffers of the emerging territorial rulers of Europe. Yet law was also an end in itself: the keeping of peace and the doing of justice were the two main justifications of royal authority, the two main sources of its legitimacy...Within months of his election Barbarossa asserted his prerogative to legislate and promulgated his first peace statute asserting royal jurisdiction over violent crimes and disputes over seisin. (488, 489)

In developing royal legislation, Barbarossa sought the assistance of four doctors of law from the University of Bologna Law School, "the greatest of the Bolognese jurists" (489), to report to him on legal rights and duties and to draft legislation. One example of Barbarossa's legislation was the Roncaglia Peace Statute of 1158. It commenced "Frederick by the grace of God emperor of the Romans" and ordered: "By this decreed law, which is to prevail in perpetuity" all subjects are "to observe true and perpetual peace among themselves" (qtd. in 497). Those who broke the law were referred to as "peacebreakers." Barbarossa committed himself to the ideals of both "peace through law and of justice through law" and believed that "the emperor's mission to secure peace and to do justice was the sign of his appointment by God to fulfill the divine plan of salvation, and in the new age introduced by Pope Gregory the VII [the age that gave birth to the Western Legal Tradition], law was the chief instrument for peace and justice that was available to secular rulers" (493, brackets mine). Similarly, the Preamble of the Royal Law of Denmark pronounced: "By law, shall the land be built" and "It is the office of the king and chiefs who are in this country to guard the law and do justice." (qtd. in 515).

The first great law book in the West, the *Sachenspiegel* (the Mirror of Saxon Law, circa 1220) pronounced, "God is himself law, and therefore law is dear to him" (qtd in Berman 521). Berman observes that at that time: "Law was seen as a way of fulfilling the mission of Western Christendom to begin to achieve the Kingdom of God on earth" (521). Implicit in the *Sachenspiegel* was the view that in accordance with divine sanction society must be based on law. In England, Glanville affirmed that the "royal power...should be adorned with laws for the governance of subject and peaceful peoples."[6] Bracton held that "the king must not be under man but under God and under the law, because law makes the king, for there is no *rex* ['king'] where will rules rather than *lex* ['law']."[7] The authority of the king was derived from law. It was *lex* that made *rex*. When the king ruled by force alone, he ceased to be king. He became a tyrant and tyrants should be "deposed." What was emerging was the concept of the supremacy of law and rule by and under law.

In England Henry II established "the first permanent, central, professional royal courts of civil and criminal jurisdiction" (444). The king's peace was administered through the royal courts and the royal justices had jurisdiction over major crimes with lesser offences tried by the bailiffs. The great expansion of the royal jurisdiction in the reign of Henry II, the royalizing of the criminal law, property law, and tort law, which had previously been a matter of custom "marks the origin of English common law" (456). However, the royal law relied heavily on custom and closely associated law with custom. Lobban writes: "Common law literature…assumed that the law was not imposed, but grew out of society" (11). Consequently, "the common law was not a self-contained science, but derived its rules and solutions from below, in a constant feeding from society" (79). The twelfth-century English Assizes, which were royal legislation "established procedures in the royal courts for the enforcement of rules and principles and standards and concepts that took their meaning from custom and usage. The rules and principles and standards and concepts to be enforced— the definition of felonies, the concepts of seisin and disseisin—were derived from informal, unwritten, un-enacted norms and patterns of behavior. These norms and patterns of behavior existed in the minds of the people, in the consciousness of the community" (Hudson 227).

The communitarian character of the royal law, its rootedness in the customary practices of the community, was accompanied literally by a community police. Community participation was "enlisted in the form of a sworn inquest of neighbors, to present to the king's justices for trial all persons suspected of serious breach of the peace amounting to a felony" (Berman, *Law and Revolution* 446). As for the common law judiciary, Lord Kenyon in *R v Waddington*, 1 East 143,157 (1800), captured its communitarian character when he observed that judges were not "men writing from their closets without any knowledge of the affairs of life, but persons mixing with the mass of society, and capable of receiving practical experience of the soundness of the maxims they inculcate" (qtd. in Lobban 80). They were community judges. The current discussion of reimmersing police, judges, prosecutors, etc. in the life of their communities echoes this older style of enforcement of the king's peace or rather this older style of law enforcement.

While the king's peace was based in the customary order (Magna Carta itself "established law on the stated grounds of recording good custom") and it was the first function of the king's law to preserve this peace, at the same time the king's law served to "develop" and "standardize custom" (Hudson 226). The common law sometimes developed by "restating custom, sometimes greatly extending existing practices, sometimes assembling supported customs which justified breaks with the past, and transformed them into more fixed, more regular rules" (227). The royal law gradually produced a "hardening of the category legal" (227) as custom was standardized in the form of statutes. The interaction between customary and positive law, however, over time produced a greater separation between the two. Hudson observes, "the changes during the Angevin period encouraged legal activity and norms to become more distanced from customary perceptions of proper social practice" (228).

Standardization can be seen as a natural aim of the new centralized state. Certain rules had to pertain now to the wider realm. This was particularly true for the law of felonies (which would be articulated in more formal positive terms), whereas lesser offenses could still be handled by the local authorities in accordance with local customs. Yet, this positivization of law that gave central officials increased authority was accompanied by a natural law jurisprudence that checked their discretion: "Another element of developing common law, therefore, was the exclusion or at least the restriction of discretion. Law was contrasted with will, kingship with tyranny. According to an early thirteenth century London text: 'Right and justice ought to rule in the realm rather than perverse will, law is always what makes right, but will and violence and force are not right.' Law should proceed reasonably, with judgment. The Angevin reforms had further restricted the exercise of discretion by Lords" (Hudson 237). Discretion, then, was tied to right. Natural law checked what the sovereign might will law to be. Berman observes that twelfth- and thirteenth-century English royal law included equity as an "integral part" of law; "the equity of the royal courts was the aspect of law which gave it, its capacity to adapt old rules to new ('exceptional') circumstances, in order to do justice" (*Law and Revolution* 519). Royal law "exemplified the belief that – all law held within itself certain purposes, which were identified as justice; these built-in purposes were to guide the interpretation and application of legal rules and techniques" (518). Royal law drew from "divine law" and "natural law" for "objectivity and generality" (516). It drew on more than just the customary law and its restating of customary law was subject to the constraints of divine and natural law.

Finally, the newly formed European cities and towns of the eleveth and twelfth centuries advanced their missions of "keeping the peace and doing justice" (393) through the enactment of charters, constitutions, and statues that secured a closely knit communal peace based on a high degree of legal consciousness. Berman observes, "without urban legal consciousness and a system of urban law, it is hard to imagine European cities and towns coming into existence at all" (363).

Hence, the king's peace and the people's peace were inextricably bound to law and in developments leading to the establishment of the rule of law. Peacebreakers were lawbreakers. The king's authority itself derived from law and was limited by law. That law was viewed integratively, it drew from custom but was grounded in reason, in divine and natural law, and was standardized in positive law through formal enactment of peace statutes. The positive law interacted with the customary law according to a dynamic that gradually evolved a "harder" more formal positive law.

The integrative jurisprudence that explained the legal phenomena and the meta-law that evaluated it were developed in the law schools that first emerged in the eleventh century—in Bologna and then elsewhere as in Paris, Oxford, and Cambridge. These schools developed a sophisticated legal science and dialectic method (known as the scholastic method) that was applied to synthesizing the various elements of law, contributing to the generation of an integrated Western legal tradition.[8]

By the nineteenth century, however, that tradition had fragmented and a positivist jurisprudence and positive formal law was in the ascendance. I shall explore this subject in the next chapters. We shall see that the rise of legal positivism was stimulated by dramatic changes occurring in the social order and the political morality through which that social order was legitimated. The social order to emerge was less communitarian and the ascendant political morality gave individual rights greater emphasis as compared to considerations of the general welfare. The dominance of legal positivism in the nineteenth century coincided with the formation of a positive police. These developments eventually yielded the narrow conception of law enforcement that prevails today.

In the latter twentieth century, however, conditions such as the rise of crime and disorder particularly in the cities coupled with increasing recognition of the importance of community and other social goods to the restoration of order and prevention of crime, point to the need to recover a broader conception of the law and the law enforcement function, one grounded in both custom and *telos* that authorizes a new problem-oriented community policing. Under these circumstances, to resolve the problem of conceptualizing the police function today requires a return to a jurisprudential perspective that is integrative. The legal history, which my brief account of the "king's peace" touches, indicates what an integrative jurisprudence looks like. In part II, I provide an elaboration and I shall focus on a contemporary dynamic in which the harder positive law is softened by an emerging customary law. I shall demonstrate how norms of the community may serve to shape and give meaning to the statutes that they particularize, bringing the legislated law into closer approximation to local customary orders. The customary/positive law that results and is enforced by the police is a product of the interaction of law posited from the top and a customary law grown from the ground up. We shall also see how the police in their enforcement practice, whether more strict or more permissive, affect this interaction.

## III

I shall take up one more subject in John Kleinig's discussion of the police role, his analogy to the role of umpires in sporting games: "Like umpires in games, who are there to enforce the rules and penalize breaches, but are expected to do so with a view to the wider purposes of the game, and its need to 'flow', police officers, too, will know that an over-attention to law enforcement may undermine the needs of an ordered and peaceable social life and their role in conserving and promoting it" (*Ethics* 91).[9] Law has often been likened to the rules governing a game. The analogy is frequently encountered in the positivist literature. The factors affecting law, however, are more complex than those affecting rules that govern the more self-contained interaction that occurs in a sporting game. Yet, even in the instance of games, positivist theory is deficient in explanatory power.

Positivists and John Kleinig see the "law" of the game as the rule book. Umpires enforce these rules. The integrative jurisprudence I employ in this book asserts that the law of the game includes the rule book, but involves much more. The degree to which the rules are to be enforced ministerially (i.e., to be applied formalistically) depends on other factors that officials must consider. Umpires in applying rules have some sense of what constitutes a good play of the game. (They might have a conception of what constitutes the best play of the game—the equivalent in Ronald Dworkin's legal theory would be a conception about what justifies it.) Officials interpret and enforce the rules with a view to that end, which contributes meaning to the rules.

This good can be quite complex encompassing a composite of goods such as play itself, physical fitness, fair competition, sportsmanship, and character development—the various reasons people take up sports and parents encourage their children to engage in sports. The rules, then, are interpreted and applied not just as ends-in-themselves, but teleologically in light of that conception of the point of the game, the goods participated in by playing it; what Kleinig may refer to as "wider purposes" and we might add reasons. It makes a difference whether this is a children's game (where the principal point may be to teach the discipline of rules) as opposed to a professional contest (where a high level of performance and competition is desired and the entertainment of fans is an important *desideratum*). However, umpires must also apply the rules depending on the particular "flow" of the game refereed. When the game seems to be getting out of control, officials may enforce rules more strictly. To enforce the rules all the time, this way, however, could involve constant stoppages, detracting from the best play. When the game is well under control, a less formal approach might facilitate a more spirited play. The rules are read, then, in light of the contexts to which they are applied and these contexts in a sporting game are highly fluid—they vary within the same game and from game to game. (Even sporting games are not discrete; there is such a thing as a grudge match and long-standing rivalries that officials ought to factor in their approach to a game). The rules then, are to be interpreted and applied with a view to their context dependency over time, that is, their historicity. ("Flow" over time is perhaps a good metaphor for what is meant here by "historicity.") Players take their cues from the pattern of official enforcement of rules that become the basis of what may be called reasonable expectations about how the rules will be enforced. For officials to move abruptly and without justification from a permissive to a strict calling of fouls would violate not only the reasonable expectations of the players, but also, and not unimportantly, the reasonable expectations of fans. It would likely offend the participants' and spectators' sense of fairness and detract from what makes for the best play of the game.

There might seem to be some disanalogy here between games and law given the relevance in games of audience to official action. Yet, law as well has an audience. The enforcement of law has a point beyond the interaction of officials and the subjects of their immediate intervention. It sends a message to the rest of the society that reinforces law abidingness and deters law breaking. It does so in part through the riveting drama of police, prosecutors, and judges performing their roles in the administration of justice. John Finnis puts it this way: "There is the need of almost every member of society to be taught what the requirements of the law—the common path for pursuing the common good—actually are; and taught not by sermons, or pages of fine print, but by the public and (relatively!) vivid drama of the apprehension, trial, and punishment of those who depart from that stipulated common way" (262). This is not just the material for television and the movies.

The decisions of officials, then, require rather complex empirical/normative judgments. This is why the best officials are often those having the most and best experience officiating. The quickness with which these judgments must be made make them seem intuitive. However, that perception belies the degree to which they are the product of an expertise that has become second nature.

What the analogy to rules of the game and umpires reveals is that the "law" has a formal dimension (analogous to the book of rules and formal reasons for obedience to them), which is understood and applied in light of a teleological dimension (analogous to a conception of the good of the game or the best play of the game in which deontological and/or consequentialist reasons figure in justifying an official's judgments) and an empirical/historical dimension (analogous to an official's consideration of context and the evolving circumstances from which the rules derive meaning and according to which an umpire is bound to modulate his or her approach to calling the game). The last includes the value of being able to rely on reasonable expectations about the order officials will enforce. All three dimensions, interact are understood in light of each other, and no one automatically trumps the others. The end(s) of the game it may be said is discernible given its rules and the way it is played—not in isolation from these considerations—and the rules and play are not discerned absent some theory about the end(s) of the game. At any given point in time, one sort of consideration may predominate over another, but that may shift over time with another consideration taking precedence. Each of the dimensions of law, then, generates normative force. When the normative force derived from reasons generated in one dimension is combined with that generated in the other dimensions, they bind an official charged with enforcing law to a particular decision. In these respects, the rules of games and the function of officials who apply them are analogous to law and the function of officials charged with its enforcement.

In sum, social peacekeeping constitutes one good among others that needs to be factored into a conception of law's *telos* that embraces all the goods sought by the legal enterprise. This teleology of police must be integrated with a conception of law's formality characterized in terms of the constraints of certain formalities associated with the rule of law (summed up in the idea of integrity in law). Finally, the teleology and formality of law must be integrated with a conception of law's historicity that addresses the good of an enduring yet evolving tradition of law (summed up in the term "prescription" and expressed in the common law conception of law as "changing changelessness"). This is accomplished through an integrative jurisprudence. In this jurisprudence, ends do not justify means, but means and ends and contexts interact together and are judged in light of each other. Law is means, ends, and contexts together. In recent times, it is particularly the importance of contexts that has been underappreciated, as it is often through the medium of contexts that conflicts between law's forms and ends are reconciled.[10]

In part II, I shall elaborate the theoretical framework of the jurisprudence that accounts for the integrative nature of law, law enforcement, and the new police. I shall do so by using the current paradigm shift from professional law enforcement to problem-oriented community policing as the point of departure. But before doing this, I shall sketch police history and the paradigms that have emerged to explicate that history and that lead up to the paradigm shift. In chapter 4, I center on the rise in England of the formal positive police. Chapter 5 addresses the American police experience.

# The Rise and Limits of the Formal Positive Police

In this chapter, I take up the question of when "police" arise. The answer to the question hinges on what we define police to be. After treating the definitional issue, I then consider the emergence of a particular species of police, the formal positive police, in the nineteenth century. I connect the development to changes in the social order and the rise of formal positive rationality in law, in moral culture, and in social organization generally. I close with a consideration of the limits of formal positive police, limits that correspond to the limits of organizing social life exclusively on the basis of formal positive as opposed to teleological and what may be called historical rationality.

Policing as a "profession" constituted by an organization of full-time salaried officers emerged in the West as a relatively recent phenomenon, that is, in the early nineteenth century. Its advent is usually identified with the establishment of the London Metropolitan Police by an Act of Parliament in 1829. The rise of formal positive police was necessitated by complex changes occurring in the nature of social organization at that time including industrialization, urbanization, the increasing mobility and rootlessness of populations, the rise of large bureaucratic organizations, and the social disorders these changes gave rise to. It was prepared for by related changes in the normative concepts by which governmental authority (including legal authority and the use of coercive force) were legitimated. These normative changes had roots in the liberal theory of the state already on the rise in the seventeenth and eighteenth centuries. One such theory was John Locke's, briefly discussed in the previous chapter. Another was Immanuel Kant's, whose formal philosophy of ethics would inspire John Rawls' *Theory of Justice* and Ronald Dworkin's *Taking Rights Seriously*, two twentieth-century works that have greatly impacted jurisprudence. The rise of formal rationality in law, however, had even deeper roots in the formation of the western legal tradition with the emergence of legal systems in the West beginning in the eleventh century. The rationalization, conceptualization, and systematization of law first occurred in the canon law of the Roman Catholic Church, which served as a model for later secular developments. The formation of the canon law (the *jus canonicum*) was necessitated by the separation of ecclesiastical and secular jurisdictions and the rise of legal pluralism, as the separation of these systems and regulation of their interaction required the increased formality. This formalization of law progressed in the development of the English common law (discussed in the previous chapter in connection with the idea of the "king's peace") and continued in a long historical development toward the modern western system of separation of powers and the rule of law. (See Berman, *Law and Revolution*.) However, the trend toward formalization of law took a new direction in the nineteenth century, when liberal theory in conjunction with the changing social conditions spawned a new individualism, which was increasingly hostile to the communitarian orders upon which the traditional law and police depended and which necessitated a new kind of police.

To maintain as many do, however, that "police" is a phenomenon born of the nineteenth century is to prejudice the analysis in favor of positivism and to reproduce the narrow conception of the phenomenon (critiqued in the previous chapters) that is still prevalent today. An example of this prejudice as applied to legal analysis can be found in the work of H. L. A. Hart.[1] One of the most dominant legal positivists of the twentieth century, Hart distinguishes between what he said might be called "pre-legal societies" and societies having law. Hart distinguishes the latter on the basis that their social orders were regulated by norms having sufficient positive formality to be validated by "secondary rules," such as a "rule of recognition." The rule of recognition, in Hart's analysis, is a master rule stipulating the standard or procedure by which social norms become legal norms. For example, a rule of recognition (ratified perhaps in a written constitution) might establish a legislature and stipulate the procedure, whereby this official institution validly enacts law. For Hart, any society lacking such formalities (i.e., lacking secondary rules) lacked law. "Pre-legal societies" had norms that regulated and ordered behavior (customs and morals—what Hart refers to as primary rules that generated obligations), but these, because they were not subject to a determinate rule that validated them, did not in his view constitute law, except in a "rudimentary" sense. By analogy, one might reason that societies lacking formal associations that we recognize as police departments (the earliest mature version being the London Metropolitan Police) lack police. However, as societies predating the development of formal positive legal systems had law— not positive law as such, but law whose formality was based on custom and perhaps natural reason—so societies before the emergence of positive police departments had police, although usually merged in customary institutions, such as the family.

An example may be drawn from English history. While the monarch in theory had ultimate authority for keeping the peace, "it had been the custom since Anglo-Saxon times for the king to delegate much of the responsibility to his subjects" (Hanawalt 32). In 899, England under King Alfred established the "Frankpledge System," which survived into the fourteenth century. It constituted a system of policing in which men of the village "had the primary responsibility for ensuring the good behavior of their neighbors and for identifying, pursuing, catching, imprisoning, and trying felons" (32). This system consisted of a series of extensions of the family, and was well adapted to enforcing the customary norms of that highly local order. Family men (who by the Assize of Arms in 1181 were required to be armed)[2] swore to respond to a "hue and cry" that a crime was committed and apprehend the offender (33). The system was organized into families of ten, which were called a "tithing," with a "tithing-man" at its head. One hundred families constituted a "ten tithing" under a "constable." Several ten tithings were under a "shire-reeve," from which our word sheriff derives.[3] The family, however, was more than a block upon which Frankpledge policing was built. It was an ordering normative conception. For example, the manorial lord's group of armed retainers who were not necessarily related by kinship to him (and who supervised the stewards and bailiffs and enforced his prerogatives vis-a-vis the villagers) was referred to as his *familia* (31). The term conveyed the type as well as the closeness and significance of their bond to the lord. So dominant was the family as an ordering conception in English history that William Blackstone in his *Commentaries* likens the state of social civility he calls "police" to "a well governed family" (Book IV 162). By the fifteenth century, however, Frankpledge was superseded by a system of local constables tied to the justices of the peace. That still comparatively local system of police, that included sheriffs, continued more or less for four hundred years until events in the nineteenth century precipitated the leap to formal bureaucratization and the establishment of police departments as we know them today (Light 99).

Analogously, there are different species of law that preceded Hart's positivist law. Sir Henry Maine in his classic treatise *Ancient Law* locates legislated law, the central case of positivist law, at the end of a long genealogy of species of law that are for the most part not positivist. (Maine identifies six stages of law. In the earliest, law largely took the form of *themistes* of "divine" inspiration. Law was spirit; it was "in the air," so to speak. Later epochs included the era of customary law—law was implicit in habitual conduct—then codified law—where it was the explicit product of enactment, followed by the stages of "legal fiction," "ideal models of law," and only then legislation.) It seems fair to assert that all ordered societies have some kind or degree of law. In traditional societies, the law was implicit in long-established social arrangements such as the family. In modern liberal and commercially oriented societies, the law is more what Lon Fuller calls "made" or "explicit" law, that is, the product of enactment by formally constituted officials (*Anatomy of Law* 43ff). It is more the product of individuals or groups pressing agendas in formal assemblies such as legislatures, conscious that their end is the enactment of law.

There seems to be no good reason, however, to deny that the ordering mechanisms typical of traditional or communitarian societies are law, or to say that it is only modern liberal and especially commercially oriented societies that have law. It is better to acknowledge that different kinds of societies have law that differs in kind; more particularly differing in the kind and degree of formality characteristic of its law. These differing forms of law may be referred to as species of the same genus, law. Max Weber, for example, classifies three ideal types of societies organized by distinct kinds of authority: traditional, formally rational, and charismatic. The law of these societies I contend will differ in not only formality, but also teleology and historicity. A formal/rational society, represented in some degree by modern capitalist society, will produce law that is more formally positivist; a traditional society will produce law that is more formally prescriptive; and a charismatic society will produce law that is inspired and inspires and is more teleologically formal. In describing this last kind of social order, Weber focuses on the personal charisma of the leader whose magnetism enables him to issue law. That charisma in Weber's view, rather than tradition or formal validity, gives legitimacy to the law of this society. A charismatic law more in keeping with the religious tradition would be the one that embodied what Aquinas, citing to the Psalmist, characterizes the natural law to be "the imprint of God's light in us" (*Treatise on Law* 9). Moses' Ten Commandments may be considered as a manifestation of this species of law. As with the genus law, the genus police will differ in species and these differences will or rather should correspond to the underlying differences in law.

Our law is more formally positivist, inter alia, because our overall society is more impersonal, dynamic, pluralistic, heterogeneous, commercial, industrial and postindustrial, and individualist—conditions less favorable not only for the formation of customary law, but also natural law formality as these conditions contribute to the rise of moral relativism, which undermines belief in a universal moral truth and an objective human good on which the natural law is based. (I shall explore the connections between positive formality in law and various social conditions in part II.) Yet, as we shall see, even our law retains in its more particular manifestations nonpositivist law to varying degrees. Lon Fuller observes: "If we look closely among the varying social contexts presented by our society we shall find analogues of almost every phenomenon thought to characterize primitive law" (*Fundamental Principles* 243). This kind of informal non-positive law still prevails in some families, neighborhoods, small towns, churches, and intimate associations of various kinds.

"Informal" non-positive law intrudes even into contemporary criminal law, which is comparatively one of the most formally positivist bodies of our law. Lawrence Friedman observes that even here formal due process is in far less use than generally believed. (This was even true in the nineteenth century, the formal century par excellence.) While formal due process is on display in sensational trials or in cases handled at the top of the system dealing with crimes carrying the harshest penalties, below that in the vast number of cases, procedures are more informal and less liable to validation by a positivist secondary rule of recognition. This is the world where discretion looms large— the discretion exercised on a daily basis by police, prosecutors, and judges.[4]

Why the persistence of nonpositive law, even here? It is partly due to the fact that the formal criminal process is expensive and slow. It is easily overwhelmed, necessitating reliance on informal mechanisms. It is also due to the fact that the efficacy of the criminal law depends upon the integrity of underlying communitarian orders that keep crime at the margins. These communitarian orders, in turn, depend in large part on customary law for their preservation. They are less well suited to regulation by formal positive law—a subject I pursue later. Nonpositivist law persists in the criminal sphere as well because there society is not always focused on retributive punishment, an end well suited to formal positive law. Goals of deterrence, rehabilitation, restorative justice, and community order are served as well and these demand more informal mechanisms at home in other species of law. While the informal mechanisms and the ends of order maintenance and crime control may raise legitimate concerns about sacrificing those goods served by formal due process, these concerns may be addressed and the price incurred as far as due process is concerned reduced as law may produce other kinds of compensating formality. Customary law, for example, can provide a useful check on the behavior of officials through its own species of formality (prescriptive formality), thereby serving the end of due process. It could be said that this formality is superior to positive formality because it already exists in the habits of people as opposed to positive formality, which is "on the books" so to speak but requires existential enforcement. (Natural law formality also checks official discretion by the constraint of justice and right, as, e.g., expressed through conscience and embodied in the principle of fidelity to law.) I shall dilate on the different kinds of formality and their operation in part II.

Our formal positivist law is seen as out of place in more homogeneous, traditionally ordered communitarian and decidedly "nonprimitive" societies such as China and Japan (although less so with the westernization of these societies), as well as other Asian societies and African societies. When in Rwanda, a few years ago, western-style due process was employed to adjudicate the enormous crimes of genocide committed there, it had to be abandoned in favor of the more informal and traditional local law, which emphasized reconciliation over formal adjudication and conviction—indicating that the appropriateness of formal positive law depends not only on the kind of social order but also on the scale of the problem that law must come to grips with. There is indication that Chinese law, which has been more informal and emphasized mediation and reconciliation, is with the increasing industrialization and transformation of the economy in a capitalist direction, acquiring more of the features of western formal positive law. As China moves more in a "western" direction, the embrace of communitarianism in the American criminal justice system (through community policing, community prosecution, community courts, and community corrections) suggests that the American system is moving more in an "eastern" direction. The future will likely produce a fusion of "eastern" and "western" styles of law and police.

That our society cannot have law and police without a relatively high degree of positivism, however, does not mean that other societies cannot have law and police whose formality is not a result of positive enactment but is a more gradual product of customary practices—or that these other societies should have our kind of law. Recognizing that there are other kinds of law and police is especially important since there is no reason to believe that modern liberal and commercially oriented society is the final form of social organization of western man, or will be the final form of social ordering for humankind, or that in modern liberal society informal implicit law does not still play a significant role in the ordering of social life, or where absent cannot be generated to provide the basis for social control and the restoration of public order. Proponents of "fixing broken windows," as we shall see in part II, endorse practices by which police in effect help generate a customary law in their localities that, in turn, supports the formal positive law in an integrated effort to reduce and prevent crime. Kelling and Coles themselves, however, do not articulate the new paradigm in these terms.

# I

Charles Reith correctly holds that every society has police, that is, some means of "securing observance of law" (*Blind Eye* 11). Police existed prior to the London "Met" and its immediate precursors. So, of course, did law. While police and law predate their positivist forms and are coterminous with each other, police and law together have changed in species over time. The "Met" represented a new species of police. How then, given this variety and historical variability, might police be defined or rather described? We might approach the issue, as Reith does, from the role of police in securing observance of law and what that entails. Law observance, Reith holds, depends on physical (military) force and moral force. These two forces require a third, police force, which serves as "a medium through which they [military and moral force] can function" (Brackets mine, 10).[5]

Law itself may be characterized as the medium or integration of physical force and moral force. Law contains the power to inflict physical violence (a capacity emphasized by positivists), but in natural law theory, law is also an ordinance of reason integrally directed to securing the human good. Police rely on both the moral force of law, which has sway with the law abiding, and the force of physical violence, which has more sway with those who are not amenable to reason or admonition. (Of the two commissioners Robert Peel put in charge of the metropolitan police, one was a military officer and the other was a lawyer.[6]) One could say that when the moral force alone is sufficient, the police as external authority are redundant. When the moral force and the police force as a medium are impotent, then society must rely on the military force—as in the postwar period in Iraq. However, as recent conditions in Iraq and Afghanistan make clear, the military force cannot substitute for the police force indefinitely, as securing order on the streets requires winning hearts and minds and consciences, and cultivating a willingness to observe law. Police rather than soldiers (or diplomats representing central governments) are necessary.

Police preserve social order by invigorating ("enforcing") the moral and the physical (material) force of law. Physical force requires the gymnasium and the field. Police academies have historically addressed the physical vigor of recruits. To be a moral force, on the other hand, the police themselves must be people of moral character, since character is at the basis of action and reasoned judgment that precedes action. Unlike the man or woman of bad character, the good person takes as his or her given a moral end. He or she only deliberates and exercises choice regarding the best means to it. This presupposes a moral intelligence, what Aristotle calls *phronesis*, a faculty that correctly discerns the good and the efficient means to it, which moral character then acts on. (In policing, this means a faculty that correctly discerns in law an enterprise committed to realizing certain real goods, summed up in the phrase—a just order—and the means efficient to the production of that end.) Moral character alone while well intended might miss the mark, either in terms of what the right end is or what the means required is or both. The choice of proper means then requires practical wisdom and moral character that guide deliberation toward achieving the right end, produce the right decision as a choice among means, and then determine the will to act in accordance with the decision.

Character, of course, must be acquired. It is not an endowment of nature. Good education, good counsel, and good habits are essential. These require institutions that inculcate them and a cultural and social milieu that sustains those institutions and the character they help form. Aristotle observed that to a significant measure we learn to be good people by imitation. Good police officers are reared on noble examples of citizen and police virtue. If these examples are to effectively serve to inspire police conduct more than just incidentally, a professional culture is needed to articulate and transmit dramaturgical narratives of police heroism and admirable behavior that excite the desire to emulate. To foster habits of law abidingness among the citizenry (which is one way the police enforce law), they must themselves provide red-blooded examples of law-abidingness.

Since the moral force is expressed not only through good deeds but also through the force of reasoned persuasion—it is a *logos* in the sense of persuasive speech—police must be able to articulate to citizens the reasons behind the law they enforce. Police practice, therefore, demands a full-throated rhetorical capacity in addition to moral intelligence and moral character. Preparing the police to be good officers and competent law enforcers then is a tall order requiring the classroom, a professional literature and culture, and more. The police academies have not begun to address all these capacities. Nor has the profession taken up the issue of promoting a professional literature and culture that inspires police virtue.

As one may refer to the dimension of law's morality, its formality, and its material force (dimensions of law I shall examine in subsequent chapters), so one may identify in the principle of police a dimension of its morality (the force of its moral authority), its formality (as in its subjection to rules and other legal norms), and its materiality (the actual force for order that it exerts on the streets with particular attention to police authority to use physical violence in securing observance of law). With respect to formality in the police principle, as with law, one may refer to kinds and degrees of formality. Accompanying these qualities of the police principle and its embodiment in persons and communities of a certain character are the means by which they are made effective in society. This involves the constitution of police authority and the various instruments for that authority to execute its duties (ranging from the relatively informal practice to formal institutionalization, and within that range let us say from Frankpledge to the Met).

## *A*

As police has existed in ordered society for time immemorial, one would expect that thinking on the subject is not only modern but also ancient. Indeed, one can find a highly sophisticated reflection on police in the thought of Plato's Socrates. The first known political philosopher, Socrates, is also (though this is generally not appreciated) the first philosopher of police. In Plato's *Republic*, Socrates constructs an imaginary city whose guardians are a fascinating version of professional police. Their composition and education form the major part of the discussion, which concerns the nature and preservation of justice, perceived as a kind of order in the soul and the city. Socrates' analysis exposes the moral, psychological, sociological, and institutional nature of the principle of police that will preserve not only justice but also the individual's and the city's freedom.

One of the guardians' primary duties is to preserve the city's just order, which may be referred to as its law. Socrates characterizes justice as the "rule," the "practice," and the "power" by which the virtues of "moderation, courage, and prudence…came into being; and, once having come into being, it provides them with preservation as long as it's in the city" (Plato, *Republic* 111). Prudence in the Socratic sense is wisdom, which discerns the good of the city and the individual and the means to their realization. Courage involves knowing what is truly to be feared, dishonor as opposed to death, and acting accordingly in defense of the city. (Aristotle understands courage to involve the proper regulation of fear, neither fearing too much (cowardice) nor too little in the service of the good, the just, or the noble.[6]) Moderation involves a mastery of desire and spiritedness by reason, producing a harmony in the soul and the city. It is the ground of good judgments and the will to act on them.

Socrates treats these moral virtues, necessary for a just order, as civic virtues in two senses. They are not only virtues of the civil order itself but also virtues of the individual citizens who comprise that order. To be preservers of the city's "freedom" and its justice, Socrates teaches that the guardians must themselves be just. They must possess an order parallel to the city's justice in their souls—an inner psychological order in which reason with the help of spiritedness governs desire. Here the operative sense of the liberty preserved is moral liberty, the freedom to will and do as one ought (in accordance with rational desire of what is good) rather than merely do as one may desire. Where subjective desire is for something that is bad, action based on it constitutes the abuse of liberty, the tradition called "license." Liberty, then, is a freedom harvested from discipline. The mastery of desire is the key to this freedom as unchecked desire becomes a "tyrant" and "enslaves" the soul, deforming reason into a kind of cleverness applied to securing the objects of irrational desire. The enslaved soul is the criminal who calculates how best to get away with crime or the corrupt official who extorts money from the criminal.

The order the guardians keep in the society is an externalization of the internal principle of police and is the foundation for the civic virtues of courage, moderation, and prudence. To have the capacity to preserve the city's freedom, Socrates reasons that the guardians must be fierce and yet also gentle, indeed they must be "philosophic"— physical force and moral force are moderated by an education in gymnastics and "music." Allan Bloom notes that Socrates treats "music" here in a broadened sense and "concentrates upon subordinating the rhythmic and melodic elements to the verbal and rational content" (*Republic*, note 38, 449). As such, it could encompass poetry, mythic tales, and even speeches accompanied by music. Today, we might include literature and other liberal arts in what Socrates refers to as the

"musical" as opposed to "gymnastic" side of the guardian's education. For Socrates, physical training when pursued to excess intensifies
the guardian's spiritedness at the expense of his philosophical sensibil-
ity. This results in a brutal guardian whose judgment is impaired and
who is a danger to the city and its laws. On the other hand, pursuing
a "musical" education for the "musical" side to excess undermines his
spiritedness. The guardian becomes too soft to defend the city. The
education and rearing of the guardians, then, should keep the physical
and musical in proper balance so as to produce guardians who are wise
and spirited. With these two principles in proper balance or tension,
with reason in charge and spiritedness its ally, the desiring part of the
soul remains moderate. These liberally educated guardians are centu-
rions of civilization and defenders of law.

Police today, as Socrates' guardians, require an education and
training that cultivates and preserves the virtues of wisdom, courage,
moderation, and justice. For the "musical part" of their professional
formation, they should be provided a humane liberal education in
law understood as an enterprise for establishing and preserving a just
order.[7] However, police training and education alone cannot bring
about moral character (which is built up from youth on) and so police
must develop means to recruit and screen for good moral character.
That task entails judgment and determination, which themselves presuppose moral character on the part of the recruiting and screening
police. Police training and education (and departmental practice and
culture) then should build on and reinforce moral character particularly as it sustains law-abidingness and the willingness to secure in the
society and among the population observance of law.

Edwin Delattre's book *Character and Cops* is a fine example of
the application of virtue ethics to law enforcement. The importance
of the moral virtues to law enforcement is also well reflected in the
International Association of Chiefs of Police 1957 Law Enforcement
Code of Ethics. Appropriately articulated in the form of an oath, the
Code in pertinent part reads: "As a law enforcement officer...I will
keep my private life unsullied as an example to all, maintain courageous
calm in the face of danger, scorn ridicule; develop self-restraint; and
be constantly mindful of the welfare of others. Honest in thought and
deed in both my personal and official life" (Kleinig and Zhang 92). It
is noteworthy that the 1957 IACP Code does not separate the public
and private life of the officer, leaving him or her in private to live as he
or she pleases. These two aspects of life form an integrated unity, as in
Socrates' account. The Code also enjoins the officer to be unbiased:
"I will never...permit personal feelings, prejudices, animosities, or

friendships to influence my decisions." (92). The officer swears never to accept gratuities.

In 1991 the IACP promulgated a new Law Enforcement Code. The 1957 Code was reaffirmed with some modifications. For example, the law enforcement officer's fundamental duty is "to serve the community" rather than "mankind" (92), and it was supplemented with Canons of Ethics. The canons, comprising eleven articles, are not formulated in the first person as was the 1957 document, which is sworn to as an oath (usually at the time of the officer's induction into the department). Rather they take the form of rules specifying the various duties the officer "shall" perform. Failure to fulfill a specified duty can be the basis for disciplinary action. The 1957 Code may be said to articulate more an "ethic of aspiration" to which an officer commits, while the 1991 Canons express an "ethic of responsibility" according to which an officer may be held accountable. (The quoted terms are borrowed from Lon Fuller, *The Morality of Law*.) Interestingly, while under the 1957 document, the officer swears "never to accept gratuities," Article 9 of the Canons states a conditional prohibition: "The law enforcement officer...should be firm in refusing gifts, favors, large and small, which can, in the public mind be interpreted as capable of influencing his judgment in the discharge of his duties" (96). This relaxing or fudging of the duty, although it might be defended as more appropriate for a disciplinary canon than for a principle to aspire to, strikes me as ill advised.

## B

Police defined not as the principle of a morally ordered civilization but as a formal organization charged with enforcing laws, arose in the nineteenth century in England with the Police Act of 1829. The London Metropolitan Police is thought to be the first legally posited or formally positivist police force in history. It is noteworthy that the Met's father, Home Secretary Sir Robert Peel, fought considerable resistance when advocating for the new police force. Opposition came partly from entrenched local interests who feared that a centralized authority based in London, at some distance removed from local interests, would put their prerogatives in jeopardy. In Parliamentary debates, opponents argued that the new police force would be a threat to the cherished liberties of Englishmen. Peel, however, in a letter to Wellington responded: "I want to teach people that liberty does not consist in having your house robbed by organized groups of thieves, and in leaving the principal streets of London in nightly possession of drunken women and vagabonds" (*Supplementary Despatches* qtd. in Reith, *A New Study of Police History* 132). Peel's advocacy for the new police acquired urgency given the growing concern about disorder in the burgeoning metropolis of London. By 1829, London had experienced a great influx of people and very extensive commercial development. With a population of a million, it was the largest city in the world. The stupendous growth, however, was accompanied by an alarming rise in crime, vice, and disorder. In the end, although Peel was unable to secure the City of London's adoption of the new police, the new force created by Act of Parliament in 1829 would have jurisdiction over the surrounding metropolitan area; hence, the name "metropolitan" police.

Peter Manning observes that conservatives who opposed Peel's reforms in the period from 1822 through 1828, while conceding that a metropolitan police might more cheaply and efficiently police London, felt it would not only "reduce their power to rule in the city" but also "be counter to traditional organic or common law modes of regulation and enforcement" (*Police Work* 77). There was considerable legitimacy to these concerns, especially the latter. It was becoming patently clear, however, that the traditional organic law grounded in the preindustrial social order was ill suited to regulating the new highly dynamic industrial society that was replacing that order.

The rise in crime, vice, and social disorder prompted Patrick Colquhoun, a utilitarian social reformer, to write the first modern treatise on formal positive police, a seminal work that influenced Peel. Colquhoun in the *Treatise on the Police of the Metropolis* writes of London, in what amounts to an expression both of pride and shame: "this Metropolis is unquestionably not only the greatest Manufacturing and Commercial City in the world, but also the general receptacle for the idle and depraved of almost every country...Gambling, Fraud, and Depredation, almost exceed imagination, since besides being the seat of Government, it is the center of fashion, amusements, dissipation and folly" (*Treatise* Preface). Colquhoun draws parallels with ancient Rome (as had Gibbon a half century earlier in his great history on the *Decline and Fall of the Roman Empire* in 1776) "immorality, licentiousness, and crimes are known to advance in proportion to the excessive accumulation of wealth" (Preface).[8]

Colquhoun opens the *Treatise* with the pronouncement: "Under the present circumstances of insecurity, with respect to property, and even life itself, this [police] is a subject which cannot fail to force itself upon the attention of all" (Preface). By "police" Colquhoun explains he means: "the correct administration of whatever relates to the Morals of a People, and to the protection of the Public against Fraud and Depredation." Colquhoun focuses on crimes against not only property and person, but also morality, as the last contributed to the other two. It is worth noting that morals legislation and its enforcement, out of favor in the west today, was in the nineteenth century still considered an important part of the solution to the disorders of the new commercial society. Traditionally, the protection of the public morality was an integral objective of the police power.[9]

Colquhoun argued for a new police designed to replace the obsolescent constabulary that had been rooted in the local orders and that enforced the largely customary English common law. The landed aristocracy, the dominant element in the local order, had provided the basis upon which "the English Common Law was interpreted in practice" (Manning, *Police Work* 64). That law reflected the "traditional English style of life...patterns of respect and behavior shaped by centuries of mutual association with shared assumptions and ideas" (64). It was administered by justices of the peace who were "well-acquainted with the personal circumstances of those they saw and had detailed, concrete knowledge of local customs and traditions of justice" (69). The traditional constabulary was attached to them. Constables acting as agents of the judges would collect fees for catching an offender and for restitution.[10] In the period prior to the 1820s, police largely took the form of "loosely organized night watches and constables who worked for the courts, supplemented by the private prosecution of offenders in the lower courts" (Monkkonen 199).

Patrick Colquhoun appreciated that a new system of police required by the new social conditions presupposed a "new Science" whose object would not be the mere catching of criminals but the prevention and detection of crimes. The new science Colquhoun insisted should be based "not in the Judicial Powers which lead to (italics) Punishment (i) and which belong to Magistrates alone; but in the PREVENTION and DETECTION OF CRIMES, and in those other Functions which relate to INTERNAL REGULATIONS for the well ordering and comfort of Civil Society" (*Treatise*, Preface. Capitalization in original). The new police should be based in the legislative power. Indeed, the new police would be created by Parliamentary enactment and would be its agent, committed to enforcing that body's legislated reforms.

Colquhoun's treatise proposes: "a 'scientific' rational, prevention-oriented police...tied to English traditions of legalism and rationality." (Manning, *Police Work* 73). Sir Robert Peel's approach as home secretary was consonant with Colquhounian theory: "His overall administrative philosophy could be characterized as making fine adjustments in social regulation by means of impersonal, rational, and preventive modes of social control" (77). These developments in England became paradigmatic of the nineteenth century's approach to police. The century saw the "transformation of responsibility for public safety from local, personal, and voluntary groups to formally devised rational forms of social control" (60).

Peter Manning sums up the sociology behind the transformation of police: "what took place was the gradual decimation of an old hierarchical order based on personal loyalty, local ties, custom and deference, where sense of place was neither questioned nor questionable. What was in the process of emerging was a capitalist order relying on imperative coordination of social segments through rational-legal administration, where economically based patterns of exchange became determinates of social relationships" (81). The new police was a manifestation of that "rational-legal" style of administration.

How might this transformation be accounted for? In the older more communitarian order, a person's identity was in large part a product of his relationship to social groups. He may have fulfilled the role of father, farmer, and town leader (or in England, perhaps even lord of the manor). These roles were not individually constructed—as lifestyle choices—but emerged organically over time and attached the person to a broader tradition and history that produced them. In fulfilling these roles, the person's disposition was not self-consciously "deferential" as if to suggest he was suppressing individual desire to blaze his own path. While it cannot be ruled out that this may have occurred with some individuals, the assumption of roles was largely unquestioned; it was considered natural and thought worthy of a good man, who assumed that it was the duty of everyman to contribute to the good of his community to which he owed much, including his loyalty. These roles bonded individuals to their communities and committed individuals to a set of norms that ordered those communities. The orders of these communities then reached deeper than observable behavior, penetrating into a person's consciousness, forming a fundamental part of his or her sense of identity. Over time the internalization of the experience of community provided, among other things, the context for those ordered memories and habits of action and qualities of character that helped sustain that identity and helped form the basis of an existential morality.

Robert Bellah and his coauthors in *Habits of the Heart* observe that a true community is "a community of memory" that not only ties the individual to the past, but also directs him or her to the future (153). Persons in community derive their sense of a life worth living largely from an historical narrative based on the lives of parents, ancestors, and persons of substance. These shared narratives provide exemplars of virtue that excite the desire to imitate. There are also stories of scoundrels, whose behavior is disgraceful and to be repudiated. Such dramaturgical narratives form a part of the curriculum of a diffuse school of moral virtue in which the community's young and old are educated. In the United States, for example, prior to the mid-twentieth century, moral formation drew on a republican tradition that celebrated the virtues of Washington and other founding fathers and a biblical tradition that taught the moral virtues.[11] Reared on this kind of moral education, a person's view of his or her future was not a spontaneous construct of his own making, but a natural extension of a collective past that was prescriptive. The individual's sense of the wholeness of life and the interrelatedness of things, then, was based on his or her ties to a community of which he constituted an integral part. Law and police reflected and enforced that communitarian order. Both legal and police principles were rooted in tradition and moral virtue.

The diachronic norms that governed these traditional communitarian orders, the organic product of a collective history, carried strong sanctions when violated. In the context of family, for example, should an individual be tempted to violate one of the community's norms, this would be resisted by the counteracting desire not to disappoint parents or to damage their reputations by wrongdoing, because your name was theirs. In the event an individual violated the norm, its exposure brought shame on the individual and on his or her family. If the violation were especially serious, it brought ostracism. The formal sanctions of fine and imprisonment were largely unneeded.

The highly dynamic industrial society that emerged in the nineteenth century, however, rent this tightly knit social, cultural, and moral fabric. Increasingly, individuals left rural towns and farms for work in the cities. Mass migration and urbanization produced metropolises, such as London and New York, where uprooted individuals had no previous ties and could live relatively anonymously.[12] The move to the cities freed the individual from the bonds of country; he or she could now choose his or her relationships, or perhaps even choose isolation over social life. No longer bound to a collective past, a person's identity was now more up to that individual. This social environment was productive of what Robert Bellah has called an "ontological individualism"—"a belief that the individual has a primary reality whereas society is a second-order, derived or artificial construct" (334).

That individualism was already prepared for by political philosophers of the seventeenth and eighteenth centuries, such as Locke, who conceived of civil society as a product of a social contract. In a "state of nature," persons are individual. They enter into civil society by exchanging natural liberty for the rule of positive law. Despite the fact that this scenario at the core of liberal individualism is a fiction (no actual society is based on a contract of its members nor is anyone born into a state of nature that is precivil society), the new social order would lend it a kind of credibility. It would only be a matter of time before the individual would think that he could choose not only his own relationships and future, but also his own norms, giving rise to a normative individualism.

With the emergence of a highly dynamic industrial society, the idea that law itself was an organic part of an existential order that was inherited and to be discovered no longer rang true; rather, law would seem to be the invention of individual wills responding to present exigencies. The law would lose its historical and natural character. Jeremy Bentham could with some credibility dismiss customary law as mere "fiction" and deride natural rights as mere "nonsense upon stilts" (*Of Laws in General* in Feinberg and Coleman 36 and "Anarchical Fallacies" line 229, respectively). The ascendant ontological, normative, and existential individualism readily coupled with a legal positivism that displaced a more natural and historical jurisprudence.

However, the romantic myth of an autonomous individual, liberated from prescriptive norms not of his or her own choosing, would be difficult to sustain, given the hard facts of life in the gritty urban Dickensian landscape. The new economy did not leave it to individuals to legislate their own norms; rather in large part, it substituted a new set of norms for the old ones. These would be of the newly formed "artificial persons," the status that the law conferred on the new corporate entities. The corporations were not natural or organic communities, outgrowths of smaller associations such as families; rather, they were synthetic constructs organized by the positing of rules and procedures (or bylaws) that coordinated the activities of their members toward the realization of the corporation's ends, whatever they were, but typically the making of profits. This governance by abstract posited rules constituted a formal rationality to which individuals in their work life were expected to conform.

Prior to the nineteenth century, wealth in England had largely been in the hands of the aristocracy and was based in land, which is fixed, immoveable, and decidedly local. The landed aristocracy served as guardians (and police) of the social order. They were bound by a prescriptive set of duties known as *noblesse oblige*. With the new society, capital (which is impersonal, fungible, and highly mobile) replaced land as the principal basis of wealth and power. Those who held capital would replace the aristocracy as the dominant element in the society, transforming the regime. The stake of the capitalists was not in communities and traditions as such, but in goods, ships, trade, technology, intellectual property, and even people, anything that constituted capital.[13] These capitalists advanced their positions by exercising ingenuity, entrepreneurship, and a potent acquisitiveness. They created profit-seeking companies whose reach extended to national and indeed transnational markets. These far-flung dynamic enterprises were decidedly not local and not governed by local norms or the norms that had been passed on by the tradition. Nor were the new artificial persons (the corporate enterprises) bound by any code of stewardship equivalent to *noblesse oblige*. In fact, the new entrepreneurial powers could be quite hostile to traditional norms and social arrangements. This shifted the "moral" balance of power. The norms associated with the commercial enterprises would take precedence over those generated by the family and traditional institutions.

The new corporate order was based on a normative structure that rewarded individual creativity, adaptability, invention, productivity, and the willingness to move and change. Norms that encouraged entrepreneurship became dominant—as did those that rewarded the capacity to find or create markets. Skills that stimulated consumer desire would be highly prized. Associations organized for economic purposes reward those who make profits. A successful businessman is rewarded not because he is a good man, a good father, or a good neighbor, but because he has brought money into the firm. Scoundrels may be rewarded, while good men lose their jobs. A man who deserts his family or a woman who does the same to pursue some economic opportunity may, if the venture succeeds, get rich—while the man or woman who refuses to do this and instead places family above work may be passed over for promotion or even lose his or her job, and the family suffers at least in economic terms—to do good is not to do well.

With the rise of the economic imperative, centrifugal pressures on the family (a traditional transmitter of morality and convention) increased, as did the pressures on organic communities generally. The constant reshuffling of people and resources in pursuit of profit maximization produced dislocations, disrupted relationships, and dissolved traditional roles. It produced the mobile protean population amassed in the cities. Survival and success favored those who were mobile and adaptable. The effects on the family were considerable. Sons and (in the last quarter of the twentieth century) increasingly daughters left hearth and home and the old neighborhoods to pursue careers, which took them to distant locales, making a diaspora of the family. This meant that the family no longer had a determinate geography or history. Familial custom and traditions that required the regular gathering of family faded. The family ceased to be the principal transmitter of morality that it had been. A common education in the virtues, which was essential to moral formation in the older society and had been transmitted partly by the dramaturgical narratives that personified the culture, was also lost. It required the support of the smaller intermediary orders, such as churches, civic associations, and sundry community organizations. But as with families these associations, rooted in the towns, were weakened if they did not disappear altogether, as the individual and his projects and the corporate entities and theirs took priority. Here profits meant enlarging markets, which in turn meant stimulating consumer desire, which is infinitely multipliable. The acquisitiveness of the new society was in conflict with the traditional value of moderation.

Accompanying the increased social compactness in cities, the rise of capitalists and the fall of the aristocracy, the new individualism and consumption orientation, and the disintegration of social bonds and traditional institutions was a new form of social interdependence reflected in the new mechanical means of production developed by the corporations. This interdependence was technical rather than affective, it was impersonal, and it was consistent with the general trend toward fragmentation of social, cultural, and moral life in the society. The assembly line, invented by Henry Ford in the twentieth century, represents a pinnacle of its development. Here we have a segmented process in which the competences of individual workers are discrete yet cumulative. Individuals need not know the skills of other persons on the line and need not know one another personally. Indeed, productivity might be enhanced by separating them to individual compartments to prevent inefficient social (collegial) interaction. What is lost, of course, is the individual's sense that he is a part of a whole, a social consciousness and solidarity with others in the pursuit of a common enterprise—what may be called an ontological communitarianism. However, this sacrifice is "justified" by the efficiency it produces and the managerial control it fosters. (What may also be sacrificed, as Charlie Chaplin evocatively depicted in film, is the laborer's humanity.) The individual competence valued is that of skill related to the segmented task, rather than skill tied to *telos*, defined as the flourishing of the human good. Nevertheless, this form of social ordering did demand a morality of its own. It does matter to individuals down the line, and certainly to management, that workers come to work sober and perform their tasks competently and efficiently, hence the period's emphasis on enforcing the utilitarian virtues in part through the enactment of temperance laws.[14] These useful virtues, however, were subordinated to the ends of a commercial material society rather than directed to securing moral goods for human beings.

What this new environment produced was a "bureaucratic monoculture" (the term is from Bellah and his coauthors in *Habits of the Heart*) in which the individual pursued material betterment, where social conditions at least in theory allowed for upward mobility based on technical competence and contribution to profit. Material betterment could be achieved as the new market economy produced more wealth, a middle class, and a consumer cornucopia. However, the culture was predicated on a disjunction. In his or her private life, an individual was more free to organize it as he pleased, but in his work life, he was bound to conform to the corporate culture. The autonomy of the individual was reconciled (if uneasily) with his submission to the corporate hierarchy, by the relegation of the former to private life and the latter to work life. The division of life into a private sphere apart from work became a matter of common consciousness. The dominant *ethos* to eventually emerge was a version of liberal utilitarianism, a coupling of what Robert Bellah has described as "expressive" and "utilitarian individualism" (*Habits of the Heart*). Expressive individualism allowed for the growth of bohemian culture and the pursuit by the individual of his or her own lifestyle. Utilitarian individualism fostered the bourgeois values prized by the corporations for their workforces. This *ethos* would be secured by the larger legal system, which sought to protect the rights of the individual and referee a fair playing field ideally based on fair equality of opportunity, with freedom of contract or rather a libertarianism (in which the corporate person could dominate) governing the economic sphere.

The normative architecture of the new society that emerged was in part based on the elevation of the new moneyed wealth, the autonomy of the individual in the private sphere, the autonomy of the corporation in the economic realm, and the increased valuation of goods associated with formal positive rationality. The new market society promised to satisfy demands whatever they were. These would be within the choice of individuals. The society as such had no determinate end. Instead, the individual determined how he was to live. The corporation would determine what ends it sought to achieve, subject to market forces (which it could nevertheless attempt to manipulate) rather than the constraints of custom or tradition. There would be no public *telos*, as there had been in the older communitarian society. Instead, what was desired was the freeing up of a private realm where individuals pursued ends of their own choosing. It was thought that this would be well served by the operations of the free market, which would ensure an economy responsive to these desires. The public sphere was to be increasingly limited in its scope and authority. The disjunction of private and work lives, then, was accompanied by a disjunction of private and public life, with the latter increasingly contracted.

What eventually emerged was a new deteleologized and historically detached public morality, whose normative architecture was truncated to serve formal positive values, accompanied by a contraction of the public authority and the police power. It crystallized in the political morality of liberal individualism, which postulated two fundamental principles: (1) a "neutrality principle" that required neutrality in the part of the state with respect to "goods" pursued by individuals including corporations, and (2) a "harm principle" that prohibited individuals in their pursuit of their own "good" from impeding others in the pursuit of their own "goods." This individualism, however, existed side by side with the new economic structure, which by itself was organized along hierarchical lines. The corporate order, more than the democratic state, would be difficult to square with liberal individualism. Employees were not treated as individuals invested with autonomy while they were at work. Quite the opposite, many could complain that they were used as instruments of management rather than respected as Kantian ends-in-themselves. Nevertheless, the new middle class that eventually emerged progressively shed traditional morality and progressively adopted this *ethos* and that lent stability to an order that otherwise might have become polarized between oligarchs and laborers (or capitalists and proletariat as Marx envisioned). Its members were largely law abiding and the law that they obeyed was the new positive law enacted by the legislatures.

Outside of the realm of personal life (where norms were increasingly up to the individual) and work life (where the norms were largely up to the company) and with the disintegration of organic communities, the regulation of the larger society would now be up to the legislatures. The legal developments paralleled that of the corporate entities. The new legal order would be the product of wholesale invention rather than the offspring organically generated from natural communities. In the nineteenth century, law became positivized on an unprecedented scale as organic communities declined and artificial associations prospered. The nineteenth century in England witnessed extensive movements to codify English law, with Bentham and Peel playing leading roles. Legislation facilitated rapid, systematic transformation of law, which the common law could not, as that had proceeded in piecemeal manner by judges deciding individual cases without necessarily considering larger implications or wholesale renovation of law. The Parliament by wholesale legislation, on the other hand, could (and did) by broad strokes reform entire bodies of law, including the criminal law. The law that emerged was the explicit expression of the will of those who held sway in the new centralized state.

Legal centralization (evidenced by the rise of legislation as the primary means of legal development) went hand in hand with the organization of social activity by formal bureaucratization. The bureaucratic form of organization offered to the legal enterprise what it offered to the corporation: "Precision, speed, consistency, availability of records, continuity, possibility of secrecy, unity, rigorous coordination and minimization of friction and of expense for mankind and personnel" (Weber, *Law in Economy and Society* 349). These were formal qualities highly prized by the new society. Bureaucratically organized work, Max Weber explains, exerts: "a steady and definite pressure in the direction of maximum acceleration of the reaction of the administration to the given situation" (350). It was well suited to the new dynamic society and the new police force necessary for enforcing order within it. In American policing, this can be seen in the Reform Model's emphasis on response time.

Professional exertion Max Weber notes is "without regard to person" and "without bias or favor" (351), virtues of formal justice, and reform policing. The new professions would be governed by "logical sublimation," "deductive rigor," and a "rational technique in procedure" (304). The professional would be "emotionally detached" and directed by the organization's rules and procedures. Formal bureaucratization maximized the "possibility for the realization of the division of labor in administration according to purely technical considerations, allocating individual tasks to functionaries who are trained as specialists and who continuously add to their experience by constant practice" (351). Sir Robert Peel's reforms of the criminal law and his establishment of a new formal positive professional police were in considerable part an instance of this formal rationalization and bureaucratization of law and law enforcement. Over time this formal rationalization, however, would produce a new positivist vision of the professional committed to precision without regard to end, as with the policeman who enforces the rules without questioning what their justifying purposes might be—a professional virtually indistinguishable from the professional assassin played by Max Von Sydow in the film *Three Days of the Condor.*

The mobility of population, the breakdown of multigenerational families and social groups, and the massing of largely anonymous individuals in cities meant that the informal sanctions of traditional societies (such as shame, public humiliation by pillorying or other forms of exposure, the censure of neighbors, and the reliance on their good will, dependent as these are on social integration) lost their effectiveness. It is no accident that the nineteenth century witnessed the rise of the modern prison, which would be offered as a substitute for the loss of the traditional mechanisms. The solicitous if oppressive scrutiny of the traditional community (of which Hawthorne's Salem in *The Scarlet Letter* provides an image) was replaced by the more technologically based observation of the modern prison, which found purest expression in Bentham's *Panopticon,* whose effectiveness derives not from its correspondence to norms internalized by individuals but instead from the capacity of technology to provide constant external surveillance.[15]

To conclude, the passing of a social order rooted in the local community had left a vacuum in the policing principle. The local community to the extent it remained intact had less and less relevance to the law legislated in the social centers and less and less relevance to the law that governed the lives of individuals. The new legal orders, however, required enforcement. A Frankpledge System, rooted in the traditional family and local community, would make little sense here. The police principle that emerged was a natural extension of the society and culture that necessitated it. It would be organized along bureaucratic lines, it would not be rooted in local communities, and it would be governed by principles of formal positive rationality that dominated the law and social organization generally. As we have seen, such an external police was very much needed. Conditions of poverty, immorality, and license accompanied by increased opportunity for crime (as individuals were in closer proximity due to the population density and lived more anonymously with much opportunity to hide in the crowds) gave rise to intolerable levels of fear, crime, and disorder.

In sum, several points should be emphasized. (1) The new society produced vast urban centers fueled by dynamic commercial enterprises that attracted large numbers of disconnected individuals without roots in community, who lived in relative conditions of anonymity. This fostered ontological, normative, and existential individualism where a person's identity would be derived (at least outside of work life) from his own spontaneous goals rather than through the natural assumption of a role he was expected to fulfill—a role that was not chosen by him, but rather for him. This was in contrast to the former society's communitarianism, which had produced a culture rich in narratives of people who lived exemplary lives rooted in community and the fulfillment of social roles. In that society, the individual's vision of a life worth living was rooted in a past, which reached back for generations and was directed by a sense of stewardship toward a prescribed future. In the new society, on the other hand, the individual was increasingly concentrated on a discrete present in which he pursued a materially comfortable lifestyle guided by his own lights and in pursuit of his individual interests as he perceived them, subject of course to the constraints of the new corporate order and ever vulnerable to the enticements of the consumption culture. The new society gave rise to a new normative architecture based on the individual pursuit of subjective ends where social interaction was regulated by the ideals of fair opportunity and fair competition that rewarded the production of profits and was based on liberal values and the utilitarian virtues necessary for diligent performance, while at the same time it sought to stimulate consumer desire at the expense of moderation. While the individual could be a "swinger at night," during the day while at work he was required to conform to a corporate role.[16] There he had to conform to a social hierarchy out of harmony with the autonomous self. This produced one of the most acute tensions in the new social order.

(2) The new dynamic society impeded the traditional mechanisms of moral formation, which were largely the product of intermediary institutions (such as family, church, and sundry neighborhood associations) and which depended on enough stability in the social order to produce customary norms, the individual habits that constitute the moral virtues, and a cultural and institutional framework for transmitting those values.

(3) As the new society frustrated traditional mechanisms for social control that depended on familiarity and the intermediary institutions that bred it, social organization whether in work life or social life more generally took the form of governance by a system of abstract rules posited in accordance with certain formalities. The positive rules bound persons subject to them and officials charged with enacting, interpreting, and enforcing them. Social life was more and more ordered by a system of formal positive rationality.

(4) The formal positing of legal norms in the legislatures substituted for their organic production from within the society itself. The

legislatures came to the fore as the principal sources of law. They would be focused on present concerns, not on keeping faith with the past. Reformers, such as Bentham, designed legislation to clear away what was seen as the dead wood of customary law. Legislation was accompanied by the formal positing of sanctions and the invention of the modern prison. The new regime substituted for informal sanctioning methods that were directed at the reclamation of character, the determinate prison sentence. The rationale for the latter was different than that for the former. Prison time served was considered payment of a debt incurred. The metaphor was well suited for the commercial mind and culture. It did not necessarily entail reform of the criminal or a restorative justice that repaired the damage to the social fabric caused by the crime, either in strict theory or practice. As for rehabilitation of the criminal, abysmal recidivism rates indicated that reclamation of character was not a serious objective of the new system of "corrections." The principal interaction was now between the individual and the state or the corporate bureaucracy. Intermediate associations played a diminished role.

(5) There were implications for the police. Policing increasingly became viewed as an external principle enforced by a formally rational bureaucracy of salaried officials limited by a highly formal positivist conception of the rule of law. Liberal individualism, which underwrote these developments, would produce increasing skepticism about the use of law to enforce morality accompanied by a disposition to contract the police power, particularly with respect to the public order and morality. While that has not yet yielded the repeal of all morals legislation, or in the United States the judiciary's declaration that all such legislation is unconstitutional, in the society the trend in personal life has been toward increasing permissiveness about morality and personal virtue generally. The immoderation unleashed has produced enormous black markets in drugs and sex that would fuel crime and various disorders. Moreover, these developments accompanying the rise of individualism and its companion moral relativism have further contributed to the decline of the family and other intermediate orders, the rise of negative communities (gangs and organized crime enterprises), and a host of other disorders. These factors have complicated the police role into the current period.[17] In addition, as character and personal virtue increasingly have been viewed as matter of private life, it would become more difficult to insist that the police themselves acquire the moral virtues of moderation and "keep their private lives unsullied" (IACP Law Enforcement Code of Ethics). This has brought the character of police into question.

Thus, the rise of formal positive policing in London in the early nineteenth century, as well as in other modern cities that arose in that century, was connected with fundamental transformations in the moral, legal, cultural, and social order. The society to eventually emerge would be dominated by a middle class/oligarchic class morality based on material gain and upward mobility grounded by a deteleologized public morality (based on abstract formal rules and focused on the deontological rights of the individual) and a new professionalism that bracketed ends and focused on means instead. What emerged was a society governed by formal positivist law that embodied these ideals, enforced by a formal positivist police that was organized as a species of formal bureaucracy. It was a limited police (subject to law and formal positive rules and procedures) that was supposed to respect the liberties of individuals.

## II

### *A*

The eighteenth century witnessed the rise of the political rights of the individual, as in the American Revolution, accompanied by the rise in the liberal theory of the limited state. This meant a new description of the rule of law and a new sense of the limited ends of government. Rights in the emerging tradition of liberalism were now at the center and could trump social interests. The rise of liberal individualism would affect the police. If the public and officials were to be checked from invading the prerogatives of the individual, this could be based on a highly formal positive law that limited official discretion. In this approach, the rule of law necessitated a high degree of positive formality in law and a correspondingly diminished discretion for officials. The idea of police as ministerial agents of law is a logical consequence. The formal bureaucratization of police, with the formal virtues it brings, is a corollary. The nineteenth century developments described in section I radically transformed the social order in such a way as to precipitate this formal positivist *ethos* for law and police.

Yet, there are certain limitations to such a formal positive profession. Too much detachment can be a liability, as became evident by the latter third of the twentieth century in the urban centers of the United States—an issue I reserve for elaboration in the next chapter. Because the more communitarian traditional norms and the institutions they supported (institutions that in turn supported them) remained essential to social order, a balance had to be struck between these and the more individualistic norms associated with the formal positive legal order and its police. While I have discussed Sir Robert Peel's approach in connection with the rise of formal positive policing, it should be acknowledged that it was more balanced than generally appreciated. Close inspection will bear out that Peel sought to balance the positive formality of police against some of the advantages associated with the earlier more informal police tied to their communities.[18]

Some balance between a libertarian and communitarian police, although not explicitly stated, is reflected in the nine principles of law enforcement Peel articulated as part of the mission statement of the London Metropolitan Police. The principles promulgated were as follows:

1. The basic mission for which the police exist is to prevent crime and disorder.

2. The ability of the police to perform their duties is dependent upon public approval of police existence, actions, behavior, and the ability of the police to secure and maintain the public respect.

3. The police must secure the willing cooperation of the public in voluntary observance to the law to be able to secure and maintain public respect.

4. The degree of cooperation of the public that can be secured diminishes, proportionately, the necessity for the use of physical force.

5. The police seek and preserve public favor, not by catering to public opinion, but by constantly demonstrating absolute impartial service to the law, in complete independence of policy, and without regard to the justice or injustice of the substance of individual laws; by ready offering of individual service and friendship to all members of society without regard to their race or social standing....

6. The police should use physical force to the extent necessary to secure observance of the law or to restore order only when the exercise of persuasion, advice, and warning are found to be insufficient.

7. The police at all times should maintain a relationship with the public that gives reality to the historic tradition that the police are the public and that the public are the police; the police are the only members of the public who are paid to give full-time attention to duties which are incumbent on every citizen in the interest of the community welfare.

8. The police should always direct their actions toward their functions and never appear to usurp the powers of the judiciary by avenging individuals or the state.

9. The test of police efficiency is the absence of crime and disorder, not the visible evidence of police action dealing with them. (Qtd. in Kelling and Coles, *Fixing Broken Windows*, 105–6)

The most quoted of these today is the axiom that "the police are the public and the public are the police," although this is often restated as the police are the community and the community are the police. So prominent in Peel lore is this axiom that it is often forgotten that when he formulated it, it was in the context of a new professional force for the first time removed from local control and administered from a central office. That "the public are the police" stands in dialectical tension with their detachment. There is then considerable irony in the use of Peel's maxim by advocates for the new community policing as against the professional law enforcement model that detached police from their communities. Yet, to invoke Peel on behalf of the new community policing is, as we shall see, quite sound.

There is tension elsewhere in the nine principles. Principle 5 that states the police owe to law "absolute" and "impartial" service in "complete independence of policy" and without regard to the "justice or injustice of the substance of individual laws" sets forth a highly formal conception of law enforcement that seems to demand a certain detachment or professional distance of police from their communities. The police are enjoined to provide a service equal to all without regard to race or social standing. Principle 8 serves this formality by restricting police to their enforcement functions. They are not to encroach on the judicial function that entails greater discretion. Implicit is the separation of powers that safeguards individual liberty. Police are to avoid vigilantism and abide by the rule of law. Yet, other principles prescribe a police service attached to the community. Principle 7 stipulates: "The police at all times should maintain a relationship with the public that gives reality to the historic tradition that the police are the public and the public are the police." They perform duties "incumbent on every citizen in the interest of the community welfare." Principle 2 enjoins the police to seek "public approval" and principle 3 directs that they are to secure "the willing cooperation of the public in voluntary observance to law" (i.e., secure the internalization of the police principle) and to secure the "public respect." These objectives would seem to presuppose an *engagé* communitarian police committed to realizing social goods. They suggest a more social welfare than individual rights orientation for the profession. Principle 9 assesses police efficiency in terms of achieving substantive ends (the absence of crime and disorder) not "visible evidence of police action" such as numbers of arrests—a criterion applied by the highly formal professional law enforcement model. In its forward looking crime prevention perspective, the Met's mission statement explicitly ties the police backward to the *historic tradition* that the "police are the public" (italics mine).

What is striking then in principle 5 are the categorical terms: "absolute," "complete independence of policy," without regard to the "justice or injustice of individual laws." A formalistic construction of principle 5, one that interprets law as a positive formality apart from its substantive goodness or rootedness in community, however, threatens to drive it in opposition to the other principles, as well as in opposition to itself, as the first clause refers to seeking "public favor" and the last clause requires police to offer "ready service and friendship to all members of society."[19] The danger of principle 5 (aside from the effects of its distorting our conception of law) is that if it were applied without due regard to the others, it could lead to too detached a police force. The professional law enforcement model that emerged and replaced the more community-based police officer in the United States in the twentieth century has been criticized for precisely this excess. On the other hand, were the new centralized police force to exercise too broad a discretion, it could threaten the liberty of citizens. As that threat was very much in the forefront of opposition to Peel's Met, principle 5 may have had to be articulated with such a high degree of "mandatory formality" at that time.[20]

If we take Peel's nine principles and read them as a whole, we see that he sought to preserve the communitarian aspect of the traditional police while at the same time establishing a centralized bureaucracy, at some distance removed from the community, that could efficiently enforce a law that was becoming increasingly characterized by positive formality; a law that was increasingly generated from the legislative center. The Parliament had become the favored institution to reform law and through Peel's instigation created the new police. The rapid and far-reaching changes in law and police were necessary to bring order to the increasingly dynamic yet disordered commercial society that was emerging. However, the new society would prove resistant to order and in the United States social disintegration in the urban centers in the latter half of the twentieth century produced levels of crime, disorder, and fear that the too detached police would have difficulty controlling. In the United States, the police had not achieved Peel's balance.

### B

The preceding discussion indicates that law and police vary in species according to social context. I shall next briefly relate law and police to social context, leaving a more detailed discussion to part II and a subsequent volume. Michael Banton in *The Policeman in the Community* observes that in 1962 Edinburgh, Scotland, there were two murders, two culpable homicides, and eight rapes compared to on an average thirty six murders and manslaughters and sixty rapes in an American city of similar size. He contends that the lower rates in Edinburgh were not attributable to better police work but to the fact that Edinburgh was a "more orderly" community than the American counterparts. Drawing from Homan's *The Human Group*, Banton reasons that social control "is a property of states of social relations, not something imposed from outside" (2). It is not something that is essentially posited. More important is the type of social order itself. What sociologists call "mass society" (in which individuals are amassed in given areas but without developing social bonds with people around them) has less capacity to generate social control internally than does a tightly knit society, where socialization is strong and identification with the community is stronger than identification as an individual self. Modern mass society then requires more externally imposed social controls, such as the formal positive police, to compensate for the deficiency of internal mechanisms.

Social control is directly related to the level of social integration in a society. It is high in what sociologists call the *gemeinschaft* society— the closely knit, small, stable, homogeneous society relatively insulated from outside influences, such as a tribe in a remote region or the Massachusetts community in Thorton Wilder's *Our Town*. In *Our Town*, people know one another, they share common values, notions of right and wrong, and there is a strong sense of continuity or history. The individual is known in connection with his or her family and the family is an institution spanning generations. The individual in *gemeinschaft* society may two generations later still be paying for the indiscretions of a grandfather; while the good reputation of ancestors may continue to reward great grandchildren. Such a social structure provides a powerful source for generating and reinforcing stable patterns of behavior and customary norms according to which individuals are punished or rewarded. Banton comments: "Law and law-enforcement agencies, important though they are, appear puny compared with the extensiveness and intricacy of these other modes of regulating behavior" (2). The policeman in such a society he holds, "obtains public cooperation, and enjoys public esteem, because he enforces standards accepted by the community. This gives his role considerable moral authority and sets him apart from the crowd socially, much as does the role of minister of religion."[21] On the other hand, where the standards enforced are not widely accepted, as when freshly minted by legislatures without regard to facts on the ground, the police who are charged with enforcing them are less supported. They come to be seen as "them" and not "us." The authority that the police enjoy is merely positive, it is the authority invested by the State.

Given my earlier analysis of law and police, it is apparent Michael Banton does not appreciate that Edinburgh had more (not less) law and police than its American counterparts. However, it was a law and police of a different species that was internalized in individuals and embodied in social institutions. Such law and police supplemented the ordering force of Edinburgh's external positive law and police. But many modern cities lack the internal principle of order (or police) of the Edinburgh that Banton describes. While governed by a largely positive law and police, if they are to reduce crime and disorder they must also be able to generate the same species of law and police produced by the smaller intermediate orders that helped sustain Edinburgh's order. The police appropriate to them will be hybrid.

## C

In developing his solution to London's problems, Colquhoun did not draw from Plato, although we may consider how he might have. When in Plato's *Republic*, Glaucon introduced luxury into the imaginary city they were constructing; Socrates reasoned that this would give rise to disorders both domestic and foreign. The acquisitive city, the "feverish city," by unleashing desire and multiplying it, produced among other ills social disorders and crime, the very conditions for which Colquhoun and Peel sought solutions in nineteenth-century London. It was these conditions that led Socrates to establish the class of professional guardians. While Socrates focused on the internalization of the principle of police and the formation of civic virtue through education particularly of the young, rather than through reliance on formal positive laws—the good city he thought would need few such laws and their proliferation in the bad city would be as futile an attempt to cure disorder as the attempt to cut off the heads of a hydra (Plato, *Republic* 102–4)—Colquhoun by contrast sought a solution to the metropolis' problems in "the general influence of good Laws, aided by the regulation of an energetic Police, [through these]…the blessings of true Liberty, and the undisturbed enjoyment of Property, are secured" (Brackets mine. *Treatise*, Preface).

Colquhoun's reliance on positive law (as opposed to Plato's reliance on a corps of elite guardians—the so-called philosopher kings and their auxiliaries) constitutes a stark choice in political philosophy and public policy. By now, however, it should be clear that Plato and Colquhoun faced rather different situations. Socrates' imaginary republic was small, comparatively homogeneous, and deliberately designed to be so. It was likely to reproduce conditions favorable to the establishment of a customary order that supported the relatively few positive laws the city needed. (Social arrangements, such as the communism of the guardians, the censorship of poets, and an educational curriculum that addressed the musical and the physical, were designed to dye the discipline of law into the souls of the guardians to discourage innovation and insure stability, unity, and loyalty.) However, the ancient Greek *polis* (not to mention Socrates' imaginary city) was a far cry from the diverse metropolis that London had become in the nineteenth century, where customary law formation was thwarted partly by the social dynamism, the conditions of anonymity of the population, and a political morality increasingly tipped in favor of the individual's autonomy and acquisitiveness (where the individual recoils at even the slightest hint of censorship or discipline).[22] This was a society where innovation and entrepreneurship were richly rewarded. The production of order there required positive laws enforced by a vigorous external police. That order and the police charged with enforcing it were limited by a legal culture increasingly sensitive to the rights of the individual, particularly negative liberty and privacy, at first in the economic realm but with time extended to the realm of moral culture.

This book argues that solutions to problems of social order depend on the nature of the underlying society. While Socrates' solution to the disorders of the "feverish city" may be criticized as inapposite to the modern metropolis, the positivist solution of the utilitarian liberal individualist by the same token may be criticized from the standpoint of smaller more intimate social orders such as family, neighborhood, and church communities—the intermediary social orders that are constituent parts of the larger impersonal society and upon which the larger social order depends, yet, which may wither under its centrifugal pressures. The challenge in the current times is (1) how to provide for the moral foundations of the public order in the absence of the social integration of the ancient city; or rather in the United States, the social integration that had been produced by the republican and biblical traditions both of which have been very much weakened in the contemporary period and (2) how to find the proper limits of social and individual goods, such as the public order and individual liberty. Intermediary associations of various sorts have an important role to play. For these social groups, the classical paradigm, which centered on the production of moral virtue, is highly apposite. It is important to see how modern societies require an approach to police that is a fusion of modern and classical elements.

Alexis de Tocqueville, the nineteenth century's astute commentator on democracy in America, recognized the importance of intermediate institutions (such as family, schools, churches, and civic associations) to the preservation of American democracy and liberty. They provided, he thought, the context for the generation of the social "mores"—the "habits of heart" and "of mind" that regulate desire and imagination, rendering them conducive to civic virtue. As liberty was increased in a democratic order, Tocqueville held, this had to be compensated by an increase in the disciplining influence of a public morality. The American framers, not to mention Tocqueville, recognized the importance of churches and religion, in particular, for preserving republican institutions. George Washington in his "Farewell Address to the Nation," for example, admonished his countrymen that their constitutional order rested on these two indispensable pillars. He was skeptical of the capacity of a secular humanism to substitute for them:

Of all the dispositions and habits which lead to political prosperity, Religion and morality are indispensable supports. In vain would that man claim the tribute of Patriotism, who should labor to subvert these great Pillars of human happiness, these firmest props of the duties of Men and cities. The mere Politician, equally with the pious man ought to respect and to cherish them. A volume could not trace all their connections with private and public felicity. Let it simply be asked where is the security for property, for reputation, for life, if the sense of religious obligation *desert* the oaths, which are the instruments of investigation in Courts of Justice? And let us with caution indulge the supposition, that morality can be maintained without religion. Whatever may be conceded to the influence of refined and educated minds of peculiar structure, reason and experience both forbid us to expect, that National morality can prevail in exclusion of religious principle.

Can it be, that Providence has not connected the permanent felicity of a Nation with its virtue? The experiment, at least, is recommended by every sentiment which enobles human nature. Alas! Is it rendered impossible by the vices?

(qtd. in Kmiec 51–2)

In the United States, the social order reflected and transmitted the morality of the biblical and civic republican traditions. These traditions constituted an important check on the individualism that tended toward autonomy and materialism. The founding fathers would, as we should, regard the disintegration of these disciplining forces in contemporary society as a matter of very substantial concern.

The formal positive police that suit a modern pluralistic commercial polity (one that like our own mixes republican and democratic elements) necessarily fuses formal and informal elements. That form of police is most effective when the underlying social order is neither too tight (where a communitarian order makes them partial to elements in the community) or too loose (where the social context is composed of rootless anomic individuals amassed in a given area where police come and go like a military force). The formal positive police are most effective when crime and disorder are at the margins. This happens when moderation in the social order is preserved. This appears to occur not when imposed from above but when generated from a pluralism of intermediate social institutions such as family, neighborhood, school, and church. These associations, however, do not arise as a matter of legislative enactment but evolve through the natural association of people who develop affective bonds over time, bonds that mature into a form of solidarity that is organic. The smaller intermediary associations build *philia* (good sons and daughters make good friends, good friends make good partners, and good friends and partners make good citizens) and these affections serve to moderate tensions that may arise among individuals, between individuals and the social group, among social groups, between the individual and the state, among social groups and the state, etc. Indeed, members of such associations think of themselves less as individuals and are more willing to fulfill social roles that secure for them social goods that the underlying associations give persons access to. One way of interpreting Aristotle's critique of the communism of Plato's *Republic* is that by absorbing family and property into the state, he destroyed the principle of *philia* that is at the basis of the city. The city is held together by a pluralism of associations. Unity is a limited good requiring, however, another limited good, pluralism, to remain good—hence, the axiom *e pluribus unum*.

The police as a profession need to play a role in mediating and moderating social conflicts and in so doing preserve the social distances appropriate to the social groups.[23] The kind and degree of formality in law and its enforcement that applies to these groups must vary with the kind and degree of *philia* appropriate to them—a subject I shall pursue in part II. Mandatory arrest in cases of domestic conflict may well undermine the family relationship and by doing so undermine the social and legal order.[24] Legislators and judges err when they apply thinking appropriate to state/individual relations to community relations. The principles proper for the regulation of the interaction of the individual and the state are different from those principles regulating a communitarian order in which the individual finds the fulfillment of his or her social nature. To impose the former on such intermediate institutions risks damaging them and ultimately the larger legal order they support. It involves a kind of totalitarianism that is opposite of Plato's (if Plato's can be fairly referred to in these terms[25]), where the city does not absorb the individual but rather the state/individual relationship and the principles that govern it absorbs that of intermediating communities displacing the principles appropriate to their regulation. Reith advocated a democratic police as opposed to the totalitarian police of the gendarmes. To be that they had to be of the community—hence, Peel's principle that the public are the police and the police are the public. However, the community is multiple and these plural communities stand in complex relationships with individuals and the state.

Modern commercial society gave rise to a social order necessitating regulation by formal positive law. In addition, by unleashing the acquisitive principle in human nature, it was vulnerable to undermining the moderation necessary for its preservation. The unleashing of desire brings with it a powerful source of disorder requiring a powerful principle of police to tame it. In the unregulated democracy, according to Socrates, it unleashes an equally powerful countervailing totalitarian force that is the germ of tyranny. As a solution Socrates, as we have seen, proposed a powerful professional class of guardians, fierce yet philosophic, that is housed apart from the rest of society to preserve its integrity. Such an institution would quite understandably generate anxiety in the liberal democratic republic. Liberal society requires a limited police, but at the same time, a potent police. Hence, its need to rely on intermediate institutions (and a moral culture that sustains them) that serves to generate an internal principle of police sufficient to moderate the individualistic and acquisitive impulses stimulated by the society's new economic and social order.[26] By invigorating intermediate institutions that provide for the formation of moral virtue in the citizenry, the desiring principle is moderated and the police principle and the legal principle at the same time are strengthened, thereby reducing the need to rely on external police and positive law. The external police, in turn, would take two forms with one aspect constituting an *engagé* problem-oriented community police assisting in the maintenance of order and the other aspect constituting a formal positive police left with the task of fighting crime at the margins. The new formal positive police would also have to be committed to subsidiarity, that is, to assisting the policed, police themselves to further reduce dependence on the external police. (I amplify on subsidiarity at the end of part II.)

The key today is to have a police that can restore order without becoming totalitarian. Community policing is careful to ground police to the community; however, when the police are not grounded to law, to morality, to the goods that we associate with our constitutional order, vigilantism may ensue. Police themselves must internalize the political morality that is the particular substance of our principle of police.

Positive law and positive police are insufficient as remedies for generalized corruption and as security for the rule of law. A corrupt society, as Socrates understood, soon demands a totalitarian (tyrannical) police. The attempt to forestall this by increasing reliance on positive laws to resolve the increasing disorders would, he thought, be to no avail; it would merely be like cutting off the heads of a hydra. Even in the absence of generalized corruption, however, positivism poses challenges for the ideal of fidelity to law. This is because positivism reads law as the expression of the will of the sovereign, whoever that may be. In societies with a strong libertarian culture, ultimately law, it is thought, should conform to the will of the individual who is to a large degree a sovereign unto himself. As Durkheim observes, however, "What my will has done, my will can undo" (*Professional Ethics and Civic Morals* 106). The dominance of the positivist conception of law may help explain why some American police did not cleave to law—it reflected the political or judicial will of those with whom the police often did not agree. Durkheim holds: "The true source of respect for law lies in its clearly expressing the natural interrelatedness of things.... It is not because we have made a certain law ... that we submit to it, it is because it is a good one—that is appropriate to the nature of the facts, because it is all it ought to be, and because we have confidence in it" (107). He concludes: "What matters, then, is the way in which the law is made, the competence of those whose function it is to make it and the nature of the particular agency that has to make this particular function work" (107). It matters that those who make and enforce law are good people committed to realizing law's *telos*, respectful of the rule of law, and sensitive to the requirements of law's historicity (i.e., its relativity to social contexts over time). These officials should appreciate the interrelatedness of these things. This means, inter alia, that our law must be to some extent depositivised, reteleologized, and be more historically rooted, if that law is to be, and be perceived as, both good and integrative of a "natural interrelatedness of things." A public conception of substantive justice must be revitalized as well as a public commitment to substantive virtues and social goods, such as community itself. This requires a commitment to a common good that is a fusion of individual and social goods, which goes hand in hand with the revitalization of community and sundry intermediary associations at the local level. The police are necessary for this revitalization. However, in order to serve it, they must break out of the formal positivist mold. To do this, they require a philosophy and an ethics as well as an education and leadership that foster the organic generation of a police culture more oriented to the good of community and productive of that fidelity, which binds police to law's service.

Sir Robert Peel's police sought to balance the formal rationality of law with the forward looking substantive ends of the law and sought to avoid the social detachment, which would eventually be heralded as the basis of professional law enforcement in the United States. As we shall see in the next chapter, under the professional law enforcement model, the limited professional police would be reactive rather than proactive, focused on retrospective criminal investigation rather than forward looking crime prevention. The model extended positive formality too far and the result was a formalistic mechanical police unable to cope with the rise in crime and disorder in the latter twentieth century—problems not unlike those confronting Peel. The current times then should harken back to Peel, particularly his dictum (and "the historic tradition") that "the police are the public and the public are the police." The times require that for solutions to crime, disorder, and community decline we look beyond the positive criminal law to more informal law that is more sensitive to local conditions, such as the law of injunctions, civil law, and equitable remedies—and beyond this to the capacity of police in conjunction with the community of persons they serve, to generate customary law. That is, the times require that we look to advance law's ends as mediated in concrete social contexts over time rather than enforce rules as ends-in-themselves abstracted from social contexts. The times require the building of a professional ethos and police culture that is, among other things, productive of those dramaturgical narratives that emerge from the life of community and provide models of admirable character, the virtues, and a substantive vision of the good life. The times also require greater sensitivity and commitment to the *telos* of law.

In the next chapter, I survey the American police experience and the recent trend favoring a community-oriented police. I evaluate the leading analytical approach taken to understand it (that of Kelling and Moore), before turning to the analytical framework that forms the structure for an integrative jurisprudence of police, from which the solutions to current problems of police may be derived.

## CHAPTER 5

# The American Police Experience and the Limits of the Managerial Perspective

The following account of American police history will be quite summary.[1] It is intended to provide some context for the evaluation of the highly influential managerial perspective Kelling and Moore have applied to that history.

Formal positive police departments emerged in the United States only two decades after the London Met. In the larger cities, such as Boston and New York, they can be aptly described as large-scale formally rational bureaucracies similar to the Met. Yet, one should observe certain differences between the American police and their British counterparts.[2] One difference is in centralization;the degree of centralization of police organizations that occurred in England was never reproduced here. American police service is delivered by nearly nineteen thousand agencies constituting what Patrick V. Murphy has called our "fragmented non-system of policing."[3] It is in part the product of a legal and political structure that has been more pragmatic than its British counterpart, one that is rooted in a revolutionary tradition that celebrates the rights of the individual formalized in a written constitution and Bill of Rights, as opposed to the English system whose constitution is unwritten.

A product of federalism, political decentralization, fear of concentrations of governmental power, a spirit of pragmatism, and dynamic social forces less rooted in tradition than in individualism, this American phenomenon poses particular problems for the student of police history. With thousands of police departments "pursuing their own visions and responding to local conditions" George Kelling and Mark H. Moore in their essay "The Evolving Strategy of Policing" observe that American police history is "incoherent, its lessons hard to read" (2).

Undeterred by this, Kelling and Moore, nevertheless, divine in police practice over time sufficient patterning to yield a periodization of that history, one that has come to enjoy widespread acceptance. American police history, they say, divides into three eras each of which is characterized by a distinct paradigm of policing. The history reveals: a Political Era (roughly from the 1840s that witnessed the first formal police departments in the United States to the early 1900s), followed by a Reform Era (beginning in the 1930s and continuing into the 1970s, as a "reaction to the political era"), and the Community Policing/Problem Solving Era (which they contend followed the reform era and continues to the present.) However, as there is evidence that professional law enforcement, the model of policing to eventually emerge from the reform era, still exerts considerable influence, it is more accurate to say that we are in a period in which the paradigm is shifting. Reform policing and community policing are supported by different values and Kelling and Moore are not neutral bystanders; they are among the leading proponents of the new policing. Under the current circumstances, to assert that we are in a problem solving/community policing era is itself a form of advocacy.

Mark Moore does note in his excellent essay, "Problem-solving and Community Policing," that no department in the country (at least as of that writing in 1993, but it is probably still true today) has organized itself entirely along the community policing/problem-oriented strategy (128). There is still some resistance to community policing among police executives and the rank and file. Nevertheless, it is fair enough to say that the new strategy has received considerable attention in the literature and among politicians. The Clinton administration backed it and the 1993 Crime Bill provided it with impressive financial support, although federal funding in recent years has largely dried up, putting the continued ascendancy of the paradigm in jeopardy. The 2009 Economic Stimulus Bill provided funding for policing and it remains to be seen how much law enforcement money will be used to fund community policing. Community policing still holds considerable sway in academic and high-level professional discussion of police, even if some police practice may remain resistant to its adoption. Problem-oriented community policing has much to recommend it and an appraisal of current policing must consider its interaction with professional law enforcement. I shall in the next three sections provide a brief description of each of the eras Kelling and Moore identify before considering some limitations of their approach to the subject.

# I

Kelling and Moore observe:

> Early American police were authorized by local municipalities. Unlike their English counterparts, American police departments lacked the powerful, central authority of the crown to establish a legitimate, unifying mandate for their enterprise. Instead, American police departments derived both their authority and resources from local political leaders, often ward politicians. They were, of course, guided by the law as to what tasks to undertake and what powers to utilize. But their link to neighborhoods was so tight that both Jordan and Fogelson refer to the early police as adjuncts to the local political machines. ("Evolving Strategy" 4)

Police service during what Kelling and Moore refer to as the "political era" was delivered largely through the cop on the beat who was often a native of the community "recruited from the same ethnic stock as the dominant political groups in the localities" (5). As a result, police officers developed strong relationships with the community. This had certain advantages. It put police officers in a better position to gather intelligence and cultivate informants. They could get to know where the trouble spots were and who the trouble makers were. However, there were disadvantages. It would be more difficult for officers to exercise judgment not biased in favor of the community's dominant constituents and those with whom they were familiar. Individuals were apt to be dealt with because of who they were or rather were not, instead of because they had committed specific acts violating positive law: "police regularly targeted outsiders and strangers for routing and 'curbstone justice'" (7). As local politics were controlled by ward bosses who held police jobs within their patronage, these bosses could exert disproportionate influence on law enforcement. The literature reports a disturbingly high level of control. Police were purportedly involved in "encouraging citizens to vote for certain candidates, discouraging them from voting for others, and, at times...assist[ed] in rigging elections" (4–5 brackets mine).

Political and biased policing coincided with police corruption—which was putatively widespread. In the NYPD, for example, certain officers provided "protection" to illegal enterprises "on the pad," that is, which had paid either the police themselves or their bosses for that protection. This seems little different from the "protection" extorted from businesses by the Mafia. New York City's "tenderloin district" (replete with gambling houses, houses of prostitution, and speakeasys) was a bonanza for an entrepreneurial police officer and apparently was a much sought after assignment (Lardner and Repetto 261–75). The principal function of the police in the political era, it is said, was the control of crime. Crime control, however, should be distinguished from the formal upholding of the law on the books. In maintaining order in their communities police were tempted if not pressured to circumvent due process of law. "There is more law in the end of a policeman's nightstick than a Supreme Court decision," was NYPD Inspector Alexander "Clubber" Williams' motto and he apparently spoke for many at the time (64–5). Williams joined the force in 1866. While brought up on numerous occasions for abuse of authority, he was consistently exonerated. Such an attitude would die hard. Even Grover Whalen, a Commissioner of the NYPD from 1928 to 1930, adopted a version of William's maxim.[4] A squad of his officers who were involved in highly publicized raids was known as "Whalen's Whackers" (206).

In the political era, communities evidently expected more than just crime control and order maintenance from their police. The police assumed responsibility for the provision of a wide array of social services: "municipal departments ran soup lines; provided temporary lodging for newly arrived immigrant workers in station houses; and assisted ward leaders in finding work for immigrants, both in police and other forms of work" (Kelling, Moore 5).

In sum, for the period generally referred to as the "political era," police were closely tied to local communities and responsive to ward bosses and others who controlled local politics. Policemen were drawn from the local community and reflected its culture and ethnicity. They often lived in the neighborhoods they patrolled. Informal political authorization and the decentralized organization of departments were well suited to upholding the local order built up around the customs and practices of the local community. The order that the cop on the beat maintained was largely determined by such local politics. This made policing appear more like pre-Peel-type policing. Minorities and outsiders could be the recipients of a rough justice. In the final analysis, the political era has been roundly criticized for its corruption and discrimination.

It would appear that the progress toward formal rationalization of the police service in the United States as compared to England was slowed by local control and the decentralization that dominated the political era. It would, inter alia, take the progressive movement with its de-emphasis on local history and its emphasis on forward looking reform to bring forth a more complete transformation of policing toward the formal positive model.

## II

Kelling and Moore observe: "Control over police by local politicians, conflict between urban reformers and local ward leaders over the enforcement of laws regulating the morality of urban immigrants, and abuses (corruption, for example) that resulted from the intimacy between police and political leaders and citizens produced a continuous struggle for control over police during the late nineteenth and early twentieth centuries" (7–8). It was from this struggle that Reform Era policing emerged. That style of policing would eventually be refined into what Mark Moore has defined as "Professional Law Enforcement"—the paradigm that today vies with problem-oriented/community policing.

The political style of policing had come under concerted attack with the arrival of the Progressive Movement bent on cleaning up government and reforming the ills wrought by industrialization. Theodore Roosevelt, a major figure in this movement, served as President of the NYPD Board of Commissioners and attempted reforms of that organization, apparently, not with complete success. Lardner and Repetto in NYPD comment "The police job had gotten the better of Roosevelt. Running the country was, comparatively speaking, a breeze" (124).

Although the authorization for police in the Political Era came in large measure from local politics, the reform era sought to curb political interference and corruption through the formal limits of the positive law and a new professionalism organized around the enforcement of that law. Police would be seen not as municipal employees who served at the pleasure of their superiors, but rather as officials whose allegiance was to law itself. Kelling and Moore observe:

> Law, especially criminal law, and police professionalism were established as the principal bases of police legitimacy. When police were asked why they performed as they did, the most common answer was that they enforce law. When they chose not to enforce law—for instance, in a riot when police isolated an area rather than arrest looters—police justification for such action was found in their claim to professional knowledge, skills, and values which uniquely qualified them to make such tactical decisions. Even in riot situations, police rejected the idea that political leaders should make tactical decisions; that was a police responsibility. (9)

I would note that by not arresting looters, the police were not necessarily refusing to enforce law, but as law now was seen in more formal positivist terms, the tendency was to perceive it that way. Reform policing entailed a formal positive law enforcement augmented by technical expertise.

This produced a narrower conception of the police function. Police retrenched into reactive criminal law enforcement, backing off from crime prevention that was the hallmark of Peel's policing. They also shed the social services: Roosevelt in New York did away with the soup kitchens and the sheltering of homeless persons. The social service work was increasingly seen as nonpolice work to be performed by other municipal agencies. Professionalization implied specialization; the police were to specialize in the detection and arrest of criminals. Formal legal authorization and the narrowing of function were accompanied by increased centralization in the organization with the bureaucracy reorganized to track the formal definition of crimes. Police division of labor was determined by formal legal categories: a fraud bureau, an organized crime unit, an arson unit, etc. The detective bureau came to carry cachet as the patrol bureau declined in prestige, signaling the emphasis on reactive crime detection rather than prevention. The "personal approach" was replaced by the "case approach" (13), citizen complaints were handled as cases. Reconceptualized in terms of formal legal categories, cases were abstracted from the social circumstances in which they occurred. Bureaucratic centralization was also accompanied by a deliberate separation of police from their communities. Police officers were not to be assigned to specific territories, as had been the case, but rather to types of crime. The professional distance achieved, it was thought, would ensure more impartial, neutral enforcement of law.

Foot patrol was replaced with the patrol car that came into widespread use in the 1930s. The patrol car became the "symbol of policing…it represented mobility, power, conspicuous presence, control of officers, and professional distance from citizens." (14) It allowed for a much wider range of patrol, disembedding officers from their neighborhoods. However, breadth shortchanged depth as police became transients. Police retreated into the "cocoons" of their cruisers. (The metaphor is Patrick V. Murphy's.)

The success of the police would be measured in terms of quantifiable criteria: numbers of arrests, numbers of passings, response time, and crime reduction as indicated in the Uniform Crime Reports—discrete data detached from social context and what is called today "quality of life." Police practice came to be under increasing regulation by formal positive rules and policies promulgated by the departments.

This progressed toward the formally rational administrative style characteristic of the professional law enforcement model. Mark Moore describes the style: "Elaborate policies and procedures are encoded as standing orders and regulate the conduct of officers. One of the most important jobs of superior officers is to see to it that junior officer's conduct accords with the standing orders. Policies typically flow from the top down and obedience is expected" ("Community Policing" 107–8). Reform policing, then, was based on a highly formal approach to practice. The individual officer was not to exercise discretion as the cop on the beat had, but was to enforce law by strict application of the legal rules and departmental regulations. This fostered a discrete approach to crime detached from social context.

I should note that the social changes discussed in the previous chapter (industrialization, urbanization, etc.) that fueled the nineteenth century trend toward formal rationality in the organization of social life generally also supported the trend toward reform policing or professional law enforcement in the United States. That style of policing was more formally rational than the more locally oriented cop on the beat style of policing it was replacing. And so from this view, some form of professional law enforcement was likely to emerge even without the progressives' political attack on corruption.

The 1960s and 1970s, however, brought considerable social upheaval, radicalization, and other destabilizing conditions. Kelling and Moore point to conditions such as "the civil rights movements, the migration of minorities to cities; the changing age of the population (more youths and teenagers); increases in crime and fear; increased oversight of police action by courts; and the decriminalization and deinstitutionalization movements" (16). One might add as a destabilizing condition that contributed to the rising levels of disorder, the general deterioration of traditional transmitters of morality: family, neighborhood, and church.

In the 1960s crime rose as did disorder and fear: "The consequences of this fear were dramatic for cities. Citizens abandoned parks, public transportation, neighborhood shopping centers, churches, as well as entire neighborhoods" (14). The social disorders that had given rise to the formal positive police in the nineteenth century, now, in their latter twentieth century manifestations, proved to be beyond the capacity of the professional law enforcement model to control. What was becoming clear was that the policing that emerged had failed to maintain that balance with a community-oriented policing that Peel had advocated. Reform policing had downgraded the order maintenance activities of police, but new research and empirical experiments, such as the Newark Foot Patrol experiment conducted by the Police Foundation, increasingly supported the thesis that police order maintenance activities undertaken in close association with the community were critical in restoring order, reducing fear, and ultimately crime. This fundamentally challenged the reform era's emphasis on detachment of police and reactive criminal law enforcement. It was becoming apparent that the reform paradigm depended on crime and disorder occurring at the margins. When these conditions became widespread, the paradigm buckled under the strain. The disruption to the social fabric wrought by the 1960s and 1970s meant that the almost exclusive reliance on formal positive law and police (the essence of reform policing) was not sufficient to upholding law and order.

Despite the emphasis of reform policing on nondiscrimination, minorities did not perceive their treatment by police to be fair. Police would be challenged by the civil rights movement, not to mention the antiwar protests. Moreover, research revealed that police still used considerable discretion despite the reform model's restrictions on discretion. The reform strategy had "failed to rally line officers" (15). It did not accurately describe the facts, it failed to provide a rationale for regulating the discretion that police exercised, and it was unsuccessful in controlling crime.

In sum, the progressive era in the United States ushered in a new model of policing. Whether called "reform era policing" or "professional law enforcement," the new paradigm elevated formal values over those determined by local politics and communities. With the reform era, a highly formal version of policing emerged that was detached from local community control, that shed the cop on the beat for the mobile patrol by automobile, and that focused on retrospective criminal investigation rather than prevention. However, corruption remained and the unequal protection of the law afforded minorities continued to be a scandal. These conditions along with an eruption of crime and disorder in the latter half of the twentieth century related to fundamental changes in the social order exposed the deficiencies of professional law enforcement, precipitating the current paradigm shift to a new problem-oriented community policing. The shift in practice has marched under banners such as "fixing broken windows" or "taking back the streets."

## III

Mark Harrison Moore in his essay on "Problem-solving and Community Policing" expresses the current skepticism with reform policing:

"We can no longer be confident that patrol deters crime..., that detectives, working only from evidence at the scene of the crime, can often solve crimes... or that rapid response results in the apprehension of offenders... Nor can we be sure that arrests, even when followed by successful prosecutions, convictions, and jail terms, produce general deterrence, specific deterrence, or rehabilitation" (111–12). In other words, we can no longer be confident that reform era professional law enforcement has the capacity to realize the *teloi* of law.

Moore elaborates: "Strategists now recognize that the reactive nature of current police strategy sharply limits its crime control potential. Reliance on patrol [by automobile] rapid response to calls for service, and retrospective investigation virtually guarantees that police efforts to control crime will largely be reactive." Reactive policing treats calls for service "as discrete incidents to be examined for serious law breaking rather than as signs of an underlying problem that has a past and a future." (112). "[I]f called, police will often cut short the encounter if there is no legal action to be taken." As a result, reactive police know little about the people or situations they encounter and the police in turn become strangers to the people they police. "Taken together, this means that the police feel distant from a neighborhood's citizens, they seem both unreliable and uncontrollable" (113). "The police gradually became cut off from the aspirations, desires, and concerns of citizens" (117). In other words, the reform paradigm's failure to fulfill its promise (its nonteleological character) was also due to its neglect of law's historicity and its failure to tailor law enforcement responses to local conditions over time.

Drawing on the recent research and experience, Kelling and Moore write:

> The problem confronting police, policymakers, and academicians is that these trends and findings seem to contradict many of the tenets that dominated police thinking for a generation. Foot patrol creates new intimacy between citizens and police. Problem solving is hardly the routinized and standardized patrol modality that reformers thought necessary to maintain control of police and limit their discretion. Indeed, use of discretion is the sine qua non of problem solving policing. Relying on citizen endorsement of order maintenance activities to justify police action acknowledges a continued or new reliance on political authorization for police work in general. And, accepting the quality of urban life as an outcome of good police service emphasizes a wider definition of the police function and the desired effects of police work. (18)

While reform policing had contracted the police function, the new community policing expands it:

> The definition of police function broadens in the community strategy. It includes order maintenance, conflict resolution, problem solving through the organization, and provision of services, as well as other activities. Crime control remains an important function, with an important difference, however. The reform strategy attempts to control crime directly through preventive patrol and rapid response to calls for service. The community strategy emphasizes crime control *and prevention* as an indirect result of, or an equal partner to, the other activities. (19, italics in original)

While law under community policing would continue to be the "major legitimating basis of the police function," in Kelling and Moore's view, it would not:

> fully direct police activities in efforts to maintain order, negotiate conflicts, or solve community problems. It becomes one tool among many others. Neighborhood, or community, support and involvement are required to accomplish those tasks. Professional and bureaucratic authority, especially that which tends to isolate police and insulate them from neighborhood influences, is lessened as citizens contribute more to definitions of problems and identification of solutions. (19)

On the corollary question of what authorizes the new community policing, Mark Moore writes, "Community satisfaction and harmony become important bases of legitimacy along with crime fighting competence and compliance with the law. Politics, in the sense of community responsiveness and accountability, re-emerges as a virtue and an explicit basis of police legitimacy" ("Community Policing" 123). Moore adds, "Thus community policing sees the community not only as a means for accomplishing crime control objectives but also as an end to be pursued. Indeed, as an overall strategy, community policing tends to view effective crime fighting as a means for allowing community institutions to flourish and do their work rather than the other way around." (123). Moore observes, "the goal of policing is not just to reduce crime but also to reduce fears, restore civility in public spaces, and guarantee the rights of democratic citizens; in short, it is to create secure and tolerant democratic communities" (131–2). Community policing, then, is not just a means (a formal rationality), it is as well committed to the aforementioned ends, that is, it has a teleology. Community policing as well entails a broadened perspective.

Community policing approaches problems in light of their history and develops solutions that provide for a desirable future. Community policing looks backward before going forward. Community policing attends to the historicity of local orders and demands an historical rationality.

However, Moore acknowledges that police activities undertaken in light of aforementioned teleology and historicity, nevertheless, must be limited by formal constraints: "None of this is intended to make the police entirely subservient to the communities and their desires. The police must continue to stand for a set of values that communities will not always honor" (123). For example, "the police must defend the importance of fairness in the treatment of offenders and the protection of their constitutional rights against the vengeance of an angry community" (123–4). Addressing the danger that community policing's enhanced discretion poses, Kelling and Moore argue that it is less vulnerable to the ills of the political era because "The civil service movement, the political centralization that grew out of the Progressive era, and the bureaucratization, professionalization, and unionization of police stand as counterbalances to the possible recurrence of the corrupting influences of ward politics that existed prior to the reform movement." (19) Community policing, therefore, benefits from the adoption of various formalities that the reform era had achieved. The new policing that Kelling and Moore advocate, then, is a synthesis of professional law enforcement and problem-oriented community policing.

I tender two points on the Keeling and Moore analysis. (1) The sundry sources of authorization for police actions that they refer to, in "politics," in "community satisfaction," and elsewhere, raise the same concerns regarding the rule of law and a police discretion that is unauthorized by that rule, that I had raised in critiquing positivist police theory and John Kleinig's normative theory of policing. Law is not merely a "tool," let alone "one among many others." Law is an end as well and a source of authority for the instruments police use and the objectives that they pursue. It is because Kelling and Moore read law too narrowly that they need to find legitimacy for the broadened function from "other" sources. What they refer to as "political authorization" needs to be reunderstood as a legal authorization, where the authorizing law is partly grounded in the community's customary order, an order that is a particularization of the law's order overall. The new police practice requires in addition recognition that law is committed to substantive goods, which the oft used expression "quality of life," only vaguely suggests. This requires reading law's *telos* (for an articulation of community flourishing) as well as law's historicity (for articulation of the law's accommodation to the requirements of local orders over time as it realizes that *telos*). Community policing should be understood as cutting across the entire spectrum of the legal enterprise necessitating analysis of the adjustments required to law's formality (which in part concerns protection of rights), its teleology (which concerns the flourishing of community, a good in which the individual participates), as well as its historicity (which ties the individual and law to an organic development). Kelling and Moore, like so many writing in the field, miss how an enhanced conception of legal authorization, through an enhanced conception of law integrated into a jurisprudence of police, provides the necessary framework for justifying the adjustments. Kelling and Moore miss this not only because of the limitations of their concept of what law is, but also because of the limitations of the managerial perspective they adopt. This leads to my second point.

(2) It should be observed that the shift to problem-oriented community policing has in large measure been argued for from an analytical perspective that is the product of the culture it challenges, and suffers from some of that culture's limitations. The modern police emerged as a species of formal bureaucracy with the rise, inter alia, of industrial society. The critical literature has come from the positivist social sciences and most recently the discipline of management. Management as an academic discipline is the academy's response to the rise of formal bureaucratic social organization and tends to prejudice analysis in favor of the formal values embraced by that form of social life. Mark Moore, for example, subjects policing to the analytical/evaluative framework from which he examines private corporations. He applies management principles to the resolution of the policing problem. However, the tendency is to underestimate how a public service such as policing requires thinking different from that which governs private commercial organizations.[5]

I shall consider some specific strengths and weaknesses of Kelling and Moore's framework. In "Evolving Strategies of Policing," Kelling and Moore articulated an analytical framework based on the concept "corporate strategy"; they appear to use the term "organizational strategy" interchangeably with it. This produced a discussion that contrasted the three models of policing along seven "interrelated" aspects: authority, function, organizational design, relation to environment, demand, tactics and technology, and outcome. In his later essay, "Problem-solving and Community Policing" Moore defines "organizational strategy as "a declaration of goals to be achieved," which includes "an account of the principal values that animate the organization's efforts and that regulate the organization's internal administrative relationships and external client relationships" (104). The strategy is "justified as a whole by explaining why the particular course of action chosen is a beneficial and feasible one in light of current environmental challenges and opportunities" (104).

Kelling and Moore assert that the concept "organizational strategy" is useful not only to "describe the different styles of policing in the past and present, but also to sharpen the understanding of police policy makers in the future" ("Evolving Strategy" 23). They argue, for example, that the analysis is helpful in explaining why "team policing" did not endure. (Team policing involved the establishment of police units having responsibility for a particular geographical territory. The rest of the department remained organized along professional law enforcement lines.) "While a strategy, presupposing its separate authorization, function, organizational design, relationship to environment, team policing was mistaken for a tactic within the reform model of policing. The result was that it never became more than an adventitious appendage to the organization, never integrated into a department-wide mission, never developed department wide support, and as a result was readily cut off" (23–4). As an organizational strategy, community policing requires a general restructuring of the department that addresses all seven aspects they identify. The insight afforded by differentiating an organizational strategy from a tactic, then, is indeed valuable as is the Kelling and Moore analysis generally.

I have two chief criticisms, however, to make of the Kelling and Moore approach. First, it is too narrowly grounded on criteria of formal positive rationality. Second, it foregoes additional insights that are gained by differentiating an organizational strategy from an *ethos*, and a philosophy. As to the first, subjecting policing to a formal positive rationality is of value because it subjects police practice, which given the decentralization and considerable discretion exercised by officers is apt to be disorganized, or ad hoc, to criteria such as consistency, logic, and coherence—producing a convergence of mission, policy, procedures and rules to practice, thereby providing for what might be called an accreditation of police practice. However, the limits are twofold. First, law is not something that is simply chosen. It is in part the product of history and tradition—as in the London Met's principle that the police must "respect the historic tradition that the police are the public and the public are the police." That principle cannot be understood prescinded from the normative significance of that history, although many who invoke the principle seem to ignore it. To an extent we do not choose our law rather our law is chosen for us as the product of our history and traditions. These have a logic, formality, and rationality of their own, different from formal positive rationality. And that logic, formality, and rationality is integral to and should receive emphasis in problem-oriented community policing. I shall dilate on this in Part II. Second, law is committed to advancing certain ends (formal goods and substantive goods) that limit choice. These include individual goods secured in part by the natural and moral rights of the individual and social goods, such as community and justice, secured partly by the natural and moral duties of the individual. These goods are entailed by the new police paradigm Kelling and Moore endorse as that paradigm involves a synthesis of professional law enforcement and community/problem-oriented policing.

A similar deficiency can be detected in economic analysis that has found its way to law and police work.[6] Let us consider an economic analysis of rights. That one has a right under an economic analysis is a determination of a market, where individuals make choices based on calculations of value: both what they value and how much they are prepared to exchange for those objects of value. The analysis ascribes value based on subjective preference; it does not ascribe objective value to goods where that conflicts with the subjective assessments made by individuals and, in their aggregate, societies. What is entailed is a formally rational scheme that achieves efficiencies in measuring and to a degree rationalizing these subjective choices. A right to liberty, for example, is derived based on a cost/benefit analysis that makes it, as a subjective choice, worth purchasing at a certain price in terms of public order or public safety. But rights are, in one tradition, thought of as securing objective human goods, liberty being just one. Jefferson in the Declaration of Independence affirms that liberty is among those rights that are "unalienable." The utilitarian John Stuart Mill holds that liberty does not include the right to sell oneself into slavery—certain rights are not to be traded away as in economic exchange. Rights, in a deontological tradition such as Kant's, are rooted in the dignity of the person, which is not to be traded away. Kant's principle of humanity holds that a person is to be treated as an end in himself, never as a means. Economic analysis fails to capture this higher teleological formality of rights. (In Kant, the formality is deontological, and in Mill, it is a rule-based utilitarian consequentialist formality.)

Furthermore, market analysis proceeds from the perspective of the individual and his or her calculation of value. It tends to short-change social goods that are not reducible to the paradigm of rational choice of individuals. Social goods, such as justice and community, are argued for on a complex basis that includes not just consequentialist reasoning at home in economic analysis, but teleological/deontological and historical reasoning. It is important to note that this is true of individual rights as well, as the US Supreme Court has tested claims of substantive rights, for example, those construed in the Fourteenth Amendment's due process clause, in part according to their rootedness in the history and traditions of the American people. These rights are also given a teleological grounding as the claimed rights are tested in terms of whether they are "implicit in the concept of ordered liberty," where "ordered liberty" is a *telos* of law. The historical and teleological aspects of law, and derivatively law enforcement, then require that we transcend the formally rational criteria that limit economic analysis and the Kelling and Moore analysis, to include criteria developed from a teleological and historical rationality where the goods pursued are not merely chosen or individual in nature. I shall provide an elaboration of them in Part II. Therefore, one cannot simply extrapolate from the individual to the public sphere or simply apply the concept of organizational strategy developed for private corporations to the public authority.

Aside from these limitations, the influence of economic analysis has contributed to a degradation of our conceptions of police and law-abidingness. This is reflected in the new vocabulary that refers to citizens as "customers" of police services. Police are seen as selling services to citizens (where public perceptions are catered to as an aspect of marketing police to their communities). This distorts their vocation; police uphold rather than sell law. They must remain steadfast when the community demands action inconsistent with its law. Preoccupation with marketing breeds the mindset that "perception is all," which undermines commitment to substance and integrity in practice.

Peter Manning, who has taken up some of the problems raised by the economic analysis of police, makes the following argument in "Economic Rhetoric and Policing Reform":

> the economic or market metaphor, which emphasizes 'choice' or 'demand', is inadequate to explain those 'services' which are not chosen by an individual but which serve the interests of the state. These include the power to regulate, to arrest, to fine, to incarcerate, and to use deadly force. The economic conception emphasizes the service, choice, and demand aspects of policing, but denies the central fact of policing: its use of force in the interests of the state (Bittner, 1990). (459–60)

It is not only the state, however, but also the public at large and communities that have interests implicated. The law enforced is not only the state's, but also the communities' and their members. And it is not only the state's use of force that distinguishes it from a private corporation, but also its duty to "establish justice" and to secure to its citizens various goods, including the rights of the individual.

Peter Manning observes that as a consequence of the new economic analysis: "The traditional bases of the police mandate—commitment to maintaining the collective good, serving with honor and loyalty, and observing tradition—are being modified (Bordua and Reiss, 1966). These traditions conflict with pragmatic concerns such as avoiding legal liabilities and civil suits" (449). The preoccupation with limiting liability and civil suits produces a defensive disengaged police less committed to fulfilling the police mission and more obsessed with limiting responsibility to the adherence to rules—as expressed in the attitude, "All I need to do is follow the rules, then I've done my job and I'm O.K." The commitment to fulfilling the spirit of law (realizing its *telos*) is abandoned. Manning has made some additional points: "The present appeal to market forces for reform, analogous to deregulation, is a retrograde step with regard to civic control over police command and police accountability" (453), and "A more pragmatic, businesslike form of policing, competing to win a market share, risks the loss of the legally granted police monopoly on force" (450). It also risks diminishing police commitment to protecting the rights of the individual and their rootedness in the historical tradition that ties them to their communities and an organically developing law. For the interests of the state and the use of force (that Manning identified) then, I would substitute the *telos* of law enforcement. Law's *telos* commits police to serve the interests of organic communities and persons, not just the interests of the positive state. It commits police to securing an ensemble of goods where that end authorizes peaceful and coercive means, depending on circumstances.

The managerial market-oriented perspective tends to distort what police do and what law is for. The reasons that militate a shift away from formal professional law enforcement require as well that we shed a conception of police that substantially reduces them to the model of formal bureaucratic organizations of the same genus as commercial enterprises.

My second main criticism of the Kelling and Moore analysis, which is related to the first, is its failure to differentiate key terms and discern their relationship. In "Evolving Strategies," each of the models is referred to as a "professional ethos." Moore in "Problem-solving

Community Policing" even refers to community policing as a "philosophy" (126). Kelling and Moore are not, however, discriminating in their usage. The goals of differentiating styles of policing and sharpening the understanding of police policy-makers could be advanced by differentiating Kelling and Moore's key concept "organizational strategy" from that of an "ethos" and a "philosophy" and relating these terms to the "jurisprudence of police." This would link the analysis of concepts to the nature, functions, and limits of the legal enterprise. And that is important partly because it is necessary for elaborating the nature and limits of police authority. To hold, for example, that community/problem-oriented policing is authorized or legitimated by "community, law, and professionalism," as Kelling and Moore do, leaves unclarified how these three sources of "authority" are linked to the legal enterprise as an overarching legitimating and limiting concept. Corporations come into existence by the positive act of incorporation and they remain subject to law. But that law is not merely posited (as in legislation), it is an outgrowth of custom, tradition, and nature. These truths mean that "organizational strategy" cannot be the key term that organizes the analysis. An examination of the three terms ("organizational strategy," "ethos," and "philosophy") indicates that each addresses a fundamental feature of the law enforcement enterprise. A term that addresses all features of the legal enterprise integratively is still needed.

Moore's key term, "corporate" or "organizational strategy," describes a method or an instrument for getting things done—a *technē*. A "professional ethos" suggests something different. Kelling and Moore state that there is "a certain professional ethos that defines standards of competence, professionalism, and excellence in policing; that at any given time, one set of concepts is more powerful, more widely shared, and better understood than others; and that the ethos changes over time" ("Evolving Strategies" 4). Sometimes the ethos is more explicitly articulated (as let us say the reform era paradigm was through Vollmer and Orlando Wilson), sometimes it is more implicit in the way the profession acts. That the ethos changes over time—that it has a diachronic character—requires historical analysis to explicate it; the term "organizational strategy" is insufficient to this task.

Ethos (or habit), Aristotle states in the *Nicomachean Ethics* (Book II), is connected to *ēthikē* from which our term "ethics" derives—ethos is the habit of doing the right thing. As it is sustained activity that produces habit, ethos refers to the consistency of our actions over time. This is important to the genesis of moral virtue. For Aristotle, we become just men, for example, by doing just things with sufficient regularity that justice becomes second nature to us. Ethos, then, accounts for the genesis and preservation of virtue in action. It is the existential manifestation of profession. Ethos modifies profession as a certain way of life (as opposed to a plan or aspiration) that is regulated by the activity of ethical norms (through the exercise of moral virtue produced by moral character). Moral virtue involves actually doing the right thing for its own sake—it is an intrinsic goodness, it is not essentially (or exclusively) an instrumental good. In the instance of justice, as Socrates holds, it is both (Plato, *The Republic*, Book II). An ethos represents an established customary (habitual) normative order. It is productive of a tradition and reflective of an historical rationality.

A philosophy is yet distinct from an organizational strategy and an ethos. It implies intellectual (not just moral) virtue—the reflective thoughtful life. A philosophy of police implies wisdom, a learned profession, committed to knowing the truths of law and police truths. Acquiring such truths requires submission to scientific criteria of objectivity as well as discretion (discerning judgment) on the part of police, if the truths are to be correctly acted on. Philosophy is distinguishable from tradition or convention. And, as Socrates knew, it can come into conflict with convention. Philosophy then points beyond formal and historical rationality to a teleological rationality.

In sum, ethos suggests the existential manifestation of the ethical basis of profession. The term "organizational strategy" suggests its form—the means by which it is delivered—the instrumentality. Philosophy conveys the way of the reflective life of a learned profession bent on acquiring knowledge of the truths of law and of law's prudent application. The three terms may be integrated within the term "jurisprudence of police," where that term conveys law's historical, formal, and teleological rationality. Rationality in these three dimensions of the legal enterprise is pursued (enforced) through three corresponding dimensions of police professionalism—its professional ethos; its strategies and tactics, methods, and forms; and its missions and values, that is, its ends. The jurisprudence of police, then, is a philosophical, ethical, and methodological (means oriented) approach to the law enforcement profession. Because "organizational strategy" as a concept is confined to the aspect of profession as instrumentality, the "jurisprudence of police" is to be preferred as the concept that provides the organizational framework for analysis and evaluation. This is because it addresses not only the methodology of the profession but also the profession's commitment to the given-ness of certain norms (norms that are entailed by law). Police are not agents of just any enterprise; they are agents of the legal enterprise that is directed to the establishment of a just order, who, nevertheless, remain bound by law's formalities. In large measure, it is the profession's commitment to establishing a just order through law that distinguishes policing from just any corporation or organization.

Management and economic analysis, therefore, are better subsumed under a jurisprudential analysis than vice versa. A jurisprudence of police has the virtue of bringing in concepts and principles from legal philosophy through an integration of natural law, legal positivism, and historical/sociological jurisprudence. This integrative jurisprudence can illuminate the bases of the legal values—including the constitutional values that Moore sees as a necessary part (although not necessarily best accounted for on his analysis) of the community-policing/problem-solving model. An organizational strategy that identifies the end to be achieved, the values to be respected, and the social environment in which these can be accomplished is derived from a jurisprudence that discerns the ends of the legal enterprise, the law's formality (its formal constraints), and law's historicity (its context orientation over time), where the overarching normative criteria are law's justice, its integrity, its prescription, and its practical wisdom. These criteria are necessary for a legal enterprise that seeks the flourishing of the human good in community—a good that is variegated and includes individual and social goods. I shall dilate on this in Part II.

Before closing this chapter and Part I, I shall clarify my position on the Kelling and Moore periodization of American police history. While the broad strokes of their periodization may slight the details, operating on the basis of Kelling and Moore's analysis is instructive. It is not best, however, to interpret the "evolution" as a linear progression. Police history swings along the shifting axes of the legal enterprise, producing more in the nature of arcs than straight lines. Simple swings of a pendulum, however, suggest a single axis in the legal enterprise. In this book, I discuss law as shifting along three axes each of which articulates a fundamental tension in law. We need to conjure with an image involving three axes where swings of the pendulum are a response to changes in each.

Community policing does not represent, nor do Kelling and Moore present it as, a simple pendulum swing back to the political era style of policing (as if one ever really repeats history exactly). Kelling and Moore argue for a community policing that is a synthesis of the previous eras: as in the political era (without the partisan and corrupting politics) and with the continuation of the "professionalism" that the reform era, inter alia, emphasized. Community policing if it is to be defended will have to entail revision of the "professionalism" and the community orientation of the political era's cop on the beat as it integrates the values associated with the other paradigms. The synthesis of the elements of the various models (presupposed, e.g., in Moore's account) reveal underlying dialectical processes. The tension in policing as evidenced in the controversy concerning models (the dispute between advocates of professional law enforcement and the proponents of community policing) are to be resolved not ultimately by the police themselves but in the give and take within the society as it strikes the proper balances of the values involved—shifting and recentering the legal axes which both affect this process of balancing and respond to it, and to which the police profession is accountable. The eras represent (and the paradigms prescriptively imply) shifts along the axes of the legal enterprise as the society searches for its center in the twenty-first century, after the tumult of the 1960s, the culture wars, a host of social disorders, and the present insecurity surrounding the war on terrorism. The position known as community/problem-solving policing is an attempt to find such a solution to the current instability and disorder in the society: a shift in the ends dimension of law toward a greater value of community (as opposed to individuality), in the formal dimension toward informality, discretion and individualization in law enforcement decisions (as opposed to formality, uniformity, and the mechanical enforcement of law), and in the historical dimension toward a greater sensitivity of law and law enforcement to the relations and contexts that affect order over time (as opposed to the exclusive focus on the discrete impersonal acts that constitute violations of a formal positive law and are the basis for arrests). It reflects a desire for more order and stability, if not the restoration of a traditional or customary order.

# PART II

# Toward a General Unified Theory of Law: The Integrative Nature of Law, Law Enforcement, and the New Police

## CHAPTER 6

# The New Police and Implications for a Conception of Law

In the effort to reduce levels of fear, disorder, and crime, policing in the United States has in certain places in recent years shifted in strategy and tactics from the emphasis on making arrests for violation of formal criminal law to more informal means of addressing the disorders and incivilities that plague contemporary, particularly, urban life. Policing has also to some degree embraced the public policy that James Q. Wilson and George Kelling capture with the phrase "fixing broken windows." This shift that many believe responsible for stunning reductions in crime in certain cities such as New York, and which is argued for on the basis of a new problem-oriented/community policing model, has called into question not only the professional law enforcement model that had been the prevailing paradigm in the United States, but also the formal positivist jurisprudence and the liberal individualist values by which that paradigm is justified.

The new policing is best understood as involving a synthesis of a professional law enforcement model based on liberal individualist norms and a problem-oriented/community policing model based on more communitarian norms: a synthesis requiring certain accommodations to the law's normative architecture, including some reduction in the positive formality of law's norms and the revitalization of the teleological and customary dimensions of law. What is needed is a theoretical framework to examine the issues. In Part II, I produce the necessary theoretical construct by integrating perspectives associated with the great schools of legal theory: natural law, legal positivism, and historical/sociological jurisprudence.

Using this paradigm shift in policing as the point of departure, Part II elaborates a theoretical framework that identifies law's axial structure and the normative balances upon which that structure rests. It argues that certain shifts in that structure follow certain patterns across law's teleological, formal, and social/historical axes. These shifts are discussed through linking the police paradigms engaged to normative models that underlie them, such as liberal individualism and communitarianism. These connections are in turn linked to fundamental features in the empirical social order. The result is an analysis that exposes the implications of the new policing for our conception of law, law enforcement, and the values underlying our law. By drawing from the perspective of the police, generally overlooked in the jurisprudential literature, the analysis affords a step in the direction of a unified general theory of law that reconciles what the legislatures and courts do, with what the police do.

# I

These are compelling times for society generally and for the administration of justice particularly. In the United States, controversy over judicial appointments has intensified in recent years, fueled by debates over the jurisprudence of the judges that have brought to the surface deep disagreements over how judges are to interpret law. The question of legal interpretation, in turn has stimulated a spate of writings in legal theory with libertarians (emphasizing the autonomy of the individual to live according to his or her own values) and communitarians (emphasizing the good of community and the individual's social duties) weighing in on a host of social issues framed in constitutional terms. The theoretical re-examination of the nature of law stimulated by the search for a theory that justifies how a judge interprets law, such as the United States Constitution, has profound implications for the relations of the individual and the society. At stake is the kind of society in which we shall live—whether or not it shall be a society that must respect gay marriage or one in which the pledge of allegiance refers to a nation "under God," and whether or not our society shall be one that shares a common morality or substantially sacrifices the "general welfare" for the "rights" of the individual. These issues concerning the scope of the police power to enforce the public order and morality have found recent expression in the battles waged over the use of municipal ordinances to address problems of disorder in our public places. In various cities, police enforcement of laws against panhandling and loitering as part of the effort to restore order and improve the quality of urban life has been challenged as violative of the free speech and due process rights of the poor and the homeless.

Policing in the United States has been in a state of ferment as well. In response to public pressure to do something about crime and public disorder, many police departments have fundamentally re-examined their goals, methods, strategies, and tactics. In New York City, for example, stunning reductions in crime, disorder, and general improvements to the quality of life have been achieved in recent years and William Bratton, the former NYPD Commissioner, credited these successes in good part to the NYPD's new problem solving/community-oriented policing.[1] Nationwide, however, there continues to be resistance to the new community policing from some chiefs and from elements within the rank and file. Some simply prefer the old ways, others feel threatened by the changes in job description, and there are those who cleave to the "professional law enforcement" model, which focuses on "crime fighting" rather than community service. Critics of the new community policing who adhere to crime control values as opposed to due process values, ironically however, fail to appreciate that "professional law enforcement" as a paradigm is conceptually (if not practically) linked to more libertarian norms than crime control norms. While police have readily embraced the crime fighting aspect of the professional police model, they have been less warm to its due process values. With federal funding for community policing now scarce and state and local governments in fiscal crisis, it remains to be seen whether departments will continue to support with their own precious funds community policing programs.

The nature of the new policing, which Bratton praised, must be subjected to searching scrutiny, not only to determine what exactly is producing the crime reductions and improved quality of life (and whether and to what degree the policing is to be credited[2]) but also to determine precisely how the new policing modifies previously held views about the nature of law enforcement and to understand the normative structure upon which it is based. The new communitarian policing must be appraised, inter alia, in terms of values with which it may be in tension (such as more libertarian values associated with more formal conceptions of the rule of law) and from the perspective of our constitutional tradition.

The new policing, we shall see, as a response to deterioration in the quality of contemporary social life linked to problems of disorder, fear, and crime challenges us to rethink what crime is and what law is. It is at the point where the new policing causes us to rethink what law is that the endeavor to theorize about police converges with the endeavor to theorize about law. While much work on the practical consequences of the new policing has been undertaken, the implications of the new policing for the concept of law itself, for our conception of law enforcement, and for the values underlying our law—that is, its implications for general jurisprudence—remains a project largely undeveloped. It is to this latter theoretical work, which may be called the jurisprudence of police, that I now turn.

# II

Police theorists analyze the new policing in terms of a shift in paradigm from "professional law enforcement" to "problem-oriented community policing." Many have had their hand at defining these paradigms and in the last chapter I provided a brief description of them. "Professional Law Enforcement," which is a descendant of the "Reform Era of Policing" that began in the 1930s, is today generally characterized as policing in the form of hierarchical, quasi-military organizations that "rapidly respond" to calls for service and engage in retrospective crime investigation. This paradigm defines professionalism in terms of the detached impartial technically skilled enforcement of laws, where police are largely inert until an offense activates them. Problem-oriented community policing, on the other hand, is prospectively focused to prevent crime. As Mark Moore puts it, "Community policing emphasizes the establishment of working partnerships between police and communities to reduce crime and enhance security" (99). The problem-solving dimension, Moore observes: "focuses attention on the problems that lie behind the incidents rather than on the incidents only" (99). Moore's thesis is that:

> The prevalent approach that emphasizes professional enforcement has failed to control or prevent crime, has failed to make policing a profession, and has fostered an unhealthy separation between the police and the communities they serve. Although adoption of these organizational strategies presents risks of politicization, of diminished crime fighting effectiveness, and of enhanced police powers, possible gains in strengthened and safer communities make the risks worth taking. (99)

This position is widely held. As I argued in chapter 5, however, problem-solving community policing is more than just an "organizational strategy," it is an *ethos* and a philosophy as well. Adopting it, therefore, will entail considerable adjustments to thinking and practice.

Those who advocate for community police generally assume community to be a good thing and argue that strong communities are positively correlated to crime reduction. John Finnis defines a "complete community" as a basic human good:

> An all-round association in which would be coordinated the initiatives and activities of individuals, of families, and of the vast network of intermediate associations. The point of this all-round association would be to secure the whole ensemble of material and other conditions, including forms of collaboration, that tend to favour, facilitate, and foster the realization by each individual of his or her personal development. (Remember: this personal development includes, as an integral element and not merely as a means or precondition, both individual self-direction and community with others in family, friendship, work, and play.) (147–8)

I adopt this as a normative definition of community and the new policing may be seen as directed toward enhancing such "community."

The changes in law enforcement theory and practice, involved in the new policing Moore advocates, require rethinking crime and law. Let us consider how. Legal positivism defines "crime" as a prohibition enacted as positive law, as in the penal code. In this sense, as Herbert Packer has said, "we can have as much or as little crime as we please" depending, for example, on what legislatures make a crime (364). Likewise we can have as much or as little law as we please depending on what is enacted as law. The conception of law as a formally posited phenomenon informs "professional law enforcement," which conceives of policing as a formally rational bureaucracy in which the administration of police practice (indeed the police department itself) is organized around the formal categories of the criminal code—hence, police departments are organized into the homicide division, the narcotics division, the sex crimes unit, the organized crime division, the fraud division, etc.

The central case of law enforcement under the professional law enforcement model is the making of an arrest for violation of law, where the central question is whether the incident responded to involves conduct formally proscribed by some posited law. The process is one of abstraction and reduction—those aspects matching the elements of the offense are isolated and treated as constituting a totality. Police resources to be allocated to the incident are then measured according to the gravity of the conduct as graded in the law book. A robbery, for example, would be more important and receive "fuller enforcement" than, let us say, a regulatory violation such as illegal street vending.

The positivist conception of law coupled with the professional law enforcement model is in turn underwritten by liberal norms associated with the rule of law. Liberal legal theory in the main limits the criminal sanction to conduct clearly specified by legislative enactment of a rule, largely to secure negative liberty (the freedom from interference by others, particularly officials of the state). The legal rule, which proscribes a discrete act (defined in terms of clearly specified elements rather than a status or relationship), is articulated in a form uniquely serviceable to limiting the sphere of official authority. Actions falling outside the explicitly proscribed acts together constitute a realm of private action in which the individual exercises "liberty" free from the intrusion of public officials. The idea of common law crime (crime as defined by the courts after the commission of the offense but grounded in social custom rather than posited beforehand by legislatures) is rejected. So is moral liberty, a concept that distinguishes liberty from license: where liberty is defined as the freedom to will and act as one ought rather than the negative freedom of not being interfered with by others where the individual remains free to indulge in vice. (Moral liberty allows for legal moralism, the use of law to enforce morals.) The criminal sanction's deployment to make a person act in ways consistent with the community's sense of his own good or to impose the community's version of the good life on individuals is generally rejected.

However, as we saw in chapter 5, a major shortcoming of policing pursuant to the professional law enforcement model was its failure to control disorder and crime in the latter twentieth century (particularly in the urban centers) and that critics attributed in large part to the model's approach to crime and disorder as discrete incidents. George Kelling characterizes the practice this way: "A chronic neighborhood problem erupts: police respond. It erupts again: police respond again. In practical terms for police, incidents have neither a history nor a future. Consistent with their reactive, non-intrusive model, police are to refrain from taking action until an incident erupts." Such constricted practice leaves police hamstrung in their effort to reduce crime. Crime actually is not a discrete phenomenon or a purely formal one, but (as the new thinking contends) the product of material processes of decay, which if caught early enough and appropriately responded to, may be reversed thereby preventing crime. Kelling and Wilson used the metaphor "fixing broken windows" to characterize this dynamic. Wilson elaborates:

> We used the image of broken windows to explain how neighborhoods might decay into disorder and even crime if no one attends faithfully

to their maintenance. If a factory or office window is broken, passersby observing it will conclude that no one cares or no one is in charge. In time, a few will begin throwing rocks to break more windows. Soon all the windows will be broken, and now passersby will think that, not only is no one in charge of the building, no one is in charge of the street on which it faces. Only the young, the criminal, or the foolhardy have any business on an unprotected avenue, and so more and more citizens will abandon the street to those they assume prowl it. Small disorders lead to larger and larger ones, and perhaps even to crime. (*Fixing Broken Windows*, xv)

As evidence seemed to justify the increased emphasis fixing broken windows puts on order maintenance, the police were encouraged to eschew the old model's 'hands off' approach. They were advised to become problem solvers and that would fundamentally alter their orientation: "Problem solving defines not merely an incident but the problem that gives rise to the incident, with its history and potential future, as the fundamental unit of police interest and work" (Kelling and Coles 163). Taking in both past and working toward a desirable future, police would expand their activities to focus on building conditions and responding to problems in a way that prevented neighborhood decay and crime.

It should be remembered that the old model's response to crime as a discrete phenomenon was required by the norms supporting the model—liberal norms that confined official action to the commission of overt acts constituting offenses, to secure negative liberty. Preventive interventions on this view violate individual liberty. It was also required by the contracted conception of law on which law enforcement authority was based. Law on this view neither has a teleology nor does it have the quality of historicity. It is a positive formality alone and that limits the authority law confers on police, delegitimizing the more preventive measures. The new policing's holistic approach to crime as a developmental phenomenon, then, requires not only a different view of policing but also an expanded conception of law and a reassessment of the liberal individualist norms that supported the old model and old jurisprudence.

Courts could have difficulty making the necessary adjustments to their thinking. James Q. Wilson puts it this way: "A rights-oriented legal tradition does not easily deal with this problem. The judge finds it hard to believe that one broken window is all that important or that the police should be empowered to exert their authority on people who might break more windows. The judge sees a snapshot of the street at one moment; the public by contrast, sees a motion picture of the street slowly, inexorably decaying." (xv) What is required by the broken windows approach and the new policing it spawns is a new jurisprudence that correctly assimilates the insight that crime is a contextual and developmental phenomenon to be approached diachronically.

Legislatures would be challenged to think differently as well. While the formal positive definition of crime may be understood partly as a device to secure negative liberty and due process values, legislatures in enacting laws pursuant to the new paradigm that reads crime as a developmental phenomenon, should frame them so as to enable police, prosecutors and judges to best address the problems giving rise to the legislation and best advance the goods sought by it. Positive law as a norm ordering human behavior should be transparent both as to the disorder it is designed to rectify and the kind of order it is intended to restore or realize. The language of law should be framed to enable enforcement actions by police, prosecutors, and courts that have reference to social experience (i.e., law's historicity) and that have reference to the desired goods the law seeks to achieve, that is, law's teleology. An example of this kind of legislation is the federal *Racketeer Influenced and Corrupt Organizations Act*, 18 U.S.C. sections 1961–68 (1976), or RICO, where the preamble authorizes liberal construction, the statutory purpose is declared to be the dismantling of organized crime enterprises, the offense is defined in terms of a pattern of conduct over time including at least two predicate offenses characteristic of organized crime activity, and penalties include asset forfeiture. These features have enabled RICO to be more effective in combating organized crime and its collateral effects than traditional criminal law of higher positive formality. In various settings, but particularly in the sphere of order maintenance, legislation would have to be less positively formal and grant greater interpretive discretion to officials, thereby authorizing them to more affirmatively intervene to help build social conditions favorable to preventing disorder and crime. The new policing, therefore, presents considerable challenge not only for judges but also for legislatures, presupposing a new jurisprudence on their part that informs the art of framing legislation and that addresses the diachronic nature of the social order.

That crime is rooted in time, place, and social contexts that shift over time presents special challenges to police.[3] It requires among other things organization of the police department and the marshaling of police resources not exclusively in terms of the formal gradations of the criminal code but with sufficient flexibility to maximize responsiveness to the many forms of crime, addressing the social contexts that produce crime and the social orders on which crime preys. It requires a division of the force in terms of community assignments and responsibilities so that officers can respond to the particular order problems in situ. The orders responded to will include organic communities (families, various neighborhood associations, businesses, etc.) each having distinct and perhaps intertwined pasts and futures. Arson is not the same crime when committed by an organized crime figure to secure power over a region, by a property owner of a failing business, or by a juvenile engaged in vandalism as a form of expression. These acts are indices of different problems calling for different responses on the part of the public authority.[4] Sensitivity to local contexts may well require major reassessments of police priorities. To illustrate, Kelling and Coles report that in the 1990s businesspeople on Manhattan's Upper West Side objected to the high priority police gave to robberies, when the more important problem for them was "illegal vending." Analysis of the social circumstances revealed that the vendors were a magnet for drug users fencing stolen property to fund their habits. These drug users congregated on the streets and harassed shoppers and pedestrians to the detriment of the legitimate businesses. Given these facts, cracking down on the vendors would put increased pressure on drug users and traffickers helping to reduce the drug presence (and thereby, crimes such as robbery). And that, in turn, would help strengthen the surrounding businesses and community as customers return to the area revitalizing its economy. Under these circumstances, illegal vending had more serious consequences for the public order and safety than the police appreciated, warranting more police resources (31).

The reconceptualization of crime and crime fighting required by the new policing, then, requires a compatible jurisprudential theory (having ramifications for judges and legislators as well as executive officials) that reconceptualizes law and provides the normative framework that authorizes and limits the new policing as it addresses problems of disorder and takes action to prevent crime. The new conception of law should read law not exclusively in terms of posited rules pertaining to discrete acts (as positivism and the professional law enforcement model had done) but as an enterprise having a history (which accounts for the relativity of legal norms to social contexts over time) and a future (a teleology in which the legal and social order matures toward a fuller realization of the human good that is both individual and communal). This broadened conception would have the capacity to assimilate the new problem-oriented/community policing in a way that synthesizes the goods it secures with those goods secured by the professional law enforcement model.

Such an integrative conception of law will be informed by the perspectives associated with the historical, sociological, positivist, and natural law schools of jurisprudence. The integration of these perspectives in turn, I argue, will be linked to teleological conceptions of the public order that are more communitarian than the individualistically oriented conception of liberal positivism. We should take stock of the implications. From the standpoint of liberal individualism, a communitarian response to crime that may be more based on who the offender is (his or her status and relation to the victim and community) rather than on what the offender has done, threatens erosion of the conduct requirement of the criminal law, and poses a threat to the liberty of the individual in part by granting too much discretion to officials.[5] On such reasoning, liberal individualism demands higher degrees of positive formality in legal norms that more narrowly circumscribe the discretion of officials to make choices about the order to be enforced in their communities. Individual liberty on this normative theory is endangered when the community has authority over determining the "quality of life" to be enforced against individuals who would live differently. The circumscription of discretion associated with liberal jurisprudence is, however, likely to be too restrictive from the standpoint of a more communitarian jurisprudence that looks to restore order and enhance the quality of civil life where these have become priorities. Liberal jurisprudence on this account sacrifices the social good and substantive justice for formal individual values. The shift in paradigm from professional law enforcement to community-oriented problem solving policing, therefore, engages argument drawn from the normative perspectives of the jurisprudence and political morality that underwrite it and those that underwrite the paradigm it is challenging, as well as argument addressed to public policy and whether individual or public goods are to be given priority. Theoretical analysis must expose these underlying normative perspectives and evaluate them.

In sum, the theoretical discussion about the new policing must be expanded to account for the implications that this new thinking about crime has for the conception of law itself and law enforcement. It cannot be based, as has been the case, on a largely implicit positivist conception of law (and law enforcement) if it is to succeed in appraising arguments for community policing in light of challenges that come from positivist jurisprudence in alliance with liberal individualist normative theory. To illustrate, criticism that the new policing cannot be reconciled to civil liberties (e.g., those of the homeless, the poor, the marginal, or the deviant), and criticism directed at the difficulty of finding sufficient authorization for police enforcement or promotion of some specific "quality of life" or particular community standard of order, must be appraised from the standpoint of balanced argument that considers the norms derived from: law's teleology (where the norms involve some synthesis of the individual and public good and the rights of the individual may be defined more narrowly to accommodate the requirements of the public order), law's historicity (where law's relativity to social context over time is justified in terms of normative analysis that takes into account the circumstances that bring law into being and shape it over time, resulting in a law enforcement more responsive to local norms), and not simply law's positive formality. The values of formal liberty and formal justice and other values drawn from a perspective on law as a formal practice having integrity (norms associated with the professional law enforcement model as underwritten by liberal theory) must be appraised against the requirements of doing substantive justice and effectively securing an enduring material order (where the relevant norms are more communitarian and linked to some problem oriented/community policing model). The justificatory arguments and the arguments concerning police authority must draw from a richer normative theory that is based, I argue, on law's triune structure.

## CHAPTER 7

# Integrative Jurisprudence:
# Law and Law Enforcement's
# Three Dimensions

I shall now sketch the jurisprudential perspective that accounts for the theoretical changes in law enforcement presupposed by problem-oriented/community policing—a perspective that provides the basis of a new science of police and a new theory of law. As Mark Moore observes, the new policing is not a rejection of "professional law enforcement" (nor should it be) but a synthesis of that paradigm with the ensemble of ideas associated with problem-oriented/community policing. I argue that the synthesis can be achieved through a jurisprudence that is integrative.

"Integrative jurisprudence," a term in legal theory, refers to a perspective on law that combines the perspectives of natural law, legal positivism, and historical/sociological jurisprudence into a single synthesis. Jerome Hall apparently first introduced the term in the 1930s referring to an integration of natural law, legal positivism, and sociological jurisprudence. Harold Berman more recently reintroduced the term and used it to refer to the integration of natural law, legal positivism, and historical jurisprudence.

Why an integrative jurisprudence? The effects of forces particularly in the eighteenth and nineteenth centuries including the continuing impact of the Protestant Reformations, political revolutions, the Enlightenment, industrialization, commercialization, urbanization, and the rise of individualism accelerated the fragmentation of the earlier jurisprudence that had constituted the Western Legal Tradition. Acting like a prism these transformative forces separated out the three distinct dimensions of law that had been merged in the earlier jurisprudence. Each of these dimensions yielded a distinct perspective on law represented, respectively, by the great schools: natural law, legal positivism, and historical jurisprudence. In the late nineteenth century, a sociological jurisprudence emerged that contributed important insights supplementing the historical school's emphasis on local and social facts. The integrative jurisprudence I employ proposes to take these refracted visions of law and synthesize them into a single perspective, thereby restoring law to full and undistorted view. Harold Berman, the leading figure in integrative jurisprudence in our times, employs an integrative jurisprudence in his widely and justly acclaimed history, *Law and Revolution: The Formation of the Western Legal Tradition.* His work, while more historical than philosophical, has nevertheless inspired and informed my present effort in integration.

Law, I argue, has three fundamental dimensions: a formal dimension, a teleological dimension, and a social/historical dimension. (The social and historical dimensions may be discussed as two dimensions, as the social order may be addressed at any given point in time and then over time. The time or historical dimension may be treated as a fourth dimension. However for the purposes of this discussion, I prefer the metaphor of three dimensions and will generally treat the sociological and historical aspects of law together.) Each of the traditional schools of jurisprudence has tended to focus on one of these dimensions—often in the process distorting or neglecting the other two. Legal positivism has focused on law's formal dimension (more precisely, its positive formality), natural law has focused on law's teleological dimension, and historical/sociological jurisprudence has focused on the dimension of law's relativity to social context over time. I should note that my analysis is different from Professor Berman's, who associated the positivist perspective with law's political dimension, the natural law perspective with law's moral dimension, and historical jurisprudence with the dimension of law's history. I do not adopt this division because the perspective of each of the schools has implications for each of law's dimensions. Hence, adopting legal positivism will have not only implications for one's perspective on law's relation to politics, but also its relations to history and to morality. Likewise, adopting natural law or historical jurisprudence has implications, in the former beyond morality for history and politics, and in the latter, beyond history for politics and morality. Law's dimensions are better characterized as formal, teleological, and social/historical and each of the jurisprudential schools must be examined for its characteristic approach to each of these three dimensions of law.[1]

While recognizing that law is a formally posited phenomenon (as legal positivism holds), integrative jurisprudence asserts that law is an enterprise that orders the lives of people over time. It is relative to the particular contexts and situations in which people live. Law is rooted in sociological and historical phenomena. The on-going enterprise of law, however, has a direction. In broad terms, law is concerned with advancing the human good providing conditions favorable to the pursuit of happiness in civil society. The specific forms of that good, however, are multiple. The US Constitution in the Preamble speaks of securing: "a more perfect union," "justice," "the general welfare," and "the blessings of liberty." To these basic goods and others that may be considered basic, law pursues numerous particular goods suggested by the term "public policy." The law's goods may be separated into categories such as individual rights and public order goods, and separated into negative precepts of justice that prohibit violation of the rights of others (as codified, e.g., in the penal code) and positive precepts that impose duties of contributing to the common good.[2] Argument from the negative precepts tends to be "deontological" in form, while argument from the positive precepts tends to be "consequentialist" in form.[3] The natural law tradition, which has placed greatest emphasis on law's teleology, has defined law as a rule directed toward the common good focusing on that dimension of the legal enterprise that is responsive to considerations of natural justice. That tradition engages reasoning that has entailed both deontological and consequentialist forms of argument.

Law's normative structure is axial; one that must balance opposing principles. There is sundry evidence of this and it is reflected in law's methodology. The scholastic method, the first method of western legal science, taught at the west's first law school in Bologna, Italy, conceived of law "as a complex unity based on synthesis and reconciliation of opposing elements" (*Law and Revolution*, 427). The method was dialectical; it involved the positing of questions concerning legal subjects and the listing of contrary propositions relating to the questions. Through critical analysis, the propositions were reconciled or synthesized and the questions answered. (Aquinas masterfully marshals the method in his "Treatise on Law" in the *Summa Theologica*.) Law's dialectical structure continues to be in evidence in judicial reasoning where opposing legal norms are reconciled by balancing them. In Constitutional jurisprudence, American judges resolve issues by balancing the rights of the individual and the interests of the state. For example, in construing the Fourth Amendment the Supreme Court of the United States in *Michigan v. Summers*, 452 U.S. 692, 700 (1967) stated that the "key principle" is "the balancing of competing interests."

Symbols of law's axial structure are all around us. It is represented in iconic form by the goddess of justice: the blindfolded Statue of

Justice at the Old Bailey in London with scale in her right hand symbolizes that justice (which guides the courts below) weighs opposing evidence and values—the way a balance weighs material goods. In her left hand, she upholds a sword, which represents the power of the legal sanction. (See the image on the cover and in "Law and Order," Dorland Kindersley Visual Encyclopedia, 154.)

Law's axial structure is represented in architectural form by the US Capital building, which constitutes a great axis connecting the two Houses of Congress. The bicameral legislature—with Senate designed to favor stability or long-term interests and House more sensitive to change and more immediate interests—was adopted to provide a balance thought necessary for preserving the virtues of our republican institutions. John Adams, who advocated the bicameralism, had held that a unicameral legislature would be more subject to tyrannical influence: "Balance, counterpoise, and equilibrium were ideals that he [Adams] turned to repeatedly. If all power were to be vested in a single legislature, 'What was to restrain it from making tyrannical laws in order to execute them in a tyrannical manner'" (Adams qtd. by McCollough 376, brackets mine). The Capital dome at the center of the building's axis gives physical form to Daniel Webster's image of the temple of justice (see chapter 1). Justice as the enterprise of erecting a dome is a metaphor for justice as the virtue that provides the axial balance as, for example, between the competing claims of the individual and the society.

Within each of its dimensions, law seeks to balance opposing norms: in the teleological dimension between the individual and the social or public good, in the formal dimension between judgments bound by rules and discretionary justice, and in the social/historical dimension between ahistorical universal norms and local diachronic norms, such as those of customary law. The dialectical tensions generated by these opposing norms are relieved in each of the dimensions by a fundamental axial principle. In law's teleological dimension the principle is justice, in law's formal dimension the principle is integrity, and in law's social/historical dimension the principle is prescription (adapting this term from Edmund Burke, I use it to refer to the principle by which a beneficent existential order endures in society. Prescription on this analysis carries normative weight.) I define these principles later. Tensions generated among the dimensions are relieved by more general principles of practical reason or jurisprudence. Given law's nature and this normative architecture, jurisprudence, then, is a principled science and the practitioners of the art of jurisprudence must possess the virtues of practical wisdom, law-abidingness, and morally good character, if they are to execute their offices well and advance law's virtue—in keeping with law's principles.

In using terms such as "axial structures" and "axial principles," I draw on Daniel Bell's vocabulary. (See, e.g., *Cultural Contradictions of Capitalism*.) Professor Bell identified discrete axial principles regulating the political, economic, and cultural realms and argued that these realms in our period are disjunctive. My work is concerned with finding conjunctions that are germane to the legal enterprise. I believe that disjunction in this area is usually the product of taking axial principles to excess in either direction of the relevant polarity. Conjunction is produced by moderation in the principle, as virtue for Aristotle consists in striking the "mean" with respect to the emotion or characteristic or action in issue. Deviations from the mean can occur when individuals or societies pursue limited goods (whether individual or social) beyond those points where they remain good. At such points, pursuit of these perceived "goods" brings individuals into conflict. For example, by reading too much individualism into the principle of justice (producing a bias toward an excessive pursuit of individual "goods" such as negative liberty or privacy) from which is derived a more formal positivist jurisprudence, law enforcement becomes disjoined from the social peacekeeping function of the police. Conversely, by reading too much communitarianism into the jurisprudence (skewing "justice" to excessively favor social "goods" such as public order or community at the expense of individual goods), due process may be sacrificed to securing the quality of life desired by the dominant element in the community. Police become community servants rather than agents of law. Vigilantism may result putting individual rights in jeopardy. It should be noted that the various social orders constituting contemporary society, however, should not strike the same balance between individual and communal goods. Families, for example, are characteristically governed by more communitarian norms than business associations. This will be explored in chapter 8. The mean or the point of virtue that strikes the right balance is therefore relative to each. This is parallel to Aristotle's analysis of moral virtue where he states that the mean between excess and deficiency is the "mean relative to us." Like finding the mean in virtuous action, finding the mean in the axial principles by which law regulates the social order requires not mathematical division but practical wisdom.

In stable times when there is a solid consensus supporting law's norms, law is hardly perceived as an enterprise characterized by axial tensions. Law's axial principles produce a balanced stable order consistent with the prevailing sense of what justice requires. In times of instability, however, where the prevailing paradigm is under attack, law's settled norms are challenged, giving rise to frank tensions and exposing law's axial structure. At these times (which appear to be our own), practical wisdom about law and moral character are especially needed by law's agents if the dialectical tensions agitated by the changes in the society are to be resolved in the best possible way through law.

Certain societies by virtue of their nature and normative structure are more given to change, while others are more given to stability. Capitalist societies that emphasize the values of individual liberty and innovation and whose legal structures are more formally rational (in Max Weber's sense) are examples of the former. Traditional societies that emphasize the value of social custom and whose norms are more prescriptive (in Burke's sense), such as Chinese and other Asian societies, have exemplified the latter, although less so in the current period of westernization in Asia. Societies and their legal orders, therefore, should be studied in terms of the characteristic balances they strike in the law's three dimensions and in terms of how these balances shift according to the particular kinetics of the society.

Aristotle thought that while constitutions varied according to convention, there was still one constitution that was best according to nature (*Nicomachean Ethics*, tr. Ostwald 132). Such a constitution strikes the best axial balances in law's teleological, formal, and social/historical dimensions, so as to best foster the natural human good and realize individual human happiness in a perfectly just community. A full analysis of the objective principles constituting this best case of law as well as systematic argument demonstrating that there is indeed a best case of law are reserved for discussion in a sequel to this volume. Here, I shall explore law's basic structure and focus on how normative shifts in that structure follow certain patterns across law's teleological, formal, and social/historical axes. In sections A, B, C, and D that follow, I shall examine the axial structure of each of these dimensions. In section A, I focus on law's teleological axis. Section B examines law's formal axis and sections C and D center on law's social/historical axis and the variety of reasons required in legal argument. In section E, I draw out some of the implications of the analysis for police.

# A

The law's axial tensions may present themselves in the form of conflicts brought to justice officials between and among individuals or between individuals and the community or state. They may be implicit in conflicts brought to the attention of police and they may be explicitly articulated in legal arguments made before the courts. In the teleological axis, law seeks to promote both the good of the individual and the community or state. An individual, however, may seek to do something that he thinks is good but violates some rule of behavior adopted by the community for the common good. The individual's claim may be framed in terms of a "right to liberty" to pursue the perceived "good" and the state may respond claiming that the legal rule is necessary for the "public order" and reject the individual's claimed right to engage in the conduct in issue.

Conflicts of this sort have arisen in order maintenance policing, which has become a battlefield for normative argument about the new policing. Here libertarians armed with formal conceptions of law (such as that of the American Civil Liberties Union) have fought in pitched battles with communitarians and others armed with, at least implicitly, more informal conceptions of law—as reflected, for example, in the "broken windows strategy" advocated by Wilson, Kelling, and Coles and the New York Transit Authority's more aggressive policy toward disorder in the subways adopted under NYPD Commissioner William Bratton. Both types of conceptions vie for acceptance by the courts. A case in point is *Young v. New York City Transit Authority*, 729 F.Supp.341, S.D.N.Y., rev'd and vacated, 903 F.2d146 (2d Cir.1990) where the issue was whether a Transit Authority regulation prohibiting "begging" and "panhandling" in the subway was consistent with the individual panhandler's First Amendment right to free speech. Also in issue in the case was the constitutionality of a New York Penal law that defined "loitering" to include remaining in a public place for "the purpose of begging."

Let us in a preliminary way address the teleological issues raised by a case like *Young*, by appraising the claim that an individual has a right to panhandle in the subways because that right secures some objective good entailed by law's *telos*—an individual good that justifies limitation on pursuit of a public good, here a subway free of panhandling and those goods attaching to such a milieu. Is it, as Young claimed, First Amendment free speech? It is difficult to see how panhandling itself is either speech or integrally connected to the good of speech. The act of panhandling does not necessarily communicate a message about poverty—or some other condition such as mental illness or some inability to access public assistance funding—that might be at the root of the conduct. Nor does it seem to be like the campaigns of charitable organizations whose appeals for donations have been considered a form of speech. The US Supreme Court has held that for conduct itself to be "expressive" and protected by the First Amendment the agent must have intended it to communicate a message and the conduct must have occurred in a context where there was a substantial likelihood that the message was understood by those to whom it was addressed. This test articulated in *Tinker v. Des Moines Independent School District*, 393 U.S. 503 (1969) is not likely satisfied on these facts. It might be contended that the conduct involved, even if not constitutionally "expressive," by making people uncomfortable draws attention to the fact of poverty and is socially useful in those terms. A society should not attempt to sweep poverty under the rug, lest it fester. If panhandling can be reasonably connected to such an instrumental social good, here a utilitarian consequentialist as opposed to deontological argument or First Amendment constitutional argument, its claimed utility must be balanced against the utility of other public order goods—such as those entailed by subways, sidewalks, and public places free of this sort of intrusion. This assessment pertaining to what promotes the general welfare, however, seems more appropriately a legislative than judicial judgment. And the legislature has already spoken having enacted the panhandling ban. Be that as it may, the argument about panhandling could be detached from "speech" and arguments about its social utility. Panhandling could be asserted a liberty as such, to which an individual has a right as an aspect of his or her self-determination or autonomy—a deontological claim that the individual might argue is based in the Fourteenth Amendment liberty clause. Such an argument links up with the claim that prohibiting "loitering" as defined in terms of subway panhandling (also at issue in *Young*) violates an individual's due process rights. However, the argument that one has a constitutional right to choose to live as a panhandler is not a clear winner. Standard due process jurisprudence would test the claimed right against its rootedness in the history and traditions of the republic and whether it is implicit in the concept of ordered liberty—a test that it is not likely to pass. Putting such jurisprudence aside, it is not clear how panhandling is consistent with the dignity of man at the basis of, at least, Kant's autonomy and the deontological right to self-determination. Under Kantian autonomy, man as a rational agent respects himself and other rational agents as ends in themselves, never using himself or others as means to his or others ends. Is not the choice to live as a panhandler, a choice to use others as means? Be that as it may, the liberty to panhandle could instead be argued an instrumental utilitarian good in the limited sense that panhandling may help the individual get by. But that good and that liberty have less weight against public order goods in a utilitarian calculation when the individual has access to welfare assistance—food stamps, shelter, and clothing—that provides for these basic needs. The utilitarian calculation, again, seems more appropriate for a legislature than for a court to make and arguably should be a legislative judgment to which a court defers, at least where society has made provision for basic human needs. (I shall take up the District and Circuit Courts' treatment of the free speech claim in *Young* later.)

*Young* also involved a New York law that penalized "loitering" where that included remaining in a public place for "the purpose of begging." Libertarians have contended that in this sphere of order maintenance legislation, that includes not only laws prohibiting "loitering" but also "disturbing the peace" and "disorderly conduct," given the greater informality in the definition of the offenses and the greater discretion allocated to officials, there is greater danger for abuse of authority and greater threat presented to the liberty of the individual. An ordinance prohibiting "loitering," especially where there is absent clearly specified instances of the conduct that constitutes "loitering," leaves open to question whether the law proscribes a discrete act or a status (that of loiterer). Such vagueness undermines the conduct requirement of the criminal law and values served by it, such as giving individuals fair notice of what the law proscribes and fair opportunity to conform their specific conduct to law, thereby assuring themselves that officials will not with legitimacy interfere in their lives. (Similar concerns have led courts to hold laws prohibiting "vagrancy" unconstitutional.) Some may also see implicated in these contexts the constitutional prohibition on *ex post facto* criminal law, as courts arguably define by clarification of the ambiguity what is criminal after the fact. In the meantime, police and prosecutors are afforded considerable discretion to act on the basis of what they interpret "loitering" to be.

Taking into account such considerations, it is contended that the balance in the area of order maintenance laws should be struck in favor of vindicating the individual's claim. Furthermore, as the offenses involved are often minor, some think it justified to strike the balance more in favor of the individual because the stakes to the public are lower. How significant to the public order is subway panhandling or loitering for the purpose of panhandling, this is an assault on what urbanologist Jane Jacobs has called the "small change of life." But is that so? A single panhandler seems insignificant but a gauntlet of panhandlers can significantly alter the social context. And even a single panhandler may pose a significant problem when the entreaties occur within the confines of subway stations, isolated stairways, and corridors, and when made at night when few are around. According to broken windows theory, conduct must be measured in light of such factors. The argument that cracking down on seemingly minor nuisances, incivilities, misdemeanor crimes, and disorders undermining "quality of life," contributes to reducing serious index crime (by cutting off processes of decay that lead to them) must also be contended with.[4] An endorsement of the libertarian position even with respect to minor offenses, it is argued, has greater cost to the public order than should be incurred.

I have undertaken this tentative analysis of issues raised by a case like *Young* to demonstrate that while the initial concern in an order maintenance case may be with law's *telos* and how competing goods are balanced, a close examination reveals that cases of this sort also turn on questions of law's formality (on how law checks the police power and how law divides discretionary authority among legislative, judicial, and executive officials) and law's historicity (as the appraisal of the goods at stake are affected by conditions—contexts—on the ground and over time). The law's dimensions are not to be treated as discrete self-contained realms but rather as different aspects of the same phenomenon. Striking the right balance in law's teleological axis will entail consideration of how the balance struck affects law's formal and social/historical axes and the goods related to them. Legal analysis must conjure with these considerations.

Judges called to adjudicate these kinds of disputes write decisions that define the scope of the individual's rights and the limits of the police power. They must strike some balance in the law's teleological, formal, and social/historical axes, determining the degree to which relative goods (of individual freedom from interference by others and of the public order and a host of goods that may be implicated such as those connected to individuality, free expression, creativity, dynamism, and diversity, on the one hand, and community, tradition, order, stability, and homogeneity, on the other hand) can be secured in a society committed to the pursuit of happiness—where the individual's pursuit of his good and the community's institutionalization of norms establishing the conditions for the flourishing of the common good (one of which is the maintenance of public order) have come into conflict. The legal analysis may center on the First Amendment but battles may be fought elsewhere—as in the Fifth and Fourteenth Amendments' "due process" clauses, the Fourteenth Amendment's "equal protection" clause or the Fourth Amendment's prohibition of "unreasonable searches and seizures," state constitutional provisions, etc.

One may step above current controversies regarding the specific conflicts between what the individual claims is good and he or she has a right to and what the society claims it may do to advance the common good, to a level of abstraction where law's *telos* seems more amenable to at least theoretical resolution. Law's teleological axis, one may say, is well balanced when it provides for the flourishing of the human person who is by nature both individual and political (in Aristotle's sense, a social animal for whom community is a natural good). Liberty is nugatory if an anarchic disorder prevails on the streets and citizens lock themselves in their apartments out of fear. On the other hand, a society that establishes order at any cost sacrifices liberty and by imposing a police state (in the pathological sense of an oppressive intrusive big brother state) deprives the individual, *inter alia*, of the goods of liberty and privacy that may be claimed as rights and, therefore, commits injustice. The right balance among the individual and social goods that we as political animals require to live well, or the balance between individual rights and the public order or just interests of the state, may be discussed as a "mean" as Aristotle uses the term to define the point of excellence or virtue where some balance is struck at the right point on a scale. Imbalances may be described as either excesses or deficiencies in some value, for example, an excess of individual freedom of action (defined as license from the standpoint of the "mean") and a deficiency of the good of public order or community. The Aristotelian "mean" in law's teleological axis is prescribed by the term "justice." Justice regulates or places limits on the freedom to do as we please, separates liberty from license, and prescribes when mere freedom is a right to liberty that the state must respect through its laws, through its establishment and maintenance of order, and through the constraints it imposes on official authority. It is a principle that relieves the tension produced when limited goods such as liberty, privacy, stability, and order are pursued beyond those points where they remain goods.[5] In its comprehensive sense, Aristotle states that justice "produce[s] and preserve[s] happiness for the social and political community" (*Nicomachean Ethics*, tr. Ostwald 113, brackets mine). The state of police defined normatively, as in the ancient Greek sense, is the condition of human flourishing in civilized society regulated by law that secures "justice."

# B

It is not only law's ends that may come into tension. Dialectical tensions may occur as well within the other dimensions of law. Consider the formal dimension. In *America's Constitutional Soul*, Harvey Mansfield described the formality of an action as "what can be separated from its end, and this separation is possible because the end can be achieved in more than one way. When one means is absolutely necessary to attain the end; no formality exists, but when a choice of means is required, the one chosen (or developed unconsciously) as 'correct' is the formality" (195). Formality, like its correlative discretion, applies to situations where choice is involved. Formality binds us to a certain choice as "correct." The formality itself, we might say, becomes an end.

Formality may be illustrated in the following case where it seems to be taken to excess. In Rhode Island, a regulation requires that whenever a school bus carrying elementary or middle school students stops, either to pick up or drop off children, the bus attendant must alight and look under the bus to make sure a child is not there. Meanwhile, traffic in all directions must stop as well. In many of these stops, given the short duration and the small number of children involved, the bus attendant's ritual seems meaningless. From an observer's point of view, the "search" is often conducted in the most *pro forma* manner imaginable (perhaps all that occurs is a slight bending at the waist and a fleeting glance toward the undercarriage).[6] It seems more reasonable to allow attendants to use their discretion when to look under the bus, but the regulation forecloses that option and that is the formality. (In criminal cases when the factually guilty are acquitted on the basis of "legal technicality" that is usually the effect of law's formality. An example is the exclusion of critical evidence because the police violated the Miranda rule.) Law's formality is more defensible when it reflects what is reasonable, but in these cases formality is less readily distinguishable from reasonableness.

Formality may arise gradually over time as the product of custom (as, e.g., in ceremonial ritual or customary law) or it may be imposed suddenly by positive enactment (as by legislation). The former I call prescriptive formality, and the latter I call positive formality. The formalities of law's norms have arisen in both ways, although in modern times for various reasons the latter predominates. (See my discussion in chapter 4.) The formality of positive law derives from the validity of the manner in which it is posited but at some level whether the posited law is obeyed depends on its effectiveness in generating support in its favor. Positive law depends on generating habits of obedience to it, that is, it depends on generating a custom of abiding by it. Freshly minted legislation requires the generation of new customs to sustain it. Positive law then seeks the effectiveness of customary norms. Habits of obedience are essential to sustaining its formality. However, positive law must also accord with *telos* as the sense of the law's justice is necessary for sustaining its legitimacy. When a law is widely perceived as unjust, that puts greater strains on the "legitimacy" it derives from its positivist validity and the normative force generated by its being consistent with custom. (Naked positive formality, shorn of the normative force of customary practice and reasonableness, is not likely to endure—absent the sustained application of coercive force.)

This suggests an additional kind of formality; it is the formality generated by the normative force, or bindingness, of natural, moral, or human rights and duties, where these take on the quality of ends or *teloi*. For instances of natural or human rights, we may think of the Declaration of Independence's "unalienable rights." In the case of a right's formality, means and ends are conflated or rather the end becomes the formality. The correct "means," as in Mansfield's definition of formality, is respecting a person as an end in himself, as a rights holder. The right precludes his or her use as a means (although in US Supreme Court practice up to that point where a countervailing social good to which the law is committed becomes, e.g., "compelling"). There is no reason, however, to confine this last sort of formality to rights. Duties are capable of generating formality, as in Kant's moral imperatives. This third type of formality may be referred to as natural law or teleological formality, where the formality or bindingness is derived from the weight of deontological reasons and/or consequentialist reasons, which the *telos* of law directs officials to give decisive weight and justifies that legal officials treat the right or duty as an end in itself. We then have three species of formality: positive formality, prescriptive formality, and natural law or teleological formality. Each limits the discretion of officials. Formality in law is at its utmost when positive formality, prescriptive formality, and teleological formality converge to support law's bindingness.

The term "formal rationality" usually refers to the logical constraints assumed in pursuing means to certain ends, whatever they may be. In organizations it is secured through rules and procedures that produce a coherent and efficient means to fulfilling the organization's ends. "Formal rationality" in the context of an integrative jurisprudence of police may also refer more comprehensively to the overall rationality generated by the legal enterprise's prescriptive, positive, and teleological formality.

Formality can be a matter of degree. Legal rules, for example, ordinarily carry a high degree of formality when contrasted with legal policies or legal principles. An official bound by rules is required to take certain action because it is stipulated by the rule. The given-ness of the rule trumps consideration of, for example, some good the official might prefer to achieve by action dispensing with it. Legal policies by contrast are of lower formality because they give primacy to consideration of the beneficial consequences to be achieved by some action. Where policy enters legal analysis, the benefits to be achieved are weighed against other considerations in reaching a judgment that entails discretion. As Ronald Dworkin contends, legal principles (which he defines as enjoining some requirement of fairness or justice rather than some objective to be achieved as in a policy) like policies have a dimension of relative weight in legal reasoning and characteristically less formality than rules. Rules on the other hand, Dworkin asserts (like the rule in baseball, "Three strikes and you are out") apply in an "all or nothing fashion" ("The Model of Rules" 140).

It should be observed, however, that even rules are not uniformly formal; some carry higher formality than others as when one rule stipulates with high precision the conduct required and another leaves somewhat open ended what may be required. (A rule prohibiting "loitering" is an example of the latter.) Even conceptions of what rules are may vary in formality; Dworkin's is not universally followed. Robert S. Summers and Patrick Atiyah observe that the English adhere to a more formal conception of rules than Americans, where the rule may be received more as a guideline.[7] Historically, the Roman jurists of the first millennium understood the rule to be merely a summary of the facts of a case. Such rules generated little formality since later cases could be readily distinguished from the "rules" tied to them. It was the twelfth century jurists that took the Roman *regulae* and interpreted them as "maxims"—the term Aristotle used for universals.[8] This more abstract conception of rules made them more serviceable as formal norms that could govern a larger set of cases (a class) having features in common with the case in which the rule was articulated. However, when rules are articulated with too much abstraction from specific conduct, they may operate more like Dworkin's principles and lose formality as officials who apply them may exercise substantial discretion in weighing them against other highly general norms.

The degree of a rule's formality may be defined as the normative inertia supporting a rule, and its limits are exceeded when the force of normative argument counter to the rule is sufficient to justify an exception. The greater the formality that a legal norm possesses, the lesser the discretion available to an official governed by it. Formality and discretion vary inversely.

The rules to which an official is bound to a certain degree prevent that official from entertaining how some action beside the rule may better achieve some policy or better correspond to some principle of fairness or morality. When legal policy and/or legal principle are in conflict with adherence to the rule, tension in law is generated. This tension may be relieved when, for example, a consequentialist argument addressed to a public policy the law is committed to or a deontological argument addressed to law's morality becomes sufficiently strong to displace the weight of formal reasons supporting the rule— formal reasons such as those addressed to consistency, predictability, or uniformity in official action. This may result in justifying an exception to the rule or its more general displacement, perhaps its reformulation or abolition. Ronald Dworkin in "Model of Rules" illustrates the phenomenon with the case of *Riggs v. Palmer*, where the New York Court of Appeals over-rode the rules pertaining to the validity of wills in order to prevent a murderer (in this case a grandson) from otherwise inheriting the estate of his victim (his grandfather). The rules of wills, underwritten by the liberal value of freedom of testamentary disposition that supported strict adherence to them, were in the case of a murder, however, trumped by the principle that "No man should profit from his wrongdoing."[9] Were the wrongdoing in *Riggs* not nearly so great, however, the rules would likely have prevailed over this principle. The law of wills will usually uphold the testator's wishes even if it means slighting substantive justice, as in the case when the testator bequeaths his estate to an undeserving son or daughter.

Legal phenomena then vary according to their degree of formality— a property that positivists, ex officio, generally have difficulty accounting for. Some legal norms, such as strict rules, are highly formal, while others, such as legal principles or policies that allow considerable room for individualized judgments, are of lower formality. In broad terms, the classic tension in the formal dimension of law is seen between the strict rule of law, which confines officials to ministerial action and the broad principle of equity, which gives officials room to choose among a number of possible actions, exercising discretion according to the equitable principle in the case. When law is seen as a body of norms of the former sort—norms of especially high formality—a more "mechanical jurisprudence" emerges. When law is seen as an amorphous mass of principles and policies having very little formality, offering little or no effective check on official authority—a view associated with the legal realists and the critical legal studies movement—the rule of law gives way to a discretionary justice. Clearly, some proper balance must be struck between these extremes if law is to have integrity. Generally, theorists who argue against police discretion do so from a perspective on law (and the rule of law) that is highly formal.[10] To reconcile police discretion to the rule of law and the duty to enforce law requires a jurisprudence that accounts for kinds and degrees of formality in law's norms.

Anthony D'Amato's essay "On the Connection between Law and Justice" examines the relative merits of a jurisprudence that is more mechanical and rule bound when compared with one that is more grounded in discretionary judgments about justice. His essay may be used to illustrate some of the tensions produced by law's positive formality and particularly the tension that can arise between law's positive formality and its teleology.[11] D'Amato constructs the following hypothetical case: Alice, while driving her car, swerves across the two solid white lines dividing the roadway to avoid running over a child who suddenly darts in front of her. A police officer stops her and cites her for violating the traffic law, which states "If a roadway is marked by double white lines (parallel lines) which traverse its length, motorists may not cross the lines."[12] When Alice protests and explains her reason for crossing over the lines, the policeman offers this judgment, which is of little comfort to her: "You did the right thing, but you violated the law." The judgment reveals something of what might be called, if loosely, the officer's operative "jurisprudence." The officer enforces the traffic law from the standpoint of a highly formal interpretation of the statute, which requires that he suspend acting on the basis of what is right because the posited legal rule in his view forecloses that option. His action may be said to presuppose a mechanical jurisprudence in that it excludes discretionary judgment. However, the action results in an injustice by punishing a person who acted rightly—an instance of a highly formal positivist jurisprudence's production of not only a separation but also a conflict of law and morals. Furthermore, it makes nonsense of the traffic law, which is enacted to protect human life but is "violated" by the action to save a life. The officer might rationalize his action on the ground that some other official up the legal ladder will have the authority to right it. (D'Amato's officer assures Alice that the traffic judge will be "sympathetic." It turns out, however, that he is not.) Decisions about discretion can turn on questions about which official, in a legal system that divides and checks power, should exercise discretion in the type of case in question. Alice, it turns out, has to wait for a decision of the supreme court to "right" the matter, as the traffic court and the court of appeals similarly adopted a highly formalistic jurisprudence and ruled against her. (This issue concerning the distribution of discretionary labor among justice officials will be pursued later.)

Can the police officer's action be considered in some sense legally wrong? Does law make available to the officer only the strict interpretation of the statute's explicit language? Legal tradition allows and may be said to require in certain circumstances that interpretation go beyond the letter of statutes. Even where statutory language is mandatory in form (as is the case with the traffic law in question) according to long established legal doctrine, it may be construed permissively when to do so avoids an irrational application. (This doctrine is called "rational interpretation" and Rutherford in his *Institutes* provides a classic exposition of it.)[13] When an officer exercises discretionary judgment by not citing Alice, he may be said to interpret and apply the statute in light of its rational purpose, that is, its *telos*. One good rationally connected to the statute would be the good of public safety, which may be construed to incorporate the principle of preserving human life. The officer who does not cite Alice (yet does speak with her and makes a deliberate judgment in light of her explanation and his understanding of the law's *telos*) may be said to enforce that law viewed from the perspective of its teleology. The officer in doing so might be said to engage a natural law jurisprudence. The officer's interpretive practice, however, should not stop with interpreting the legal rule in light of a particular law's rational purpose, although as a practical matter that may be sufficient for the resolution of the particular case. Ideally, the officer must be prepared to see this legal rule's relationship to other legal rules, principles, concepts, indeed, the entire *corpus juris*, and apply it so as to advance the law's overall rationality.

The officer's decision under this analysis does not resolve the problem by doing justice instead of law, but rather resolves a tension in law through law by striking a balance in the formal axis different from Anthony D'Amato's police officer. The relaxation of positive formality in the case is justified legally via argument from law's *telos*—which binds the officer as it generates teleological formality. The officer looks behind the positive formality for teleological reasons that justify it. He might reason that as a rule, that is generally, the traffic law is to be applied to speeders uniformly and predictably. This formality serves the law's end of public safety. However, cases such as Alice's may arise that justify relaxation of the positive formality codified in the traffic law in order to advance that same end. Furthermore, the officer may observe that formal justice—the principle that requires treating like cases alike—is not violated because Alice's case is different in a relevant respect.

Integrity is the principle of law's formal dimension that relieves the dialectical tension generated by law's norms by striking a balance between uniformity and individualization of judgment, legitimated by a balance struck (as in Alice's case) between the norms supporting law's positive formality and the norms supporting its teleology—which generate legal formality by their teleological (including deontological) rationality. Integrity in legal interpretation and action does not permit resolution of the problem by elimination either through reducing legal action to ministerial action (dispensing with law's teleology) or expanding it to constitute "discretionary justice" (dispensing with law's formality). I have not taken up Alice's case in terms of how the officer's discretion might be consistent with the traffic law's historicity (where focus may be on such things as patterns of traffic and driving habits) nor have I stated how it may involve a kind of reasoning Aquinas referred to as a *determinatio*. The law's prescriptive formality and the kind of rationality supporting it is a subject I take up in sections C and D. I take up *determinatio* at the end of section C.

"Integrity" comes from a Latin word meaning wholeness or completion. The virtue of law's formal dimension is then also a constituent part of law's *telos* as that connotes the condition of law's completion—its flourishing mature state. Law's wholeness and completion, moreover, could not occur without its existential efficacy—its material endurance or prescription. These three virtues of law cohere. Integrity in the rule of law, therefore, is achieved not simply when the law generates positive formality but when it generates full teleological and prescriptive formality—and officials act in ways that conform to that formality.[14]

Not citing Alice is a sound practical judgment of law enforcement consistent with a sound jurisprudence of police and the duty to enforce law. In not citing Alice, the officer has played the role of law's *animateur*. When the police officer accepts Alice's account of her actions as valid justification, she is affirmed in considering law to be a rational enterprise rather than made into a cynic who views law and legal officials as unjust and even stupid. She is affirmed in law abidingness rather than alienated from a law that is hypocritical. Alice now sees the police officer as an official of sympathetic understanding, as practically reasonable. But in order for law to be effectively enforced, she must see the officer as law's agent. Alice should not assume that the officer has granted her a dispensation from law or that the officer has the authority to do so and the officer must make that clear. While recognizing that police officers have legal authority to exercise discretion, it is important at the same time to stress that they are not authorized to act outside of law. They remain bound to the duty to fully enforce the law. Alice is confirmed in the duty to abide by law when she comes to understand that her departure from the legal rule was legally justified and consistent with the police officer's duty to enforce the law. Likewise, the police officer's fidelity to law is affirmed when that officer is able to enforce law in a way that reconciles law's positive formality with its teleological formality, thus doing justice according to law. Where the enforcement of law commits the officer to acting contrary to what he knows is right, strain is put on that fidelity. The principle of integrity in law works in conjunction with the principle of fidelity to law.

Proper law enforcement may require stricter adherence to formality than is generally the practice. Police frequently extend "professional courtesy" to other officers and waive the writing of tickets for traffic and other violations. It is very difficult, however, to square this practice with the duty to enforce law. Two famous cases help make the point. One day Ulysses S. Grant was stopped by a Washington, DC, police officer for speeding. The officer, who happened to be the first African American policeman in the department's history, hesitated when he saw that the man he had pulled over on 16th street was the President of the United States. Grant reassured him: "Do your duty officer." The President was fined twenty dollars, his buggy was impounded, and he had to walk back to the White House. Woodrow Wilson demonstrated a similar propriety. When the police officer who stopped his car said: "It's all right Mr. President, I didn't know it was you," Wilson reportedly responded: "On the contrary, I of all people must obey the laws." Both presidents reinforced the rule of law by their example. Police who submit to the penalty of the traffic laws, by the same token, reaffirm their duty to abide by law and seize a valuable opportunity to educate the public (and especially members of their own profession) on what it means to be governed by the rule of law.[15]

A police officer violates the duty to fully enforce law by exercising an unauthorized "discretion," as when the officer decides to give Alice a dispensation from law because he or she believes in treating women with special leniency. This "discretionary" act violates law's teleological and positive formality. I put "discretionary" in quotation marks because I use the term not to mean the effective power to get away with something as Kenneth Culp Davis does (*Discretionary Justice* 4), but rather to mean the authorization by appropriate norms that a person has to exercise judgment to do something (or nothing). By violating law's *telos* and formality, that is, the sources here of the appropriate norms, the act given this usage exceeds the officer's discretion.

How might this be argued? First, when the police officer dispenses with law in a situation to which law applies, the act in and of itself undermines the rule of law as the policeman has deprived the law of his agency. The specific basis here, an inclination to grant leniency to women, may be addressed as follows. Along one line of analysis, one that is more rights based and construes the teleological axis in more "deontological" terms, the officer's action exceeds his discretion because it denies the equal protection of the law by discriminating against men. Along a separate consequentialist line of argument, the officer's enforcement leniency reduces the law's deterrence with respect to the permissively treated group (female motorists) and is thereby inconsistent with the good of public safety. It may further erode the rule of law by making men generally cynical about law and more inclined to evade it. Hence, one can produce utilitarian support for a rule requiring between the sexes the equal enforcement of the traffic law. In either form of reasoning, "deontological" or "consequentialist," the officer's nonciting of female motorists (unlike his nonciting of Alice) may be called a failure to fully enforce the law.

Because the principle of equality under law is an issue in this case, standard forms of constitutional reasoning come into play. The justificatory arguments involved in construing the Fourteenth Amendment of the United States Constitution's equal protection clause are dialectical in form, involving both deontological and consequentialist reasoning. In the context of gender classifications, the clause is construed more as a "deontological" right carrying high formality, where it seems only an "exceedingly persuasive justification" addressed to the public good may override it a justification that is not likely to be found in the instant case. The US Supreme Court's classic three-tiered review—rational basis, intermediate review, and strict scrutiny—constitutes a scale of increasing formality where deontological justification increases in weight relative to consequentialist justification. The more recently minted "exceedingly persuasive justification" test seems to fall somewhere between intermediate review, which requires that the state demonstrate "an important governmental interest," and strict scrutiny, which requires the demonstration of "a compelling state interest."[16]

A police officer is better informed about his or her duty to enforce law and, therefore, better able to make sound enforcement judgments, if he or she has access to a perspective that synthesizes law's teleology with the logic of its formality. The law is undermined not only when it is disregarded in favor of the officer's private judgment—a frank violation of the duty to enforce law—but also when it is applied according to its letter yet irrationally, without regard to legally legitimate reasons constituting justifications or excuses.

D'Amato's hypothetical reveals the tension between a positivist conception of legal formality that severs law's form, postulated as an end by itself, from its ends and an integrative conception that interprets law's formality in light of its rational ends. The rule of law as a formally positivist and teleological principle (both together) is not advanced by unqualified strict adherence to law's letter. It may be argued, however, as was suggested earlier that the discretion to consider Alice's reasons would be better left to the traffic court—where the doctrine of rational interpretation may be more safely applied. The formality in the police action to cite her, so the argument might go, is defensible at a higher level in terms of a doctrine of the separation of powers (here between courts and police) that serves to limit abuse of power by police by reserving discretion to the courts. It seems more prudent to place discretion there. After all, police exercise discretion often beneath the radar of enfranchised public scrutiny. Judges, on the other hand, must justify their decisions in open court and are subject to appellate review with written rationale. Judges, moreover, are generally more highly educated in law and arguably better able to make the formal/teleological judgments required. This is not to say, however, that judges would be better at assessing the relevant social/ historical reasons that go into some determination about what order the police are to enforce, a subject taken up in sections C and D. A police embedded in the community would presumably be better at ascertaining the relevant facts and norms.

Beyond this question of the relative discretion and competence of judges and police (not to mention the discretion and competence appropriate to prosecutors who may decide whether and how to prosecute) is the question of the allocation of discretion and competence between courts and legislatures. How much discretion should the courts exercise in interpreting law and how much deference should they show to legislative judgments? These are questions that have arisen in the context of the highly charged political debates over judicial activism. Argument over how much discretion courts may exercise in interpreting law engage broad and deep issues in jurisprudence, including the basic question about what law is. The natural law conception of what is law, centered as it is on law's teleology, arguably results in interpretive judgments that overall strike a different balance in law's formal axis than those that are the product of legal positivism. Natural law on one account allows for more discretionary interpretation of law in light of its substantive justice. A naturalist judge on this account exercises greater discretion in interpreting such law than a judge who holds to a more positivist conception of law itself. The positivist may exercise greater discretion, however, if he or she construes the judicial role to allow a judge to generate fresh legal rules—to exercise what Ronald Dworkin called "strong discretion" where the case is not covered by existing rules ("Model of Rules" 144). But not all positivists would allow judges such law making authority. It should be observed that a naturalist may hold to a theory that is quite restrictive of the authority of judges, preferring naturalist judgments to be made by the legislature on grounds that "strong" judicial discretion is not consistent with the formality of a democratic constitutional order based as it is on a principle of legislative supremacy (within constitutional limits), and is less conducive to advancing the common good, that is, such "strong" judicial discretion is not justified in light of the operative conception of the law's teleological formality.

Distinct arguments must be made regarding the nature, scope, and limits of the discretion delegated to police, prosecutors, judges, corrections officials, and legislators, respectively. The balances in the formal/discretionary axis regulating their decision making must be struck at different places given their different roles and competences. Legislators, for example, must in crafting legislation arrive at the right formulation of the statute they enact, strike the right degree of formality in the statute's language, one that correctly delimits the discretion available to executing officials or courts. In maintenance of order legislation, the right degree of formality is arguably a linguistic formula of "low interpretive formality" to allow for the greater discretion that is necessary when dealing with problems of disorder, where the end is remedial and progressive, let us say, the restoration and invigoration of a communitarian order as opposed to retributive punishment.[17] Maintenance of order laws are generally articulated in open-ended language. Legislators, however, take direction from the courts regarding how much informality is permissible in legislation. Proposed legislation may be too vague and grant too much discretion and on that account violate the US Constitution. The Congress, for example, is not under the Constitution permitted to delegate lawmaking authority itself to administrative officials or to delegate discretionary authority that violates, for example, "due process" through "vague" laws.[18] In the case of traffic laws, on the other hand, a linguistic formula of high interpretive formality would seem best as clarity in the norm and uniformity in application is closely related to the end of an orderly flow of traffic and public safety—accordingly, the categorical formulation of D'Amato's traffic law that motorists are not to cross the double solid lines and the absence of language granting exceptions. However, even with traffic laws police officers in appropriate cases, as Alice's, exercise discretion and treat highly formal legislative language with lower formality in order to do justice and give effect to law's *telos*, which they are duty bound to do. Judgments about formality, then, must consider the relevant *telos* of the law in question. Where the end is peacekeeping, as opposed to the safe flow of traffic, low interpretive formality would seem preferable, since peacekeeping as we shall see in the sections that follow requires judgments of greater sophistication and sensitivity to contexts.

Allow me to close this section with consideration of an actual case involving George Kelling. Here is his account of it:

> On the New Hampshire Expressway, I was stopped going 72 miles per hour when the limit was still 55. When the officer approached me, he made the typical request for my license and registration but asked me as well: "Was there any reason why you were going 72 miles per hour?" I said: "No, I was just smelling the barn and eager to get home. I have no excuse." He replied: "I just can't give you 17 miles over the limit—7, sure. Maybe 10. But not 17." I understood and told him so. He wrote the ticket for 64, which was nine over the limit. I didn't like getting the ticket, but I had no sense of injustice or anger. His opening question, which I heard as a sincere request for information about whether I had some justification for speeding, acknowledged his discretionary authority and acknowledged as well, that I might have had a good reason, and he was prepared to consider it. The respect with which the officer treated me engendered my respect for him. (*"Broken Windows" and Police Discretion*, 16)

The officer appropriately asked whether the motorist had a reason for speeding and appropriately ruled out Kelling's as a legally justified excuse. (Kelling himself did so.) Up to this point, the discretion appears to be legitimately exercised. What is problematic, however, (and an issue Kelling elided) is the officer's adjustment of the facts. He records a false speed presumably in exercise of a quasi-judicial discretion to mitigate the punishment in Kelling's case. Many motorists including myself might appreciate (I am not sure what he means by "understand") such a dispensation, but the problem would seem to be that it is a dispensation from law. The source of the problem may be at the legislative level where fines might be draconian, but Kelling offers no information at that level so that we might appraise this issue. If fines are excessive and unduly burdensome that raises concerns that they are inconsistent with law's *telos*, because the punishment is not proportionate to the offense or goes beyond levels necessary for the deterrence of speeders or falls short of the law's objective in some other way. It may be that the state or municipality is improperly using the traffic law as a kind of tax to raise revenue. An officer should consider these teleological questions and police when indicated should bring them to the attention of legislative authorities and when indicated petition for change. There may be, however, reasons perhaps of the historic/contextual sort (i.e., a culture of dangerous driving that needs to be changed) that justify more severe penalties. However, the officer's handling of Kelling's case seems merely to override—or nullify—the legislative judgment without explanation. And not bringing it to the attention of police executive and legislative authorities means that the issue will not be deliberated at the appropriate levels and that officer discretion will remain below the radar, giving rise to concerns about misuse of discretion. The reduction in the speed recorded seems arbitrary. This is, therefore, not a case like Alice's where the facts themselves were irregular and not citing her was reconciled to law's *telos*, as well as its formality. Kelling has no excuse addressed to law's *telos*, nor is there justification provided for the officer's dispensation from the legislated fines (an apparent departure from law's formality). It is particularly troubling that the officer falsified a public record in order to do what he thought was right. All we have is Kelling's admission that he had no excuse that might indicate in the future he will abide by the speed limit.

## C

Patrick Atiyah and Robert S. Summers in their enlightening book *Form and Substance in Anglo-American Law: A Comparative Study of Legal Reasoning, Legal Theory, and Legal Institutions* identify two kinds of legal reasons: formal reasons and substantive reasons.[19] The latter largely overlap with what I have called teleological reasons. What I have said above regarding Alice's case is to some extent consistent with their dualistic perspective. If, however, proper inferences are drawn from the new policing's emphasis on the significance of the social context and history of acts constituting offenses for the purposes of the enforcement of law and the prevention of crime, legal reasoning is not dualistic but triune. Reasons of social context and history constitute a third kind of justificatory argument. I argue that soundly made discretionary judgments of law (I shall focus on the police in their law enforcement judgments, but this will hold true for legislatures, prosecutors, judges, and corrections officials as well) must be derived from a synthesis of teleological, formal, and social/historical reasons that officials are bound by law to consider. These judgments must be informed by consideration of law's social/historical axis and the tensions generated in this dimension of the legal enterprise.

Reasoning about the axes and the balances to be struck in them will take a variety of forms: deductive, inductive, dialectical, and analogical. This section describes the several forms of legal reasoning, centering on the social/historical axis of law. Elucidating that axis will also require I take up custom—its normative architecture and its relevance to law. In section D, I elaborate on the normative significance of custom for law and police, considering particular cases where police are drawn to the application of custom in their law enforcement work.

The social/historical axis of law generates tensions between universal and particular or local norms that are relevant to the question: how is law enforced here and now and over time? The answer to which gives normative weight to the consideration of past and future anticipated enforcement practice. Aristotle observes that in matters of action where things may be other than they are (which would be the bulk of affairs with which justice officials are concerned) judgments about action require understanding the universal norm applicable to the case in terms of its "ultimate particulars." This involves judgment that measures the significance of the particular contingent facts of the situation in terms of the realization of some universal norm implicated not merely in the case at hand but also in like cases in the future. The focus is on the local and diachronic nature of the norm.

In *Young v. New York Transit Authority*, judgment about ultimate particulars involved first understanding whether the panhandling in question indeed constituted "expressive conduct" that implicated the First Amendment—a jurisprudential judgment of considerable sophistication. The District Court and the Circuit Court of Appeals disagreed on this very question. The District Court Judge Leonard Sand understood "begging" to be like solicitation by charitable organizations, which the Supreme Court had held constituted expressive speech protected by the First Amendment: "although the beggar's entreaties may be more personal, emotionally charged and highly motivated, the substance is in essence a plea for charity." *Young v. New York City Transit Authority*, 729 F.Supp.341, at 352 (1990). Judge Altimari on the other hand, writing for the Circuit Court of Appeals, did not see begging as "inseparably intertwined" with speech: "Whether with or without words, the object of begging and panhandling is the transfer of money. Speech simply is not inherent to the act; it is not of the essence of conduct." Individuals, he thought, beg to collect money, not to express a point of view. Judge Altimari held that it was not "expressive conduct" implicating the First Amendment and criticized Judge Sand's opinion for its "exacerbated deference to the alleged individual rights of beggars and panhandlers to the great detriment to the common good." *Young v. New York City Transit Authority*, 902 F.2d 146, at 154, 158 (1990). His construction of the universal norm (the First Amendment of the Constitution) yielded a narrower right that the ordinance prohibiting panhandling in the subways did not violate. Judge Altimari in his decision struck different balances than Judge Sand in law's teleological and formal axes, balances that in his view favored securing the "common good" over the individual's choice of "good" and permitted greater informality in laws regulating the social order by limiting the sphere of rights. The general effect of a jurisprudence allowing greater informality in laws pertaining to order maintenance is to authorize greater discretion to law enforcement to take into account local contingent factors affecting the public order. This might, for example, involve among other things applying George Kelling's factors of "time, location, number or aggregation of events, condition of the victim/observer relative to the perpetrator/actor, and the previous behavior/reputation of the perpetrator/actor" (*"Fixing Broken Windows" and Police Discretion* 35), in determining how much a threat to the public safety a particular "disorderly" act is.

Particulars give rise to universals, as Aristotle stated. In one sense, this occurs through implication, as in *Young*. The facts must be grasped as implicating a general legal norm that covers the case. The appropriate action to be taken is deduced from the general norm. If begging is under the circumstances expressive conduct, then the ordinance banning panhandling is unconstitutional. On the other hand, if panhandling is not First Amendment speech and there is no ordinance on panhandling, the applicable universal may be the one implicit in the ordinance prohibiting "disorderly conduct." Such an ordinance requires a conception of that "order" and whether panhandling violates it. The normative "order" presupposed may be discerned by a process of induction from patterns of conduct observed that constitute the "order" to be enforced. Moreover, the "order" may differ from place to place. Police officers must grasp the customary norms establishing such orders as legitimate specifications of the general legislated norm. It should be noted that these customary norms are not static but subject to change, complicating the question of their legitimation. They will be affected by police acts of enforcement going forward, by the habits of people over time and other changes in circumstances. Customary norms then constitute a second case of what Aristotle calls "universals arising from particulars."

Jurisprudence, then, may involve both deductive and inductive reasoning. A situation must be appraised to determine whether it implicates a universal norm (such as First Amendment speech). The universal norm must then be applied deductively to the facts. A given set of facts, however, may implicate a "universal norm" that is discerned more inductively as a binding custom, as in the order implied by an ordinance prohibiting "disorderly conduct." A case may entail two conflicting "universals"—as would have been the case in *Young* were begging construed to be First Amendment speech. In that case, the constitutional norm (the right to free speech) as a higher ranking norm would trump the local customary norm (the customary order implied in the disorderly conduct ordinance), and control the judgment in the absence of a sufficiently strong countervailing state interest that may justify infringing free speech. It should be noted that the identification of constitutional norms themselves may require inductive and other forms of reasoning—as when an implicit right under the Fourteenth Amendment is discerned based on the determination of its rootedness in the history and traditions of the republic. Even First Amendment speech in the instance of "expressive conduct" requires reasoning that is context sensitive. In *Tinker* the wearing of black armbands by students acquired meaning given that it was at the time a generally recognized way to communicate protest of the Vietnam War. For the school to prohibit this conduct, then denied them their right to free speech.

But why can a customary norm be binding? Adverting to the normative force of custom, John Finnis asserts "there are direct 'moral' arguments of justice recognizing customs as authoritative (e.g., arguments against unfairly defeating reasonable expectations or squandering resources and structures erected on the basis of the expectations" (243). Or, I might add, that customs are authoritative based on argument that they are necessary for securing social goods. Finnis observes that when customary rules are treated "as authoritative, they enable states to solve coordination problems—a fact that has normative significance because the common good requires that those coordination problems be solved" (244). Finnis also states: "the general authoritativeness of custom depends upon the fact that custom-formation has been adopted in the...community as an appropriate method of rule creation" (243–4). Customary norms then, draw authority not only based on their being necessary for securing human goods and their natural justice, but also based on their being adopted. However, adoption need not be by explicit act. It will more typically be implicit in action. I reserve fuller discussion on the normative significance of custom to law and police for the next section.

When can a custom be legally binding, that is, exert legal formality? In *Natural Law and Natural Rights*, John Finnis provides a detailed analysis as to when a legally binding customary norm exists with respect to a certain kind of behavior. His discussion addresses the normative architecture of customary law. I shall examine it here and consider its applicability to law enforcement. The conclusion that a binding customary norm exists, Finnis argues, rests on a combination of empirical judgments (as to facts) and normative or practical judgments (as to an action's conduciveness to real human goods).

According to Finnis, there are two practical normative judgments predicate to the conclusion that a binding custom exists: (1) that it is desirable in this area of conduct that there be some "determinate, common, and stable pattern of conduct and corresponding authoritative rule" and (2) that "this particular pattern of conduct is (or would be if generally adopted or acquiesced in) an appropriate pattern for adoption as an authoritative common rule" (242). I would note that these normative judgments are predicated on two sorts of goods: the goods of stability and order (implicit in patterning) and the host of social and individual goods for which stability and order are a pre-condition, such things as community, the pursuit and completion of long-term projects, and liberty itself. These goods provide justification for the normative judgments that is it desirable in this area of conduct for there to be a common customary norm as an ordering mechanism and that the norm under review is appropriate for that task. These practical judgments, in turn, if they are to be at the basis of a conclusion that a binding custom exists, must be accompanied by two empirical judgments: (1) there "is widespread concurrence and acquiescence" in the rule of conduct (or pattern of conduct) to which the practical judgments above refer and (2) it is widely subscribed to by officials (242). Finnis adds: "states" generally, accept this rule and therefore according to law, conduct violating it is prohibited. He refers to "states" rather than officials here because he is applying the analysis to the context of international customary law—where customary law is most recognized today. Finally, to justify the conclusion that a binding custom exists requires an additional practical judgment holding that the combination of the above practical and empirical judgments are "sufficient to warrant the judgment...that there is now an authoritative customary rule requiring and prohibiting the behavior" (242).

I have two points to make here regarding the Finnisian analysis of what makes a custom a legally binding practice—if it were to be applied to legal officials operating within a particular state. First, what lies beneath the more immediate practical and empirical judgments that are to be made is law's deeper axial structure. The practical judgments as to the rationality of determining that a particular pattern is binding custom are themselves governed by the formal, historical, and teleological rationality that determines how law strikes the right balances in each of the three axes of the legal enterprise. To illustrate, the appropriateness of a given pattern will depend on whether a constitutional order is more liberal and dynamic, as that order gives less relative weight to goods such as order itself and stability and more weight to goods that are not context specific such as the fundamental rights of individuals to liberty, defined negatively. A more traditional communitarian constitution, however, will lend more weight to goods of order and stability and this will affect the practical judgment concerning what an appropriate pattern is. Therefore, law's deeper normative architecture must be exposed in order to reveal why the more immediate practical (but also empirical) judgments under Finnis's analysis are made. The practical and empirical judgments about when a custom is a practice that binds officials cannot be made independent of law's axial structure, if they are to be called legal judgments and if the custom is to be considered legally binding.

Second, Finnis' analysis is with the proper modifications applicable to domestic legal officials, such as police, engaged in the enforcement of law. An example would be a police officer's determination that a pattern of conduct constitutes a legally binding custom that gives concrete meaning to the term "order" underlying enforcement of an ordinance prohibiting "disorderly conduct." The custom provides the basis for identifying conduct as "disorderly" and for making arrests under the statute. Yet, the determination of the particular custom must be consistent with practical/empirical judgments made at the legislative and adjudicative levels and at the level of the legal tradition, as particular customs should be consistent with general custom and the *ordo juris*, which includes constitutional law, statutes, the decisions of the judiciary, and the prescriptions of the legal tradition. In cases of conflict, for example, when an individual claims a right to freedom of expression that conflicts with the community's customary order (as discussed earlier with respect to First Amendment speech), the community's custom cannot be dispositive but must be factored into an integrative analysis that synthesizes the competing claims in terms of a coherent theory about what the constitutional order requires. The legitimacy of a customary norm depends upon its being in accordance with not only the prescriptive but also the positive and teleological formality generated by the law that officials are duty bound to enforce.

Therefore, where police maintain order the word "maintenance" presupposes that there is an underlying order (pattern) that is the basis of the empirical judgment. The order needs to be squared with a practical judgment that this order is binding—a judgment drawn from an analysis of law's teleological, positive, and prescriptive formality. However, police do not always maintain an order; in neighborhoods where order has disintegrated, they may act to restore or help create order. Here an empirical judgment that there is no existing order, when coupled with the practical judgment that an order is needed and may be achieved by customary norms, may require that police be catalysts of custom formation. In such a case, this will necessitate that they work to build a consensus in the community as to the customary norms that are to govern the order to be established. Consensus building is important practically in legitimating the emerging norms of conduct (it produces normative support for them as the norms are squared with goods of free choice and consent at the basis of the right to political liberty embodied in the constitutional order) and empirically in making the norms effective. The customary norms must be capable of solving the order problem in a way consistent with the *ordo juris*. Police must move the community toward a customary order that advances law's overall virtue (its justice, integrity, prescription, and prudence).

The legal tradition had developed certain criteria for a custom to become law. Carleton Kemp Allen in his classic treatise *Law in the Making* identified in the English Common Law precedents, several of them.[20] His discussion is helpful as we search for the criteria that govern customary norms today. Allen observed that a local custom, "which in some respect is an exception from the ordinary law of the land" should (1) not conflict with a fundamental principle of the common law, (2) not be mere habit, practice, or fashion (I take this to mean that the custom should have normative weight), and (3) should have existed from time immemorial "whereof the memory of man runneth not to the contrary." The custom must: (4) be continuous not interrupted, (5) "have been enjoyed peaceably" and the right exercised "neither by stealth nor by revocable license," (6) be public, like a posited rule of law, (7) be regarded as obligatory, supported by what has been called the "*opinio necessitates*," (8) be certain, subject to limitation rather than to open caprice, (9) be consistent with other customs, (10) be reasonable: "fair and proper, as such as reasonable, honest and fair minded men would adopt," and it should (11) be consistent with the common good. These traditional criteria reflect the integrative jurisprudence of the earlier period from which they developed. A custom is legitimated according to criteria that are associated with formality (certainty, consistency, predictability, fair notice, and nonarbitrariness), teleology (substantive justice, right, common good, and reasonableness), and history (continuity and prescription). The customs referred to are normative patterns of long standing. (All quoted language from Allen, 130.)

These traditional criteria may well require adaptation to the kind of society in which the custom is to be enforced. For example, while criterion (3) requires that a custom be prescriptive in the traditional sense—that it has existed from time "immemorial"—the criterion originated in the more traditional land-based jurisprudence of pre-industrial society (having features described in chapter 4). The more dynamic industrial and postindustrial society, while still requiring customary norms, will find it more natural to construe "prescription" more flexibly.[21]

Prescription is the product of law's having met the criteria for its beneficent enduring, and this requires that we apply the full range of assessments, including the practical and empirical judgments (that Finnis identifies), which are at the basis of binding custom. What is to endure in the modern commercial society, however, is the thinner flexible order that is dynamic. Nevertheless, the prescription that this society requires must be sufficient to maintain an order that sustains the liberty and those other goods (individual and social) to which its law is committed. This, in turn, may well require the maintenance of smaller more intimate social orders, such as the family, whose prescription more approximates the traditional criteria for custom described by Allen. When the question, on the other hand, involves generation of customary norms to restore or create order, the criterion would have to be the potential of the norm to be prescriptive in the relevant sense. And that assessment, which demands prudence and circumspection, would have to include appraisal of the proposed norm's historical rationality. A norm may be too novel to be eligible. Prescription, then, depends on the nature of the social order as it persists over time. (I dilate on the relativity of law to social context in the next chapter.) Broadly speaking, the relative weights accorded the formal, teleological, and social historical criteria that enter into a judgment that a customary norm is prescriptively binding are determined by the balances struck in and among law's formal, teleological, and social historical axes.

Criteria for the evaluation of custom were developed early in the West by the canonists of the eleventh century during the formative period of the Western Legal Tradition. As much of the law had been customary, the newly emerging states and the relations among these and the ecclesiastical orders required new means for law's emergence and that was achieved partly by a ranking of sources as in Gratian's hierarchy. In his *A Concordance of Discordant Canons*, Gratian holds that existing customary law would under certain circumstances have to yield to a higher natural law. By accessing natural law in a form of reasoning that was dialectical, scholastic jurists modified existing customary law. The modified or new laws would, however, have to acquire over time the prescriptive formality necessary for sustaining them. They presumably already had the natural law formality at the basis of the revisions, the positive formality attaching to the positive authority of the officials who promulgated them, not to mention the prescriptive formality that may have been left over from the customs that they had revised.

Arranging law in terms of a ranking or hierarchy had the necessary effect of de-sanctifying customs (they required validation by standards distinguishable from themselves) and that prepared the way for reform of law by way of a more formal positive law—a species of law reliance on which would be increasingly necessary for regulating the more dynamic plural orders emerging in the West. However, it should be remembered that these formal positive orders were built on the foundations of communitarian orders that produced the customs increasingly under modification. The positive laws they generated would still require a form of support to be found in custom and the stable orders that generate them.[22]

In the modern period, with the ascendance of the legislative power and the rise of the bureaucratic state and its police (a subject I examined in chapter 4), positive law by and large replaced or at least put heavy restrictions on customary law. Today, in the aftermath of the collapse of local communitarian orders in many places, what is required is a "de-sanctification" of the formal positive law, a restoration of the distinction among the sources of law, and recognition of the legitimacy of custom and local material orders for the formation of law. This includes recognition that the formal positive law itself (enacted in the legislatures) is legitimated in part according to legal orders that emerge on the ground and these require preserving or creating conditions necessary for fostering the generation of customary orders. The customs produced help rebuild the communitarian foundation necessary for supporting the structure of formal positive law. The reconciled customary and positive law must as well be tested against criteria provided by a *jus natural* (natural law), which then underwrites them.

The reinvigoration of a customary and naturalist dimension to law will bring with it in the twenty-first century a renewed sense of a law rooted in history that is teleologically animated. Police enforcing such law will in part become "street corner judges," as William Muir put it, and in part legislators; this will open them up to the importance not only of legal principle, as Mark Moore suggested, but also all those normative features we have associated with law's customary and teleological dimensions. This enlarged role will require that they cultivate an integrative jurisprudence.[23]

To summarize the discussion of legal reasons thus far, they may be said to be of three kinds: teleological, formal, and social/historical. The forms of reasoning involved in law's administration, including its enforcement, are at least threefold. The legal reasoning involved in law enforcement may be deductive (the application of general norms to particular cases), inductive (the induction of general norms from patterns of particular conduct that emerge or have emerged as binding custom), and dialectical, where the relevant norms (local and universal) are in tension and need to be resolved in terms of some synthesis (which may occur through the weighing of competing norms, through the use of more abstract principles, concepts, and doctrines, and through their arrangement in some hierarchy as with Gratian). The dialectical form of reasoning had been critical to the formation of Western legal systems that was precipitated by fundamental changes occurring in the social order during that formative period. Jurists responded with the development of the highly sophisticated method known as scholasticism (Berman, *Law and Revolution* 131–51). In contemporary societies where there is much dynamism, producing frequent shifting of the legal axes to accommodate changing balances among goods pursued, dialectical reasoning becomes predominate as a form of legal reasoning. Today, dialectical reasoning is much in evidence in the reasoning of courts on controversial issues of constitutional law. As we saw in First and Fourteenth Amendment jurisprudence, judicial decisions have involved the balancing of deontological and/or consequentialist arguments—as when rights are balanced against state interests. Dialectical reasoning will be critical going forward in resolving the tensions arising from increasing polarization in our social life.

Legal judgment may also involve a fourth form of reasoning (which may partake of the other three but principally involves analogical reasoning), which proceeds by what Aquinas referred to as a determination (*determinatio*). He likened it to "the way that craftsmen in the course of exercising their skill adapt general forms to specific things"

(*Treatise on Law*, Hackett, 47).[24] A sailboat maker, for example, adapts the general form of the sailboat to the particular requirements of the sailor whose order he is filling. An official making a determination of law exercises a discretion that discerns how, given the particular circumstances of the case, that law may be provided a concrete implementation. The police officer who does not cite Alice eschews mere deductive reasoning from the traffic rule (not to cross the lines) to take into account that law's practical reasonableness—as one rule in a scheme of rules enacted to secure a certain order of traffic, where the resolution of this case is by analogy to a standard or model order that the scheme of traffic laws is directed toward establishing. Here teleological and customary reasons may be discerned to support that general scheme of traffic law. Reasons aimed at securing an ensemble of goods such as public safety, the efficient flow of traffic, taking into account the driving habits of people and what can be reasonably expected from them on the roadways. By deciding not to cite Alice, the police officer makes a determination from that law giving it a concrete implementation. His determination is that the law was not violated by Alice and therefore a citation was not warranted.[25] His resolution is a specific implementation of (rather than a deviation from) the scheme of traffic law. Police make determinations of law when they interpret and enforce disorderly conduct ordinances, by giving concrete implementation to an "order" the statute directs them to enforce.

A determination of law also occurs when a judge prescribes a specific penalty to an offender that is based on a more general precept that punishment be proportionate to the offense. Reasoning proceeds to a specific sentence via analogy to a standard proportion, taking into account the complex rationality of the criminal sanction. While securing goods associated with crime prevention, the criminal law is also concerned with goods related to securing due process, retributive justice, and even restorative justice and rehabilitation, among other things. Police may exercise such quasi-judicial reasoning when they resolve some dispute brought before them according to some sense of what is proportionate justice, making analogy to a standard of practice embodying the law's rationality. The informal punishment of a juvenile who has vandalized a shop (where the police officer in conjunction with shop owner, parents and the juvenile, adopt a plan of work that not only commits the minor to make amends to the shopkeeper but also constitutes a kind of punishment that educates him in the values of respecting property and abiding by law) can be considered an example of this kind of quasi-judicial determination that involves a synthesis of the ends of the criminal and juvenile law.

Our written constitution of 1787 may be said to be a determination of that scheme of ordered liberty partly reflected in the Declaration of Independence and the legal tradition and natural rights it refers to. A legislature makes a determination of constitutional law when it enacts statutes that give specific form to the political morality that underlies the constitutional order, such as laws preserving liberty and securing the domestic tranquility—goods specified by the US Constitution's Preamble.

To conclude, the preceding analysis reveals that judgments required in the enforcement of law go well beyond ministerial judgments determined by a formal deductive logic to include discretionary judgments that engage a more complex empirical practical reasoning where the goods sought by the law are construed in light of actual practices and commitments made by people. All told the enforcement of law requires cultivation of a rather sophisticated faculty of practical reasoning.

## D

As we have seen, the relativity of law's formality (as in the relativity of positive legal rules) is a function not only of relativity to *telos* (as in Alice's case strict adherence to the traffic rule prohibiting crossing the solid lines gives way to the requirement of advancing the traffic law's purpose of protecting lives) but is also a function of relativity to the facts of social order (as adherence to positive rules, e.g., is interpreted in light of the customary norms according to which individuals regulate their interaction). Let us pursue the second kind of relativity further, the relativity of law's formality to social context, by considering this hypothetical drawn from Lon Fuller's work. Imagine a police sergeant who has to interpret and apply an ordinance "there shall be no vehicles in the public park." How does the sergeant know what the word "vehicles" means? What if he or she receives a complaint (by a pacifist let us say who is offended by anything military) that a veteran's group has put on a platform in a prominent place in the park a World War II jeep as part of a monument to GIs who served in the war. The complainant insists that this monument is in violation of the ordinance as the Jeep is a prohibited "vehicle." Assuming that there is no controlling legislative history, the former synthesis of formal/teleological considerations would suggest resolving the case from the standpoint of what a rational legislature would be presumed to have meant by the term "vehicle" in the ordinance. A legislature could be presumed to enact the ordinance to protect the public from the dangers of moving vehicles in the park, a danger not posed by the stationary Jeep. Accordingly, our sergeant may construe the statutory norm as not implicated in this case and so need not take any action against the veterans, although it would be wise to consult with his or her commanding officer concerning the situation and to consult with park officials. On this account, the sergeant would not be violating the general duty to fully enforce laws. The complainant if he or she chooses might then seek an injunction in court.

Summers and Atiyah take up Fuller's case of the Jeep and the ordinance "there shall be no vehicles in the park," in the context of differentiating how an American and English judge would approach the interpretive question. (They do not consider how a police officer might have approached it.) They maintain that an American judge would likely find no violation holding "to a broad teleological conception of a rule in which its purposes are part of the rule … Accordingly, the defendant would be held not guilty because what he did had no adverse effect on park safety and quiet" (92). The English judge, on the other hand, they assert, would construe the legal rule as having higher "interpretive" and "mandatory formality" and find the defendant guilty. The English judge's jurisprudence would preclude him from having reference to the substantive purpose of the rule itself. Each judge is supposed to decide how to read the law from a point of reference on the formal/substantive axis, with the English judge adopting a position closer to the formal end and the American judge a position closer to the substantive end. (It goes without saying that some American judges would adopt the more formal positivist jurisprudence, which Summers and Atiyah attribute to the English judiciary and vice versa.)

Fuller, in the essay from which the Summers and Atiyah hypothetical is drawn, "Positivism and Fidelity to Law," insists that it makes sense to read the ordinance in light of its rational purpose (which need not have been expressed in the legislative intent or by some higher official in the legal system). Fuller's point is made in reply to Hart's essay "Positivism and the Separation of Law and Morals" and in the context of the debate between natural law theory and legal positivism. It is natural for Fuller there to look to demonstrate that a teleological perspective is internal to law as a counter to Hart's positivist denial of that premise. Summers' and Atiyah's dualism of form and substance makes most sense in the context of this debate between natural law and legal positivism.

Fuller, however, would later take up the problem of enforcing the ordinance prohibiting vehicles in the park in his undeservedly neglected book, *Anatomy of the Law*, where he took the analysis to another level

(57–9). Summers and Atiyah, surprisingly, do not reference it. There, in discussing the subject of implicit elements in made (posited) law, he uses the same ordinance "no vehicles shall be brought into the public park" to reveal an interpretive principle, which, I would say, is not teleological but rather contextual or historical. In construing the ordinance, the interpreter in certain situations will not center on the word "vehicle" (a positivist focus) nor adopt the perspective of the reasonable person who must determine what is consistent with public safety in the park (a teleological focus), but will instead concentrate on the term "park" and the meaning of that term in light of the social context in which this park constitutes an institution in the lives of the community whose park it is (a social/historical focus).[26]

In drawing out the implications of this analysis let us imagine, as Fuller does in *Anatomy of the Law*, our sergeant facing more typical questions of construction than the one involving the war memorial. For example, the police sergeant may face cases where it is necessary to consider whether the term "vehicles" in the ordinance prohibits only motorized vehicles on the ground that these are more dangerous than, say, manually propelled conveyances. Motorized go-carts on this interpretation would be prohibited, while baby carriages would not be. But are motorized vehicles always more dangerous? A motorized wheelchair arguably poses less danger than a fifteen-speed racing bicycle.[27] Should the ordinance be construed, then as prohibiting all fast carriages: skateboards as well as bicycles? But aren't cycling and skateboarding activities typically found in parks? Isn't a park arguably a place for vigorous play? Isn't it also, however, a place for repose and the quiet commune with nature? Pursuing these questions does shift attention from the term "vehicles" to the term "park," as Fuller indicates. The key to applying the ordinance is found not in linguistic analysis focused on the term "vehicles" (such as H. L. A. Hart's focus on a term's core and penumbral meanings) but in empirical/practical analysis focused on the meaning of the term "park" as an institution in the lives of the people whose park it is—analysis that leads to a practical judgment about what behavior is proper in the "park." The meaning of the ordinance is determined accordingly.

Fuller observes: "The troublesome cases are in reality resolved not in advance by the legislator, but at the point of application. This means that in applying the statute the judge or police sergeant must be guided not simply by its words but also by some conception of what is fit and proper to come into a park; conceptions of this sort are implicit in the practices and attitudes of the society of which he is a member" (*Anatomy of the Law* 59). The perspective of the reasonable person by itself a more abstract perspective, is modified by that of the reasonable person as an integral member of the particular community. One may refer to the historicity of the meaning of the term "park" in the ordinance by observing that the meaning of "park" may shift over time, that it has a diachronic quality. The shift may be not only a product of changes in community practices but also the interaction of legal officials (police enforcement practices) and the community's practices, each shaping the other, over time. Fuller observes:

> [T]he social institution "park" and the legal regulations relevant to it may be expected with the passage of time to influence one another reciprocally. A lax administration of the law excluding "vehicles," may gradually change the cultural meaning of "park." Conversely, a wholly extralegal change in the uses made of parks may gradually bring about an alteration in the meaning of the statute. (59)

The ordinance draws meaning from the contexts to which it is applied. "All this adds up to the conclusion that an important part of the statute in question is not made by the legislator, but grows and develops as an implication of complex practices and attitudes which may themselves be in a state of development and change" (59). As Fuller maintains, "In any modern legal system, illustrations like that of the park and vehicles could be multiplied many times over" (59).

Centering attention on the term "park" then pulls the analysis beyond the dualism of the Summers and Atiyah teleological/formal framework. The police sergeant must look to interpret and enforce the statute by understanding what the "park" is, not as an abstract idea (not considering *telos* in the abstract) but as an institution and social context in the lives of the people who use it, whose meaning in significant part develops over time at the grass roots level. This park may be more a place of repose, while the park on the other side of town may be a place for vigorous exercise. A third park might be both—where the park has developed distinct uses at different times or perhaps at the same time though possibly relegated to different areas within its borders. The park, on the other hand, may be less than orderly and conflicting uses may generate frank tensions. Here the "enforcement" judgments of the sergeant, whether they be more permissive or more strict, play a role in shaping the order that emerges. And that order itself is not static, requiring over time necessary adjustments on the part of police enforcement practice. The term "park," therefore, has normative significance, generated among other things by the binding customs that arise within it.

Let us now consider how a customary practice may form and become normatively binding in a particular situation. The relations of individuals interacting with one another over time may build what Fuller calls "stable expectancies" among them—predictions about the behavior of people that may be relied on as a basis for continuing interaction. A neighborhood comprising both families with young children and college students, for example, must come to terms with when and how student parties may be accommodated. In the beginning, this process of custom formation is informal. Some parents begin to tolerate late-night parties on weekends, but not weekdays, when they complain to the students and threaten to call police. Eventually the affected students discontinue the weeknight partying with the expectation that the parents will extend greater tolerance to them on weekend nights. Late-night parties on weekdays become rarer as more and more parents and students act with reciprocal restraint. Eventually, there arises the general expectation that in this neighborhood late-night parties on weekends, but not weekdays, are acceptable and future plans and actions are coordinated on this basis. With time this informal restraint gels into a common habit. It makes sense to refer to it as a normatively binding legal rule or standard of practice when it is widely adopted, relied on, generates a feeling of obligation to act in accordance with it and when it is effective in coordinating action, is reasonable (the students should find it more conducive to their academic work), is consistent with law's norms overall, and is accepted by officials, as in, police will enforce it in resolving conflicts. Under these circumstances, a custom has come into being as a legally binding standard practice—it has acquired prescriptive formality. Similar standards may also emerge with respect to noise levels at parties and other behaviors requiring coordination among students and other residents. These customary standards then have legitimate claim to provide the basis for a determination that an individual has violated an ordinance prohibiting "disturbing the peace" or "disorderly conduct." Sometimes the police must play an active role in the process of custom formation because the people involved are unable to produce a stable order or one that is consistent with legal norms. In doing so, they may employ a variety of ordering techniques from persuasion, mediation, administrative direction, and even the use of contract where police assist the parties who enter into a written agreement as to the conditions they will observe, which then facilitates the formation of a customary norm. The resultant customary order provides additional authority to police enforcement judgments consistent with it. The written contract alone, it should be noted, would not be sufficient to solve the community's normative problem because it does not bind individuals not a party to the agreement. (For an interesting use of contract, see Dayton Police Chief Igleburger's "Guidelines Related to Student and Nonstudent Residents" in George Kelling's *"Fixing Broken Windows" and Police Discretion*, 28–30.)

The normative force of custom, as compared to the normativity of discrete acts of consent between individuals, however, is complicated by the fact that it is a product of a cumulative and collective will. It is not produced by the meeting of individual wills at a given point in time, nor is it grounded on the actual consent of each individual who is or will be bound by it. From the standpoint of an individual (particularly an outsider or someone at the margins of society or a newcomer, someone removed from the diachronic process of the custom's formation), a customary norm may seem to reflect more conforming than voluntary behavior and so seem lacking in normative force. Consequently, liberal individualism that proceeds from the perspective of the individual will has been skeptical of the proposition that custom has normative force. However, liberal individualism, which is typically predicated on the counter-factual assumption that man is by nature an individual (that the state of nature is a presocial state), skews the moral calculus to favor individual goods or goods that are independent of social contexts. Because the human person is not only individual but also social by nature, rational desire directs him or her to pursue social goods such as friendship, social play, community, public order, and public morality.

Social goods have a character different from individual goods. Consider the good of community. Community is not the construct of individuals, it is not established by contract nor is it the aggregate of individual choices. It is greater than the sum of its individual parts. At any given point of time, the social good of community that an individual may experience has a history that no individual can claim authorship of. Community is the organic product of bonds that grow among persons over time, bonds that give them access to a host of additional goods such as friendship, social play, good will, trust, solidarity, order, stability, and the fulfillment of a role in which the person is embraced by the wider whole of which he or she is an integral part. Community is a good into which individuals enter and must spend time participating in, if they are to experience its goodness. This experience of community's goodness transforms persons from being individuals to being members disposed to qualify their pursuit of individuality in order to participate in this very substantial social good. Community, then, is an entity where individuals as members are understood to be persons who rationally—constructively—will their good to be a constituent part of a collective or common good in which they participate on an on-going basis and which gives them access to a host of additional goods. From the diachronic perspective of the socially embedded person committed to securing such social goods (rather than that of the asocial individual), the concept of a collective will and the proposition that custom carries normative force make sense.

The social goods are too substantial and too integral to human flourishing to be blocked by a deontologically derived right to negative liberty that trumps customary law. The securing of social goods that reflects and fulfills our political natures requires a will that rationally submits to social arrangements necessary for securing social goods. If one is to have friends and keep them, not just anything goes. The securing of social goods requires compromise, cooperation, and coordination of action over time, and that means according custom, which has the flexibility necessary to accommodate such interaction, normative force over time. It is reasonable then to construe a disorderly conduct ordinance giving effect to reasonable expectations based on past cooperative action that have become binding customs. Individuals must respect these customary norms if not only individual goods are to be favored by law.

The generation of customary orders based on the actions of people over time responding and accommodating to them, orders that give rise to reasonable expectations upon which individuals may rely, provides a normative solution to the problem of disorder, in that it yields the existential social goods desired—order, stability, community, etc. However, it should be stressed that it also provides conditions necessary for the realization of individual goods, such as liberty, that presuppose an underlying order and stability. No one has liberty when anarchy prevails.

Other reasons may be adduced to support the proposition that custom carries normative force. As customary norms are the product of people's actions over time, and as action reflects a form of consent, its draws normative force from the fact that it has been consented to. Here actions speak louder than words or mere lip service on the subject of what orders are acceptable. Customs also have more claim to democratic legitimacy, than an independently derived legislative enactment, where that legislation reflects only the will of elected officials: "For if a people is free, that is, self-governing, the consent of the whole people, which custom indicates, counts more in favor of a particular legal observance than the authority of its ruler, who only has the power to frame laws insofar as the ruler acts in the name of the people"

(Aquinas, *Treatise on Law* 67). Aquinas observes that, "custom avails very much for the observance of law" as custom reflects the interior disposition and acquired habits, which law abidingness in the fullest sense entails (65). Think of the enforcement difficulty when a positive law contradicts widespread customary behavior. This was encountered with the Eighteenth Amendment to the US Constitution (known as the Prohibition Amendment) and the Volkstead Act designed to implement it. The Amendment had to be repealed (the first time that had ever occurred to an Amendment of the US Constitution) because attempts to enforce it, given the widespread habit of drinking alcohol, were spectacularly unsuccessful and counterproductive. Prohibition made criminals out of an alarmingly large number of individuals. Custom can have the effect, as Aquinas puts it, of "abolishing" law (66). Finally, customs may well provide the only practical solution in many situations to the normative problem of what order the police are to enforce.

While the consent implied by customary norms may be considered consistent with the will of the people as expressed over time through their actions, it must be tested over time as well against a standard of reasonableness. People on skateboards and go-carts running amuck, mowing down pedestrians, per se, commit disorderly conduct because such behavior cannot be squared with any acceptable version of a park's *telos*. Skateboarding at some level may be consistent with customary use, but, when individual skateboarders behave recklessly, they may be cited for "disorderly conduct." The standard of reasonableness, however, may be particularly difficult to apply where it is the otherwise reasonable pursuit of goods by different people that brings them into conflict. To illustrate, participation in the good of vigorous play may come into conflict with enjoyment of the good of repose as when a strolling couple of senior citizens make a complaint about teenagers traversing the area on their skateboards, endangering no one but disturbing the tranquility of nature, especially the ducks on the adjacent pond. Preserving that idyllic milieu may require a ban on skateboarders for starters. Participation in the various goods that parks afford may vary demographically not only in terms of age groups but also in terms of culture. Certain cultures are noisier, less orderly, etc., than others. The circumstances may put police in sensitive situations of enforcing an order that allegedly discriminates against choices typically made by a racial or ethnic minority. Yet, an order that discriminated against minorities as such could hardly be reconciled to law.[28] Here reasonableness would seem to require that law enforcement seek accommodations to resolve the conflict. If the conflicting activities

cannot be relegated to different times or places, it would seem that
the police should engage in mediation with the objective of producing among the affected parties some settlement on the order to be
enforced rather than apply what Fuller called "managerial direction"
that imposes an order. (The choice of medium and ordering technique such as persuasion, managerial direction, mediation, contract,
custom formation, use or threat of arrest or force, legislation—or what
combination of them should be applied as they need not be mutually
exclusive—will depend on facts that may vary from situation to situation. I shall examine these and other mediums of law enforcement
and their application in a subsequent volume.) Compromises, then, in
situations of legitimate conflict may be sought and fair limits reached
on the acceptable pursuit of goods. To this end, the police may deploy
dialectics in the double sense: (1) the form of reasoning applied will
be dialectical as it seeks to reconcile otherwise acceptable pursuits that
are in tension and (2) dialectics in the ancient Greek sense of the
art of "friendly conversation" will be the rhetorical medium through
which the police may approach the parties involved. Such dialectics
should go a long way toward relieving friction. Police in addressing
such disorder problems, however, should also keep in mind the bigger
picture and longer time frame and consider how the settlement of the
particular conflict has broader implications for the overall order of the
park. The stakeholders here are not just the immediately affected parties, but the broader community and even future generations of park
users. The use of more informal customary norms and the more informal techniques such as mediation allows for incorporation of such
considerations over time. The exclusive use of highly formal positive
mechanisms such as contract or legislation, on the other hand, makes
adaptation to changes over time more difficult and contract fails to
bind parties not participating in the agreement—a problem generally
ignored by social contract theorists.

Our police sergeant in construing the ordinance prohibiting "vehicles" must reach some judgment (about what is a reasonable expectation regarding proper conduct in the park) that takes into account
*telos* and customary uses, and at the same time respects the formal
constraints imposed by law. These constraints would include the rights
of the individual to the equal protection of the law, free speech, and
freedom of assembly. A speech by a citizen may cause a disturbance in
the park, but that speech must be tolerated where the Constitution in
its First Amendment—as a higher ranking legal norm—requires that;
the practical effect being to permit a degree of disorder that the customary norm of the park would not itself endorse. That customary

norm is subject to revision as the higher law of the land is reconciled to the law that has emerged on the ground. Where the conduct in issue is "begging," a court (as we have seen) may decide that it does not implicate Constitutional norms and give decisive weight to an ordinance prohibiting "begging" or in its absence, the requirements of the customary normative "order." Where the court, on the other hand, finds that the First Amendment is implicated as in some planned political demonstration in a park that is a public forum, it may nonetheless uphold "reasonable time, place, and manner restrictions" that serve a substantial governmental interest: perhaps prohibiting the use of loud speakers after midnight in the areas abutting residential streets or denying permission to demonstrate in the park's formal gardens—provided a reasonable alternative location is made available, such as one of the open fields. The police must appreciate that the restrictions have to be content neutral. The decision to change the venue of speech may not be based on any desire to suppress its subject matter or viewpoint. This assumes, of course, that the speech is protected by the First Amendment. The Supreme Court has historically held that certain categories of speech are unprotected. Obscenity and speech directed at inciting—and likely to result in—imminent lawless action are examples (consult *Roth v. United States*, 354 U.S. 476 (1957) and *Brandenburg v. Ohio*, 395 U.S. 444 (1966), respectively.) Hence, customary use and *telos* play a role in restricting formal norms such as individual rights.

In traditional "public forums," it should be observed that the Supreme Court has given great weight to First Amendment formality, requiring that content limitations on free speech be justified based on government's demonstrating a "compelling state interest"—a burden that reflects a high deontologically formal balance of the interests involved. In this category of "public forums," that the area is a "public forum" is the product of the tradition that has designated it as a place for speech. Customarily, public forums have included public squares, public streets, and public parks. *Perry Educational Association v. Perry Local Educator's Association*, 460 U.S. 37 (1983). The formality attaching the right to these particular places, then, can be said to be prescriptive. Public forums may also be "designated" by government officials rather than be "traditional." Here, the resulting formality attaching the right to the particular place can be said to be positive. In the instance of a "designated" forum, the government has some authority to limit the forum to certain purposes and thereby to subject matter but not to discriminate in terms of viewpoint.

In the 1970s, the Police Foundation sponsored the "Newark Foot Patrol Experiment" and observed a dynamic which when viewed from the analysis above resolves into cases of law enforcement officers participating in the formation of customary norms that then become a basis of the order they maintain and enforce when, for example, they make arrests for "disorderly conduct." George Kelling, who conducted the study, found that despite the diversity of neighborhoods covered by foot patrol, officers acting without directions from superiors and independently of each other (but in collaboration with the policed community) were consistent in developing "rules of the street," which varied from neighborhood to neighborhood:

> Over time, through daily transactions, citizens and police came to know each other and to recognize their shared interest in the peace and order of the streets. Eventually police and citizens negotiated a 'disorder threshold' for the neighborhood, and rules of conduct that would be applied when that threshold was breached. While the officers' immediate involvement in the process was key, their activities may also have helped to develop a consensus regarding appropriate neighborhood conduct strong enough to persist even during times of police absence, thus heightening the effect of actual police presence. (*Fixing Broken Windows* 19)[29]

That "heightened effect" may be seen as customary law in the making. Police in these situations then participated in the generation of law's norms. Police may be catalysts in the development of community standards that become the basis of a legally binding customary order enforced through maintenance of order laws, so long as that order is legitimated according to law's norms overall. The authoritativeness of the standards is not derived as is sometimes supposed from the mandate given by the community, as that mandate itself is subject to legal criteria regulating the formation of customary law.

## E

When police exercise discretion in a way that assists in the formation of customary law (or the customary dimension to positive law) or when they interpret rules in light of more general principles or policies, some may say (like courts when they do the latter) that they make law. The discretion that police exercise in these instances seems quasi-legislative and quasi-judicial. Police discretion of this sort, according to some, violates the separation of powers and is not consistent with our constitutional order.[30]

Queasiness about the legitimacy of police discretion may partly explain the historical reluctance of police to be open about the discretion that they in fact exercise. There are several grounds, however, for rejecting a strict theory about the separation of legislative, judicial, and executive powers that renders police an entirely ministerial agency. First, our constitutional theory does not mandate nonoverlapping powers. James Madison defended the Constitution against critics who objected to it precisely because of its overlapping of powers. In Federalist 47, he argued that in none of the constitutions of the several states were the executive, legislative, and judicial departments "kept absolutely separate and distinct," and this he asserted to be true of the English Constitution, which Montesquieu had so admired. Madison argued that Montesquieu, the political philosopher most associated with the doctrine of separation of powers, objected to the uniting of legislative and executive authority in one person or body, but did not endorse the absolute separation of functions. Madison quoted this language from Montesquieu: "When the legislative and executive powers are united in the same person or body, there can be no liberty, because apprehensions may arise lest THE SAME monarch or senate should ENACT tyrannical laws to EXECUTE them in a tyrannical manner."[31] The exercise by police (as agents of the executive authority) of some quasi-legislative/quasi-judicial functions then need not be seen as per se violative of our constitutional order. Indeed, the overlapping of powers rather than their complete separation contributes to the scheme of checks and balances. The President's participation in the legislative function via the veto, for example, is a check on the Congress's power to make law. Police/community development of customary norms that, for example, constitute specific determinations of the order to be enforced under maintenance of order laws (provided they are subject to review by courts) may be defended as a necessary exercise of a quasi-legislative function, that supplements and to a degree checks the prerogatives of legislators to determine the order on the streets and is consistent with the principle of popular sovereignty.

The historical record reveals the gradual distilling of distinctive but nevertheless overlapping executive, legislative, and judicial functions. The early English Parliament was perceived as an "adjudicatory or law finding body" whose role was not to make law but find it, typically in custom. It would only later come to be perceived as a law creating body.[32] In "creating" law, however, legislatures should respect the normative force of custom and if they are to act inconsistently with it provide prudent justifications for so doing, perhaps by accessing teleological reasons. Conversely, English courts early on did not see their roles as subservient to Parliament and hence could correct legislation when it failed to correspond to what "law" required. Rational and equitable construction allowed courts to add to or subtract from explicit language in statutes. Courts also had authority to identify common law crimes, that is, offenses to customary law. (Today, this would be seen as a form of criminal lawmaking by the judiciary.) Eventually, the legislature would become the chief lawmaking authority and the courts the chief law interpreting authority, with courts retaining in exceptional cases the authority to engage in rational and equitable construction. (In the twentieth century, the US Supreme Court, however, would repudiate the doctrine of common law crime. The repudiation seems particularly defensible when prescriptive custom—sufficient to give citizens notice of the behavior proscribed and sufficient to constitute a discernible objective constraint on official judgments – is unavailing.) Nevertheless, the authority of legislature and court remains subject to the authoritative force generated by law's teleological, positive, and prescriptive formality.

Historically, the police were attached to the community and with the advent of the justices of the peace to the judiciary. The Police Act of Parliament that established the London Metropolitan Police one might say attached them to the legislature. Eventually, they would be seen as executive officials, a separate branch of authority, yet serving both the legislative and judicial enterprises through the duty to faithfully execute the laws. While primarily officials of the executive authority, police nonetheless have exercised powers that are quasi-legislative and quasi-judicial, necessitated by the role they fulfill in the prevention of crime, in order restoration or creation, and in application of law that requires discretionary judgments of interpretation. While fulfilling the duties that arise from the police role requires that police exercise considerable discretion, where appeal is made to broader principle and policy or local customary norms rather than narrower rules, that necessity should not diminish the vigilance with which a society guards the values associated with the rule of law. In engaging powers that are quasi-legislative and quasi-judicial, police must be held to formal norms necessary for preserving their fidelity to law. At present, the need to find limits particularly for the enlarged discretion of a problem-solving community police makes all the more pressing the development of the integrative jurisprudence that provides critical analysis of the normative criteria limiting the police function and that provides the theoretical basis upon which a limited police bound to the rule of law is established in practice. The rule of law, according to that integrative jurisprudence, is not just based on the positive formality generated by rules, but is also based on the binding formality generated by law's prescription as well as its *telos*.

Why must police exercise these enlarged powers? One reason is that the legislatures and courts are institutionally ill-equipped to make judgments that are highly sensitive to events that take place on the ground and evolve over time, that is, judgments sensitive to the historicity of the law. These judgments are particularly necessary in the sphere of order maintenance. Legislatures enact general ordinances abstracted from particular cases of which they lack specific knowledge, that is, the knowledge of what Aristotle calls the "ultimate particulars." It is from these facts, however, that law enforcement decisions must be made. When the question is when to arrest for disorderly conduct, police on the scene must be allowed the discretion necessary to determine the relevant order to be enforced.[33] It is the police who must grasp the facts in terms of the universal norms of law implicated by them, subject to review by prosecutors and courts. This may well require, however, a greater sophistication with constitutional law than they generally have had.[34] Police must be prepared to answer questions such as, is the speech made in the park indeed protected by the First Amendment or does it fall within the judicially designated category of speech "unprotected" by the First Amendment? If conduct is involved, is it "expressive conduct" within the First Amendment's protection? Are there valid and applicable time, place, and manner restrictions on constitutionally protected activity justifying an arrest? It would help if the officer were familiar with the First Amendment doctrine of "public forums," places traditionally used or specifically designated for free speech, where the courts have exercised a high level of scrutiny in reviewing governmental restrictions on expression. It would further the ends of law enforcement if police were able to articulate to the citizenry the rationales for these doctrines when they are the basis for their enforcement decisions. In other words, police should be conversant with First Amendment jurisprudence in such a way as to understand how the actions they take make coherent sense of the various rules, principles, policies, and doctrines that together form the *ratio* of the First Amendment. Police in order to fully grasp that *ratio* must also appreciate the philosophical basis supporting so high a value on free speech, that is, how the First Amendment right to free speech secures for human beings real goods by contributing to the search for truth about government, society, and the self, and by protecting the expression that is essential to a nature that is communicative, self-directing, and creative. However, police must be conversant with the jurisprudence of all the law implicated in the situations they respond to, not just the First Amendment. This means that police should also be familiar with factors indicating when practices that are customary have claim to legal bindingness. An officer should have sufficient familiarity with the local facts to answer the question whether skateboarding in some instance is consistent with reasonable expectations regarding conduct that is permitted in the park. When customary norms are needed, police must know how to facilitate their generation. All of this means that the police officer should know the law that he or she enforces and this requires much more than rote knowledge of legal rules. It requires knowledge of the relativity of law's rules (and other standards), that is, the relativity of the formality of legal norms to their teleology and historicity.

As for the limitations of the courts, judges render individual decisions with respect to the parties before them usually to rectify past wrongs, but in maintenance of order interventions the judgments affect multiple people not in court and should be crafted to promote an order into the future. Solutions to problems of disorder must be monitored over time, calling for more administrative than judicial expertise. The police are in a better position than the courts to make the necessary judgments.[35] Nevertheless, police discretion may be insufficiently formalized leaving too much to the individual judgment of patrol officers (who unfortunately are often ill-equipped in training and education to make the best judgments). Where policy is unwritten, the absence of documentation frustrates effective review by courts. Kenneth Culp Davis argues that the recognition of police discretion requires the articulation of appropriate policy and formulation of administrative rules that serve to "confine," "structure," and "check" the discretion lest police abuse their authority and act outside of law (*Discretionary Justice*). In order that police practice be made more open to public scrutiny and subject to effective review by the courts, Wayne LaFave recommends that police administrative rules be subject to a "hard look" review by the courts—establishing a level of scrutiny that will balance the benefits of allowing police discretionary authority to act based on their professional expertise against the public interest in checking that authority ("Police Rule Making and the Fourth Amendment" 211–77). Finally, as the courts could not possibly handle all the complaints made to police, necessity dictates that at least some, if not most, be resolved by police.

On the hard look review by courts of police rules, LaFave endorses the standard set forth in the leading administrative law case: *Motor Vehicle Manufacturers Association v. State Farm Mutual Insurance Co.*, 463 U.S. 29 (1983). While in *Youngberg v. Romero*, 457 U.S. 307,

323n.30 (1982) the Supreme Court stated that courts must show deference to the professional judgment of qualified administrators, in *State Farm*, the Court maintained that the burden remained on the agency to "cogently explain why it exercised its discretion in a given manner." The agency must demonstrate to the court that the administrative rule adopted "was the product of reasoned decision-making." More than the minimum rationality necessary to satisfy due process is required: "the agency must examine relevant data and articulate a satisfactory explanation for its action including a 'rational connection between the facts found and the choice made.'" The Court stated that an administrative rule would not survive judicial scrutiny "if the agency relied on factors [it is not allowed to consider], entirely failed to consider an important aspect of the problem, offered an explanation for its decision that runs counter to the evidence before the agency, or is so implausible that it could not be ascribed to a difference in view or the product of agency expertise" (qtd. in LaFave, "Police Rule Making" 253, brackets in original). I would add that when police enforcement judgments rely on local customary norms, courts should test these against criteria identified for a custom to be binding. When police act on rational interpretation, as opposed to law's letter, courts should test to see if they have based their decisions on reasons the law authorizes them to consider.

LaFave advocates that police act on written as opposed to unwritten rules and points to specific benefits of rulemaking. LaFave's points are followed by my commentary: (1) "*Rule making enhances the quality of police decisions*" by focusing the department on the policy being made (217, italics in original). Rulemaking "increases the seriousness with which police face up to the implications of their practices for the efficiency of law enforcement and the liberty of citizens." (218). In developing rules, police adopt a teleological perspective making self-conscious the objective being sought and the suitability of the means to achieve it. If experience is to be prudently generalized from, this entails looking backward as well, to consider how past facts and law enforcement responses to them should shape law enforcement practice going forward. This involves adopting a perspective on law's historicity. This process of deliberation over the rules to adopt and promulgate, therefore, encourages both looking backward and forward—such a broadened perspective is necessary to sound law enforcement. (2) LaFave observes that "*Rule making tends to ensure the fair and equal treatment of citizens*" by providing "uniform standards" for police action, which may broaden to profession-wide standards if adopted by other departments (218, italics in original).

Focusing on uniform standards and a police practice that adheres to them inclines toward respecting the principle of formal justice. The process of adopting rules focuses police on fulfilling criteria of formal rationality as the rules adopted should be consistent with each other and the department's mission—bringing overall coherence to their work. When the rules become the basis of the custom and practice of the department, they produce in addition a prescriptive formality, which may then constitute a best practice, leading to a profession wide standard, etc. (3) The articulation of written rules makes police decision making more visible (and therefore better subject to review and public discussion). Publicity and promulgation (producing transparency) are important features helping to tie official practice to the rule of law. (4) *"Rule making offers the best hope for getting police consistently to obey and enforce constitutional norms that guarantee the liberty of the citizen* because rules made by police are more likely to be obeyed" and enforced by them; as opposed to rules posited (imposed) from above (218, italics in original). This serves the rule of law by promoting convergence of official action with the rules, when of course they are consistent with law. It is important here to involve patrol and command staff together in the deliberation concerning the rules to ensure: that the deliberations are well informed, the rules adopted are empirically grounded, that they are endorsed by patrol, and consistent with the larger mission and policies of the department. A problem that I have often observed with police administration is the disconnection between patrol and command staff with the latter out of touch with the realities confronted by patrol, and the former in their daily practice disregarding the directives of the command staff (as the latter have far from perfect capacity to supervise patrol officers). The solution is not likely to be found in further surveillance as the more command officers attempt to subject the activities of patrol to an imposed panopticon, the more distrust and resentment is bred in the organization. It is better to incorporate a collegial approach in developing departmental policies and rules to reduce dependence on supervisory scrutiny and its negative effects.

The American Bar Foundation Survey of the 1950s advised: "The development of police expertness should be encouraged, and its existence should be recognized where appropriate" by "the development of an 'administrative law' in the enforcement field" (LaFave 248). Why administrative law as the model? Because law enforcement will put police in situations where one could not stipulate in advance the precise factors, given their infinite variety, upon which officials must base their decisions. Legislators, therefore, need to delegate what is akin to law-making authority to police. Kenneth Davis describes the process of administrative rulemaking this way in *Discretionary Justice*:

> A legislative body sees a problem but does not know how to solve it; accordingly, it delegates the power to work on the problem, telling the delegate that what it wants is the true, the good, and the beautiful—or just and reasonable results, or furtherance of the public interest. Then the delegate, through case-to-case consideration, where the human mind is at its best, nibbles at the problem and finds little solutions for each little bite of the big problem. Creativeness in the nibbling sometimes opens the way for perspective thinking about the whole big problem, and large solutions sometimes emerge. (20)

This Davis observes is like "the basic process of the creation of the common law" (21). What emerges to the extent that general rules are forgeable is something like the development of the common law or rather the customary law—police interact with community in the generation of customary norms that can then be incorporated into departmental rules and policies. What needs to be clarified, however, is the limited nature of the authority delegated. The departmental rules police promulgate must conform not only to the prescriptive formality generated by the legally binding customary norms developed on the ground, but must also conform to the requirements of positive law, not to mention be in accord with law's teleological formality. Police are not authorized to pursue "the true, the good, and the beautiful" independent of these constraints. This analysis has special relevance for the development of police rules and policies with respect to the maintenance of order where conditions are generally favorable for administrative rulemaking.

The foregoing discussion on the limitations of legislatures and courts and on the need for police to assume quasi-legislative and quasi-judicial functions also indicates why a community policing is necessary. The detached police of the "professional law enforcement" paradigm are ill equipped to make the informed judgments police must make to fulfill these tasks, particularly in maintenance of order cases. A more *engagé* police is necessary in which officers grasp the local contingent facts, appreciate how law's norms are implicated in them, and deploy the necessary professional expertise through judgments and actions that make these legal norms real. Law enforcement requires a common sense informed by experience of the particular orders policed, which should be united with a common reason inferable from the law itself, grasping the universal norms and the particular norms of law in a single understanding that is then the basis of law enforcement judgments and actions. Clearly this is far better than simply "flying by the seat of your pants"—a predicament that officers have historically found themselves in, given the absence of clear instruction regarding the nature of police discretionary authority and the normative structure that regulates it.

In sum, the foregoing analysis suggests the following disposition regarding the allocation of competence and discretion among the legislative, judicial, and executive authorities. The legislatures enact laws of more or less (e.g., interpretive) formality depending on the ends sought and the contexts involved. If the end is to protect a fundamental human good, such as life through enactment of a criminal statute, the law should entail high formality. Lower formality in criminal law (as in RICO-type legislation) may be appropriate when dealing with offenses committed by organized crime enterprises. If instead, the end is to secure a local order, the statute should be of relatively low formality, to accommodate customary norms. This, in turn, effects the degree of discretion available to judges who interpret the law enacted and police who enforce that law. In the case of a criminal statute both have less discretion, than in the case of a maintenance of order statute. In the United States, the judiciary is also required to test these laws against standards of the Constitution, thereby effecting the discretion exercised not only by police but by the legislature as well—whose enactments may be declared unconstitutional because violative of an individual's rights. Judges, however, have disagreed over what these rights are and the formality attaching to them; indicating deeper disagreements over the *telos* presupposed by our constitution, as well as the requirements of the social order. These disagreements may extend beyond constitutional rights to legal norms more generally.

The courts formally adjudicate disputes among specific complainants where they may apply more or less formal remedies, depending among other things on their reading of the law's ends—whether, for example, it is to punish retributively or to effect some restoration of order in a community—adopting equitable or less formal remedies where necessary to achieve the latter. Police and prosecutors in their enforcement actions may find themselves in a position to choose more or less formal law—perhaps formal criminal law, or more informal municipal ordinances such as disorderly conduct regulations, or perhaps civil injunctions—depending on whether their ends are, for example, more retributive (and match aspects of the criminal law's *telos*) or more restorative (and match the *telos* of order maintenance legislation).

The police in conjunction with the communities they serve fulfill an indispensable function both enforcing the law enacted by the legislatures and adjudicated by the courts. However, the police, in addition, in partnership with the communities they serve, play an indispensable role in regulating (and even facilitating the formation of) the customary orders that emerge on the ground and evolve over time. These orders must be reconciled to the law developed in the courts and the law enacted in the legislatures. That reconciliation is part of an interpretive practice where the law to be enforced by the police is read and applied in the varying social contexts, which the police officer confronts, according to the more particularized customary norms that justify the existing or threatened or emerging order—norms that are legally binding when they satisfy the criteria associated with law's teleological, positive, and prescriptive formality.

Whether a given set of facts implicates a general norm of law or is a set of facts from which may be inferred a customary norm that is a more specific determination of the law's order to be enforced or whether under the circumstances legal norms are in tension requiring dialectical resolution is a complex question requiring practical wisdom (what Aristotle called *phronesis*—which involves intelligent, sympathetic, and equitable understanding).[36] To fulfill their duty to enforce law, to act consistently with what the law commands, the police must unite such understanding with moral virtue, the firm and constant will to do what duty requires, that is the product of ethical character. It is the same species of will to act according to duty that US Grant encouraged the Washington DC, police officer to exercise, even when it meant citing the President of the United States. Law enforcement engages this kind of character, discretion, and action.

Police must understand both what the law's universal commands and how that universal may be realized in a particular law enforcement action, which may be an act demonstrating the proper degree of deference to a rule of law while at the same time exercising a discretion that advances some legal principle or policy or local customary norm. Police also require the firm and constant will to follow law, that is, they must possess the virtue of law abidingness if they are to act according to what they know the law requires—and hence reject bribes and treat friends and strangers impartially. This constitutes a jurisprudence of police (a practical wisdom about law) through which universal and particular norms are reconciled and the law is made real.

To fulfill their duty to enforce law, to make law real, police require technical skill, theoretical knowledge, and practical wisdom. Martin Ostwald observes that *sophia* (theoretical knowledge) originally indicated technical competence and skill (as in handicraft) but came to be used for scientific competence and theoretical wisdom.[37] The shift from a technocratic vision of the nature of policing, policing as a set of techniques (as in the professional law enforcement model) to a more humanistic political vision, where policing is more a vocation committed to pursuit of certain ends that are good and governed by certain principles and truths (as in a policing grounded in an integrative jurisprudence that balances the rule of law with the pursuit of a just order), involves a shift from *sophia* as craft to *philosophia* as abiding wisdom and commitment to realizing the justly ordered *polis*. Entailed is the operative sense of the term "philosophy" to be employed in discussion of the paradigm shift in policing as a shift in "philosophy."

Given the irregularity in human affairs, necessitating departures from general rules, and judgments individualized to particular situations, Aristotle understood that political science (which is at the basis of legal science that encompasses legislative, judicial, and police science) requires discretion (*Nicomachean Ethics*, Book I, chapter 2). Knowledge of law and its enforcement requires, among other things, knowledge of the political morality underlying law and (what has gone under-appreciated) the enforcement of that law requires cultivation of the art of rhetoric, that is, the art of rational persuasion, as the law is enforced best when citizens are persuaded of its reasonableness. The police officer's speech to Anthony D'Amato's "Alice" should constitute law enforcement rhetoric in the best sense. The professional law enforcement model has been associated with the view that the police are to be tight-lipped, avoiding whenever possible conversation with the public. The community policing /problem-solving model, on the other hand, assumes a more gregarious communicative officer. It therefore gives rise to the question of the rhetoric appropriate to the new police. Work needs to be done in developing the science and art of this species of rhetoric.[38] Lastly, as we have seen in this section, knowledge of law and what its enforcement requires depends on knowledge of the social facts and particularly, knowledge of the nature of the social orders policed, and the historicity of the legal norms appropriate to those orders.

## CHAPTER 8

# The Relativity of Justice, Law, and Police to the Social Bond

Liberal jurisprudence conceives of the rule of law as consisting of rules that set limits individuals must observe in their social interaction, leaving them within these limits free to pursue their own "good" in their own way. Such a scheme, Lon Fuller observes, "means that the law must deal with defined acts, not with dispositions of the will or attitudes of mind. The rule of law measures a man's acts against the law, not the man himself against some ideal perceived as lying behind the law's prescriptions" (*Principles of Social Order* 244). Fuller takes the view that the regulation of the social order by such a formal jurisprudence is "a basic necessity" within what he refers to as "the larger impersonal society." A formal professional police may also be considered a basic necessity to enforcement of the law of that society. However, Fuller recognizes that American society is composed of a plurality of social orders that are to varying degrees quite personal—orders for which, I argue, such a kind and degree of legal formalism is less apt. The formal positive police are required as well to maintain these orders on a daily basis. Fuller acknowledges: "it would certainly be a rare policeman who routinely—and without taking into account the nature and the circumstances of the offense—arrested every person he believed to have committed a crime" (245). An example is George Kelling's New York City police sergeant who did not arrest Joe, the squeegee man, in spite of his commander's order to "crack down on squeegee-ers," because he knew Joe, a war veteran, to be a gentle nonthreatening person (*"Broken Windows" and Police Discretion* 36). The sergeant seems to have construed that more formal positive order equitably, reading it as directed to a context in which the principal problem to be addressed was aggressive and intimidating solicitation. Fuller notes that with respect to minor offenses (although in light of recent broken windows theory, these may take on increased significance) a police officer uses judgment that "is inevitably affected by his perception of the kind of person the suspected party seems to be" (245). And one might add, the relation of that person and his or her conduct to the kind of order the officer is bound to maintain. Such discretion, however, cannot be accommodated to the purely liberal jurisprudence aligned to the larger impersonal society; nor by the same token should it be exercised where the social context of the officer's actions has shifted so as to render such discretion inappropriate.[1]

In this chapter, I argue that the correctness of law enforcement judgments in varying social contexts depends on the nature of the underlying social orders enforced. Where the underlying social order is more communitarian, that is, more personal, the adoption of a highly formal style of professional law enforcement and a highly formal criminal justice (that mandates arrest in all cases where a posited rule explicitly prohibits a defined act or nonintervention in all cases absent formal explicit authorization to act) may be criticized as insufficient to the end of social peacekeeping. Where the social order enforced is more individualist, or "impersonal" as in Fuller's sense, an informal interventionist style of policing may be criticized as inconsistent with civil liberties. As police encounter social orders varying from the personal to the impersonal and sometimes instances where impersonal and personal orders rub up against each other, they must be prepared to vary or modulate their responses, in effect adopt at times more the style of professional law enforcement and at other times more the style of community policing. Police, therefore, must be able to appreciate how the enforcement of the law is affected by relativity in the social orders they are called into.

Adjustments to the style of policing necessitated by different social orders are justified because as police confront these different orders they are faced as well with different principles of justice and law. I shall begin considering the relativity of justice, then law, to social contexts that vary in significant ways. As discussed in the previous chapter, law is relative to customary norms that emerge in social context. Certain social orders, however, are more amenable to the generation of custom, while others impede the formation of custom. Therefore, analysis of the relativity of law (and justice) must go deeper to see the correspondence of both to certain types of variation in the social contexts. I focus on variation in the social bond that holds people together—what Aristotle calls *philia*. I intend to isolate five features of *philia* that vary with social contexts and suggest how these variations have significance for both law and justice.[2] I shall conclude this chapter with some implications for the police.

# A

Aristotle asserts that justice varies with *philia*, the bond that holds people and states together. (Martin Ostwald in the quoted passages that follow translates *philia* as friendship, although *philia* is a term broader than friendship in the current sense and may refer, e.g., to the common interest uniting business associates.) "Friendship is present to the extent that men share something in common, for that is also the extent to which they share a view of what is just" (*Nicomachean Ethics,* Ostwald tr. 231). There is much that human beings share in common. There is a nature that all human beings share and that includes biological needs and certain basic human goods that we all seek to obtain or participate in. By nature we have various attributes and capacities in common, although these may be possessed to varying degrees because of differences in native endowments and differences in what we acquire due to our efforts or others' contributions. While human beings share the natural capacity to speak, we are not all equally articulate. While all human beings have language, not all share the same language. Moreover, we do not occupy the same land, share the same experiences, families, associations, institutions, culture, history, and so on. Human beings may, therefore, have more in common with some human beings than others. Men share friendship but that likewise is of different kinds. There is not only the thin friendship of all human beings (bonded by a common human nature), but also the friendship of those who prove useful to each other, those who are pleasant to each other, and those who act for the welfare of each other. Friendship then is not only a universal human good but also a relative good based on what draws particular friends together and holds them together. We may note that the pursuit of common goods that are finite, inter alia, means that one of the things that men share in common is the need of justice to regulate their actions with respect to these goods. However, if men have some things in common universally and some things in common relatively, and if what Aristotle holds about the connection of justice, *philia* and what is common is true, not all justice is universal, some is relative.

Aristotle states the relativity of justice to *philia* this way: "It is natural that the element of justice increases with <the closeness of> the friendship, since friendship and what is just exist in the same relationship and are coextensive in range" and so "the gravity of an unjust act increases in proportion as the person to whom it is done is a closer friend" (231).[3] Aristotle observes that the murder of a father is more "shocking" than the murder of a stranger. In elaborating Aristotle's point, we might observe that patricide violates bonds of particular intimacy: bonds at the level of biology and psychology, bonds based on special duties owed by offspring to fathers because of benefits bestowed, such as not only life itself but also maintenance and education. Likewise, it is an offense against the mother denying her, among other things, the *philia* and *consortium* of her husband. It is also an offense against the children and others who depend on the father. It is an offense that strikes at the heart of the family, an intimate form of community and a fundamental social institution on which other social institutions depend. Not all murders on this account are equal. Of course, a biological father who has abandoned his family—as opposed to the family man—is more like a stranger. A purely formal positivist jurisprudence (that is focused on the conduct alone) makes no distinction, however, between the two types of fathers (or between related and unrelated persons) in its responses to crimes committed against them. From that perspective, it is likewise difficult to support certain penal codes that designate murderers of police officers as murderers in the first degree, while murderers of ordinary citizens are murderers in the second degree. The discrimination rests on consequentialist argument addressed, for example, to the increased societal harm involved in the killing of police, given their public role, rather than deontological argument drawn from the formal equality of all human beings.[4]

I shall isolate five characteristics according to which *philia* may vary. We may begin by observing that Aristotle distinguishes *philia* in terms of the good sought by the relationship, that is, teleologically (*Nicomachean Ethics,* Book VIII). In the pros hen or central case of friendship, the good sought is that of the friend himself. Friends seek their friend's welfare without regard to selfish interest. (Family members in the tradition may be considered friends in this strong sense.) In business associations, however, the associate as such is only instrumentally good to some other end, such as the making of profits. Business associates stand farther apart from one another than friends. As Broadway Danny Rose puts it: "In business, friendly but not familiar."[5] Commercial transactions are better kept at arm's length as friends are disinclined to insist on getting the best value in trading things they have; instead, they often make gifts to one another. A bond based on this sort of utility requires some social distance, as in the relations of what Lon Fuller called "friendly/strangers"—a middle ground between intimates and enemies. Fuller observed: "A guess may be hazarded...that it is to the intrusion of the true outsider—'the stranger' in Simmel's famous essay that we owe, not only the invention of economic trade, but the more general discovery that it is possible for men to arrange their relations with one another by explicit contract" (*Principles of Social Order* 220).

The teleology of some social relationship, then, may be understood in terms of the social distance it establishes among its members. Participation in certain goods (such as pros hen friendship, family, and community) corresponds to more closely knit social arrangements. The securing of other goods (such as privacy, negative liberty, and commercial profits) corresponds to more loose arrangements. This analysis applies to the overarching social arrangement, a society's basic way of life (what Aristotle would have called its "constitution") and the ensemble of goods it is organized to secure. Aristotle's approach to this subject in his *Politics* suggests a conception of the *polis* as a whole composed of a series of social circles of increasing radii-associations characterized by extension (and thinning) of the bond holding members together. The larger communities are necessary because the smaller more intimate associations (married couples, families, kinship groups, villages, etc.) are not self-sufficient. They do not provide the full array of goods that human beings require if they are to flourish—goods that correspond to a nature that is not merely physical and social but intellectual, moral, and political. The cultivation of the intellectual, moral, and political virtues requires the resources of a social ordering that is more urbane. Aristotle holds that the human quest for widening association, with each social order building on the one before it, reaches an end in the all-round association— the *polis*, the city-state (*Politics*, Book II).[6] Aristotle understood the city-state to be a more tightly knit social order than the state in the view of contemporary libertarian theorists because he believed that it was constituted not merely for the purpose of mutual defense or commercial exchange, but as well, and characteristically, for the virtue of the citizens (*Politics* 80–2). A libertarian state committed only to mutual defense or commerce did not constitute a city in his view.[7] The cultivation of moral virtue requires that the citizens share a full-bodied public morality and this involves a constitution that enjoins the citizens to be virtuous. In the night watchman state, the citizens have far less in common. The *philia* characterizing a social order including a constitutional order, then, may vary according to the ends sought and the social distances established.

It should be further observed that the teleology and social distance of association are also relative to time. The more closely knit friendship requires time to develop. Friends, Aristotle asserts, must "eat the required measure of salt together" (*Nicomachean Ethics*, Ostwald tr. 220). While John Finnis acknowledges that community may be referred to as an "entity," he characterized community as "an ongoing state of affairs, a sharing of life or of action or of interests, an association or coming-together" (135). A communal order binds its members to reciprocal social roles that are the product of individuals interacting over time in ways that are to their mutual benefit. As individuals live together, these roles mature and become prescriptive. (As we saw in the previous chapter, when individuals interact over time certain patterns of behavior emerge, which may give rise to reasonable and stable expectations about the behavior of others, expectations upon which individuals rely. Reciprocal reliance eventually yields customary norms. When they are acknowledged as enforceable, they become customary law involving rights and duties. The customary law enforces the stability necessary for communal life.)[8] The *philia* of social orders, therefore, may vary not only according to the goods sought, the characteristic social distances established, but also according to their characteristic prescriptiveness as the interactions among persons may be more discrete and dynamic or more diachronic and stable.

This suggests a fourth feature of *philia* that is variable. We may observe that while business transactions may be discrete and presume no social commitments, intimacy, and continuity of relations in community give rise to a web of interconnectedness. Here the interaction of two individuals often has far reaching effects on others whose lives in various ways are intertwined with theirs in an order that Lon Fuller calls "polycentric." Fuller likens action in a polycentric order to the movement of a particular point on a spider's web that is then transmitted throughout the entire structure:

> A pull on one strand will distribute tensions after a complicated pattern throughout the web as a whole. Doubling the original pull will, in all likelihood, not simply double each of the resulting tensions but rather create a different complicated pattern of tensions. This would certainly occur, for example, if the doubled pull caused one or more of the weaker strands to snap. This is a polycentric situation because it is many centered—each crossing of strands is a distinct center for distributing tensions. (*Principles of Social Order* 112–3)

A battery on father that leaves him seriously disabled is not a discrete matter between him and the offender, but is a matter for wife, children, relatives, his longtime employer, and so on, where the harm to them is not measurable in discrete terms but in relational terms according to the natures of their interrelationships. It is a violation of a polycentric *philia*. The *philia* of social orders, therefore, as well vary according to the degree to which the social order is more bipolar or polycentric.

Finally, social orders differ in the quantity and quality of what individuals hold in common. Where relations are closer, more long term, and more polycentric, individuals are increasingly bound together in pursuit of common goods. Here, there is greater homogeneity to the social order. However, there is a complexity that needs to be observed. The pursuit of a common end may require the collaboration of individuals whose differences complement each other and make, among other things, a division of labor sensible and the fulfillment of a role obligatory. Where the social bond is based on complementary differences, Durkheim describes it as a form of organic solidarity. (He thought, rather too simplistically, that the degree to which a society was based on this kind of order could be determined by the quantity of its civil law.) Where the bond is based on common norms or what makes individuals the same, Durkheim states it constitutes a form of mechanical solidarity. The degree to which the social order was dependent on this kind of bond, Durkheim supposes, would be reflected in the quantity of its criminal law (*The Division of Labor in Society*). I might add, what is criminalized, whether violations of the person, property, or even morality as such. I intend to examine the deficiency of this twofold division in a subsequent volume. Where individuals increasingly pursue diverse as opposed to common goods, on the other hand, they act more independently and less is held in common. The social order, then, may vary in its homogeneity or heterogeneity (its uniformity or diversity), that is, in terms of its degree of plurality. A fifth characteristic of *philia* is its accommodation to pluralism.

Where pluralism consists of relatively autonomous heterogeneous social orders, social reality is not analogous to a series of concentric circles in which the social bond is diluted but still built upon the previous orders. Instead, it may involve the coexistence of orders at each of the levels (families, wider associations, etc.) that vary considerably in the qualities we have traced in this analysis. Some families, for example, may be more communitarian and others organized more along individualist lines where the relations may be based more on the utility and/or pleasure of members who retain a strong sense of their individuality and self-interest. A person from a loosely bound or dysfunctional family may have stronger bonds to some club or other association (perhaps a gang) that does not build upon a family bond as the concentric circle schema would have it. The description of *philia* across a wide swath of society may be rather complex, looking more like a Jackson Pollock painting than a pattern of concentric circles.

These various entities may be held together—to the extent they are bonded at all or their interactions regulated to the extent they occur at all—by a variety of kinds of *philia*.

The different sorts of tensions produced by conflicts within and among the diverse social orders constituting contemporary social reality complicate the analysis of justice, law, and police. When police are put into social orders varying significantly in the characteristics traced above, they will be confronted with different principles of justice and law. As a result, they will have to adjust their style of policing. (Legislators and judges will also have to make adjustments when the difference in principles manifests itself in their respective jurisdictions.) I intend to briefly treat the relativity of justice and law to social context before drawing some implications for the police. But before turning to that, I shall briefly sketch the nature of contemporary social interdependence.

It should be observed at the outset that much modern social interdependence does not presuppose (and is not directed toward) a communitarian order. Alan Wolfe observes in "Whose Keeper? Social Science and Moral Obligation": "To be modern is to face the consequences of decisions made by complete strangers while making decisions that will affect the lives of people we will never know" (qtd. in Clear and Karp 64). A society may experience an increase in population within a given physical space, as well as an increase in interdependence, without experiencing a corresponding increase in familiarity that may lead to personal friendship and community. An obvious example is the urban and industrial society of nineteenth century London. Indeed as the interdependence of individuals may increase, their familiarity with one another may decrease. Modern technological society has made possible an infinite number of impersonal disembodied interactions. As a result, individuals may derive benefits from one another without getting to know one another and commit harms (such as identity thefts) without any personal contact with victims.[9]

One dominant feature of modern social interaction is its dependence on technology. In both work and social life, we have come to rely on technologies that others invent and that are so esoteric that we necessarily depend on the competence of others to make them fit for our use. In traditional societies dependence on others went all the way down, so to speak, explaining the emphasis in these societies on the moral virtue of citizens. In modern society partly due to the technology, dependence on persons does not go down nearly as far. The assembly line model, discussed in chapter 4, can again be used to illustrate this point. On an assembly line my safety, let alone the success of the business that employs me, requires that other workers before me on the line—whom I may not even know—come to work sober and apply their skills diligently. For this reason both I and the company depend not only on workers having the requisite skills but also on certain virtues of character: sobriety, discipline necessary to due diligence, etc. In the period of industrialization, temperance laws were passed in part for this reason. The *telos* of such "morals" legislation, though, is quite thin. It is directed to ensuring the integrity not of a person as such, but of one segment responsible for a discrete task in a process of production that is linear. The "concern" for others, marked by enforcing temperance in this particular context, is only as extensive as the limits of the technology necessitates. (The integrity of the process could be secured by simply replacing people with machines that will never get drunk.) The interdependence of persons involved does not presuppose their moral character beyond the utilitarian virtues (and not even to that extent if the technology has rendered these otiose). It does not presuppose a concern for the welfare of others. It is possible to imagine not just work relations but social relations generally, organized along such process-oriented utilitarian lines. This kind of social order, then, does not require the full range of moral virtue, which Aristotle holds to be essential to the *polis*. It may be regulated largely on the basis of contractual principles based on mutual self-interest—those embodied in classical liberalism—coupled with the state fulfilling a night watchman function and enforcing contracts.

By contrast, the social interdependence that characterizes intimate personal associations such as the family and is also a part of modern life (though perhaps less and less so as more and more families have succumbed to the centrifugal forces of modern life) presupposes and is directed toward fostering a communitarian order. It is concerned with the welfare of its members. The interdependence here is less like a chain and more like a supporting web. Communitarian orders develop and enforce norms that uphold webs of interconnections in which individuals are bound in complex roles and relationships rather than discrete segmented tasks. The end of their social interaction is not more production of a discrete good but rather the realization of community—a good encompassing an ensemble of goods in which nonfungible persons participate in an on-going form of life in which all flourish. Moral character running all the way down is essential to sustaining this kind of order.

Modern social interdependence is composed of a multiplicity of associations falling within and around the individualist and communitarian range described above. Let us consider the relevance for principles of justice. Philip Selznick in "The Moral Commonwealth" observes: "As we move to association, and from association to community, mutuality reaches beyond exchange to create more enduring bonds of interdependence, caring, and commitment. There is a transition, we may say, from reciprocity to solidarity, and from there to fellowship" (qtd. in Clear and Karp 70). What Selznick describes is a transition from a liberal individualist order (based on individual interest and a *philia* based on the usefulness of the association) toward a communitarian order (based on the good of community and a *philia* that is based on the good of others). Laws enacted to maintain a communitarian order are derived from a conception of justice that goes beyond principles of contract and mutuality (where individuals look to advance the interests of a self) to include principles of stewardship requiring individuals to work for the benefit of others and for the good of community. Clear and Karp characterize stewardship this way:

> It asks not simply that citizens treat each other fairly (equality); that citizens take their own and others' membership in community seriously (inclusion); and that citizens coordinate their own interests with the collectivity (mutuality). Stewardship also asks that citizens step into the shoes of others, show concern for the welfare of the community, and even be willing to sacrifice some of their own desires in the pursuit of the common good. Thus, stewardship is a principle that emphasizes moral development, pressing individuals to think of themselves as members of a community, with duties as well as rights. (*Community Justice Ideal* 124)

A community of stewards will produce laws more fully and authentically directed toward "making men moral." Community policing's objective of enhancing community—understood as this kind of order—commits it to a thicker conception of justice, which in turn is tied to a thicker social and legal order.

The shift to this species of communitarianism has implications for the approach to crime. Conflicts generated and offenses committed in the context of closely knit communities have "polycentric" as opposed to "bipolar" effects—touching not just the two parties immediately affected but having reverberations throughout the social order constituted as an ongoing form of social interaction involving reciprocal responsibilities. Where the social order is more polycentric, rectificatory justice arguably consists in the restoration of a status quo ante requiring that justice officials provide redress to the full extent of injury caused. This is not just harm to immediate victims or the violation of some abstract legal entity called "the state," but harm to the community at large, restoring the full-bodied good of community that had existed before the offense was committed. A closely knit community may be expected to require that an offender do more than provide restitution to foreseeable victims and repair damage to the fabric of community. It may seek reclamation of his character because (1) it expects its members not merely to avoid doing harm to others but also to fulfill roles, including the role of good citizenship—where the citizen is a steward obligated to positively contribute to the public good and (2) it seeks the good of the offender himself. There are implications for what is made a crime. Legal moralism and legal paternalism would be ruled in.

When coercive sanctions are so tailored as to advance such a *telos*, they seem not only to violate liberal values that require strict adherence to formal retributive punishment but also to violate Aristotle's injunction that corrective justice does not consider whether the offender be a good man or a bad man.[10] In Aristotle, however, corrective justice appears to involve not punishment but compensation or restitution. A highly formal liberal jurisprudence tends to resolve questions of punishment into compensation—as in the case of strict liability, which removes from consideration the question of the moral culpability of offenders. However, Aristotle need not be understood to endorse such a formal theory for punishment; nor should he be, if the claim that justice increases with *philia* is to be reconciled with the principle of justice applicable to punishment. Were punishment to be understood as an aspect of what Aristotle calls distributive justice, the appropriate punishment is proportionate to the relative merits or rather demerits of offenders. Punishment then considers the character of the agent and his action. The offender is punished not strictly on the basis of the *actus reus*, but by taking into account the necessary measures to correct him.[11]

A more communitarian jurisprudence corresponding to the more personal nature of closely knit societies would treat punishment as an aspect of distributive justice that seeks among other things to rehabilitate offenders into good citizens, measuring the proper amount of punishment with a view to transforming them into people who do not just mind their own business but who also actively assist in advancing the common good, which includes the good of community. The offender deserves a punishment that, in Plato's view, "cures his soul" and restores him to the healthy condition of being a good productive citizen. This less formal principle seems to better comport with Aristotle's principle that justice increases with *philia*, where the social order is more communitarian, than the formal rule behind Aristotle's corrective justice, which is more appropriate to regulating social orders composed of more impersonal and discrete interactions. This analysis has implications not only for corrections officials but also for officials such as police at the front end of the justice system, as the decision whether to handle some disorder formally by arrest or informally by means short of arrest, for example, is affected by what purpose the criminal sanction is supposed to serve. A juvenile shoplifter may be better lectured to (and in the presence of his parents) than arrested; thereby advancing law's, in this case the juvenile law's, *telos* of reform rather than retributive punishment. (This is not, however, to preclude some form of punishment that serves an educative function.) Needless to say, handling matters informally in a discretionary manner generally raises the specter of abuse of power and the corresponding loss of liberty for citizens, goods given priority in the more formal individualistically organized society.

In sum, the movement from a more individualistically oriented order toward a more communitarian order involves the increased embrace of social goods (such as not only community itself but also the moral virtue of citizens necessary for that and other goods), the closing of social distances, increased polycentricity and prescriptiveness of human interactions, and decreased diversity in the social order. This has implications for the principle of justice. Justice is increased from a formal essentially negative reciprocal principle based on mutual self-interest to a more substantive consequentialist principle, enjoining individuals to disinterested actions and long-term commitments that positively contribute to the welfare of others—an instance of what Aristotle referred to as justice increasing with *philia*.[12] Conversely, the movement from a more communitarian order to a more individualistically oriented order involves the increased embrace of individual goods (such a privacy and negative liberty, that is, freedom from interference by others), the increasing of social distances (individuals interact more as strangers), increased bipolarity and discreteness of human interactions, and increased diversity in the social order. The principle of justice correspondingly is transformed from a more substantive consequentialist principle to a more formal deontological principle. Because contemporary social reality is not analogous to a series of concentric circles in which the social bond is progressively thinned or diminished but rather at each of the levels of social life (families and wider associations) there is variation in the *philia* that bonds (some families are more communitarian, some more individualist, etc.), the regulation of the social order will not be through a continuous progression from a more substantive to a more formal justice and from a more informal to a more formal law. A political community will characteristically contain all three species of Aristotle's *philia*[13] and its multiple orders will display variation in the several characteristics affecting *philia* that I have isolated. Its justice will correspondingly reflect the various principles discussed above. But so will its law and police.

I shall now briefly draw some implications of this analysis for law generally. Law's normative structure will correspond to the distinct teleology, social distance, polycentricity, dynamism, and plurality of the social orders that it regulates. The closely knit *gemeinschaft* society is more communitarian in its *telos* and this will be reflected in the ends sought by its law.[14] The end of its criminal law (assuming a state of development in which there is a Penal Code) will include restorative in addition to retributive elements, where the objectives will include having the offender reconciled to the persons and community offended and not merely fined or imprisoned according to some table legislated in advance. This has implications for the law's formality. Justice officials must have recourse to discretionary authority to tailor their dispositions to the complex task of reconciliation. *Gemeinschaft* society's legal norms, therefore, will be more informal. Moreover, *gemeinschaft* law will be implicit in the largely customary order that governs the stable life of this kind of society. It will not be the product of wholesale legislation. By contrast, the more loosely bound diverse *gesellschaft* society will be more individualist in its *telos*. Its more formal positive justice will be concerned with the vindication of the individual's rights and the observance of due process rather than the achievement of some end state or particular substantive justice. The deontological rights-based structure of its legal norms will facilitate the more diverse and dynamic orders that constitute its life. The social order will be less a web of inter-connectedness and more an open plane, including a vast private realm, where individuals are freer to innovate through entering into and out of more discrete bipolar contractual relations. Here there will be greater mobility and the pace of change will be palpable. This society, if less cohesive and less orderly, will be dynamic and creative/destructive. Explicit legislation rather than custom in the main will provide for the generation of its law's norms. As modern society contains within it elements of both *gemeinschaft* and *gesellschaft* social orders (though the latter predominates), its law will reflect that.

As for the police, when a society moves from a more communitarian to a more individualistic order, policing moves from a more socially embedded principle (as in the Frankpledge system described in chapter 4) to a more formal positive principle detached from local contexts. This occurred for the first time quite strikingly with the establishment in 1829 of the London Metropolitan Police, a formal bureaucratic organization at some distance removed from each of the localities policed. What eventually emerged was the normative model known as "Professional Law Enforcement" that constituted the dominant paradigm for police up to the recent past. High crime and social disintegration, however, have produced a shift in values in the current period with restoring public order and improving the quality of communal life taking priority. The corresponding shift toward a communitarian culture has carried with it sufficient momentum to shift the law enforcement culture, at least to some extent, to embrace problem-oriented and community policing.

The correspondence of *philia* with justice, law, and police raises the question, what happens when *philia*, law, and police are mismatched? Lon Fuller holds that: "law and its social environment stand in a relation of reciprocal influence; any given form of law will not only act upon, but be influenced and shaped by, the established forms of interaction that constitute its social milieu. This means that for a given social context one form of law may be more appropriate than another, and that the attempt to force a form of law upon a social environment uncongenial to it may miscarry with damaging results" (*Principles of Social Order* 237). I would amend Fuller's remarks to state: justice, law, and police stand in a relation of reciprocal influence with social environment. I pursue the problem of mismatches in a subsequent volume but shall use an example to illustrate it here. When the justice, law, and police of larger impersonal orders (that is roughly: the principles of liberal individualism coupled with the reliance on formal positive laws and formal positive police to enforce them) are applied to more personal closely knit social orders, we will have a case of mismatch and potential miscarriage. An example is the use of formal positive contract and mandatory arrest laws in regulating marriage relationships. Pre-nuptial contracts put the couple in an arms-length posture from the very start as they look to shield assets from each other. Distrust is sown. Where the contract defines what either spouse's respective duties or rights are (who is to do the dishes and so on), it will likely fail to anticipate the many contingencies and unforeseeable circumstances that arise in such a diachronic relationship. That failure may give rise to conflicts.[15] Moreover, when disputes arise and police are called in, mandating arrest rather than allowing police discretion to use mediation may do more harm than good. The possible outcome of the mismatch is to make marriage more like a social order whose conditions are suited to regulation by formal positive norms—an order that is more individualist and less enduring, in which interaction is more impersonal and discrete—a social order similar to that of the larger society. The resulting family will be less stable, more transitory, and less conducive to the nurturing of children. Family dysfunction and domestic disorder may be expected to rise, resulting in more calls to the police.

Contemporary social reality is composed of plural social orders varying considerably in the factors affecting *philia*. Because the business district downtown is different from the inner city neighborhood, and both of these are still different from the suburb (and because within each there will still be variation in the factors affecting *philia*), the new police paradigm must provide for a protean police capable of responding in one situation along more professional law enforcement lines, in another along more community policing lines, and in a third in terms of some variation of either. This means that community policing itself will not be the sole solution to the challenges facing law enforcement in the current period. What is required is an integrative policing.

To conclude, the current paradigm shift in policing, requires major reassessments at the level of our conceptions not only of policing but also of justice and law itself. The effort to rebuild communities in part to reduce crime, fear, disorder, and improve the quality of life requires adjustment in the underlying law enforced by police and the underlying conception of justice that underwrites that law. The law will have to authorize more official discretion and, therefore, be more informal than the law authorizing professional law enforcement, and the justice that legitimates that law will have to shift from an emphasis on the rights of the individual interpreted deontologically to an emphasis on positive duties to advance the good of community interpreted consequentially, with full recognition that the shift toward communitarianism involves a price, a reduction in those goods (such as self-determination, negative liberty, and privacy) that have primacy in a liberal individualist conception of justice. The increase in law's informality by the same token entails increased danger of abuse of discretionary authority, or short of that, the costs associated with poor judgments made in the exercise of that authority. This danger, however, can be reduced by the generation in law of prescriptive formality (through binding legal customs) and teleological formality (through invigoration of a natural law perspective that secures officials' fidelity to law's *telos*, perceived perhaps as a binding commitment to law's spirit). Both together serve to check official discretion.

## CHAPTER 9

# Summation and Closing Reflections

In closing, I shall first review how police might approach disorders generally from the standpoint of an integrative jurisprudence and then provide some concluding reflections on the integrative nature of law, law enforcement, and the new police.

## A

Given the pluralism of contemporary social reality, police must be prepared to enforce an ordinance prohibiting "disorderly conduct" by interpretation and application that takes into account and respects the plurality of orders existing in the society they serve—orders varying, inter alia, in *telos*, social distance, polycentricity, dynamism, and diversity. This is likely to produce distinct styles of policing. (The "varieties of police behavior" identified by James Q. Wilson in his book of that title may be re-examined in these terms.)

The social order of the suburbs is different from that of the inner cities and requires a different form of policing. The bedroom "communities" surrounding our cities are not fully communities but places where relative strangers reside on patches of ground divided often by fences, whether visible or invisible. Disputes there are more frequently bipolar and formal positive law is typically more appropriate to their resolution. The model of professional law enforcement and its more formal style of law enforcement is more appropriate to them as well, and more consistent with citizens' desires and expectations. However, where relations involving polycentric communities are infected by deeply rooted hostilities, more informal law is necessary. Most complaints about professional law enforcement have come from urban residential areas, which in the latter part of the twentieth century in America became hotbeds of ethnic and racial conflict and crime. It is here that the more informal problem oriented/community policing is most in demand and holds forth the most promise.

Yet, even in the suburbs when more closely knit *gemeinschaft* associations are at stake (such as a strong neighborhood association or domestic order), a more engaged policing (than the 911 rapid response policing typically offered) may be necessary. Likewise in the cities not all associations are *gemeinschaft*, calling for a standard type of community policing. If order is to be restored in Bryant Park in New York City, for example, law enforcement authorities must consider that the park is bounded by corporate and commercial enterprises, as well as the main branch of the New York Public Library. Those who use it are business people on lunch break, shoppers, visitors to the library, and tourists in mid-town. The park is not the extension of a full-bodied *gemeinschaft* association. The more stable stakeholders are the businesses and the Library, not families, friends, and neighborhood associations. A key solution to the problem of disorder can be through creation of a Business Improvement District, including the Library Board, in alliance with the police department. Formal positive law, a posting of dos and don'ts at entrance areas, supervised with the assistance of private security, kept clean by sanitation crews provided by the local businesses, and enforced by the public police, should do the trick in transforming an open air drug market where visitors are continuously harassed by drug dealers into an oasis in mid-town for readers, shoppers, and business people on lunch break.[1] However, a park bordering a residential community uptown plays a more intimate role in the life of the community surrounding it. There, the local residents are the stakeholders: families, friends, neighborhood groups, church associations, and the like. When relations are strained here, more informal mechanisms such as mediation are called for.

Special problems, however, are confronted when the social order is hybrid. This can occur, for example, when transient populations are mixed with more permanent populations–populations differing in their *teloi*, characteristic social distances, and rootedness in the community—as in town and gown tensions in the neighborhoods surrounding university campuses. They are particularly resistant to resolution. The police must be prepared to assist in the establishment of an order that can constitute the organic product of the life existing in such places. The solutions are likely to be hybrid, involving formal and informal mechanisms, perhaps contract, mediation, the production of customary norms over time, as well as the use of arrests when indicated.[2] Solutions will take time, ingenuity, dialectics, and a midwifery worthy of Socrates.

The orders appropriate to parks will vary to a large degree according to the same factors affecting the circumjacent communities.[3]

Where a park is frequented by a largely homogeneous group that is stable over time, its order will likely follow the development of custom and be more prescriptive. These conditions may be met by the smaller parks tied to *gemeinschaft* neighborhoods—parks where children and families play and commune. The jurisprudence of police will draw on the customary norms immanent in the stable order existing in and around the park. When, on the other hand, a park is frequented by a population that is more shifting and heterogeneous—such as the larger urban parks of contemporary cities (Central Park in New York City for example) its more kinetic order will be secured by more formal positive law that leaves considerable elbow room for diverse uses. The law of the park may be ordained more according to the harm and neutrality principles of liberal individualism and the corresponding jurisprudence of police will take the form of a more permissive style of law enforcement, tolerant of diverse uses so long as overt harm to individuals is prevented. Yet, these larger parks may develop plural orders within them. Sections may become identified with more homogenous communities that may be tied to them and be governed by more communitarian standards—resulting in a quiltlike pattern. In these large parks, however, the more formal jurisprudence may be invoked by civil libertarian groups, such as the American Civil Liberties Union, to resist attempts to enforce the more homogeneous orders. In New York City, recent attempts in Central Park to restrict use of the Great Lawn have been challenged as violative of principles of liberty and free expression. In tension is the view of the park as a place for quiet repose with nature or an esthetic ecology and the view that it is a place for expression of diversity and a public forum for exercise of First Amendment rights. Similar issues may also arise in a relatively small urban park, such as Washington Square Park near Greenwich Village. Surrounded by New York University and a vibrant intellectual and artistic community, it is a place for Frisbees and chess matches, not just demonstrations, countercultural expression, and the recherché urban contact with nature. Police are likely to be called into situations where these diverse uses produce conflicts. If they are to deal with them constructively and in a way that fulfills their duty to enforce law, police must have recourse to a variety of means of legal ordering including: informal mediation, persuasion, administrative direction, use of contract, custom formation, and formal arrest or threat thereof.

In sum, the relativity inherent in the police enforcement of the plural and diverse orders comprising contemporary social reality and to various degrees desired by contemporary people must be reconcilable to the more abstract conception of the "public order" implicit, for example, in the legislature's enactment of some "disorderly conduct" ordinance. That conception, in turn, must be reconciled to an over-arching conception of "ordered liberty" conceived as the *telos* of our constitutional order. A jurisprudence that interprets order mainte-nance statutes in this way provides legal authorization for what may appear to be reliance on highly particularistic "community standards" in making enforcement decisions. The key is to demonstrate how the locally relative solutions to the problems of order, decisions which in one place back a more restrictive order and in another a more permis-sive order, are justified not independently of law through community standards (which per se determine what the specific "quality of life" to be enforced will be), but according to law, making the case by marshaling teleological, formal, and social historical reasons drawn from law's norms. The order enforced is legitimated according to reasoning (whether deductive, inductive, dialectical, by determina-tion or analogy, or some combination of these) derived from law's triune normative structure.[4] Such reasoning requires an integrative jurisprudence.

Bringing legal integrity to the resolution of problems confronting contemporary police, however, will be difficult. Today, there remains confusion over the nature of the *telos* to be achieved (how commu-nitarian, how individualist?), confusion over the nature of the law's formality to be enforced (how much discretion, e.g., are the police to legitimately exercise?), and confusion over the normative implications of the sociology and historicity of the plural orders involved (e.g., what are the local customs and what degree of normative force is to be given to them? How are conflicts among customs to be resolved? Or in the absence of custom, how is custom to be formed?). These confu-sions lead to judgments and actions whose haphazard effects ricochet throughout the social order, further complicating police work. This is to be expected in a period of re-examination and fundamental shift-ing. We have yet to reach an equilibrium in which the various values pursued by the legal enterprise are reconciled in a way that garners a consensus.

The current shift in the paradigm of policing from professional law enforcement to problem oriented/community policing may be understood as a response to the incapacity of 911 reactive policing and the formal jurisprudence that underwrites it, in certain places (particularly the urban centers over the past several decades) to pre-serve a satisfactory order. The preservation of order today in many places requires the reinvigoration or creation of customary normative orders, which provide the more stable communitarian order necessary, among other things, for the flourishing of liberty and the pursuit of happiness. For the police, the preservation or restoration of order will not be a matter of enforcing formal positive norms to the exclusion of customary or natural norms. One reason is that the formal positive norms are geared more to the individualistic *ethos* that has failed to sustain the social capital necessary for strong intermediary associations. Nor, however, will it be a matter of enforcing local community norms exclusively, as these may be inconsistent with law's norms and enforcement of them may take the form of a vigilante "justice" that violates the legitimate rights of individuals. Instead, it will be a matter of enforcing law understood as an order derived from a synthesis of natural, positive, and customary norms in which individual and social goods are held in proper balance.

# B

The preceding analysis is predicated on a conception of "law enforcement" that is more complex and is empirically and normatively richer than the generally operative largely positivist conception of law enforcement prevalent in the literature and in practice. Law enforcement according to general usage is the making of an arrest for violation of some posited law. It is not social peacekeeping or maintenance of order, activities that may have the effect of improving quality of life, enhancing community, and ultimately preventing crime. Because formal arrests constitute a smaller percentage of police activity than maintenance of order interventions, some have argued that police are not law enforcers as much as they are peace officers. This way of speaking rings true only if the term "law enforcement" is construed "positivistically" as tended to be the case in the professional law enforcement model. When the term, however, is construed "integratively," which I believe is what the new policing requires, the peacekeeping and order maintenance activities of the police constitute part of the fabric of law enforcement. These activities enforce law in the sense that they make law vigorous by instantiating goods of peace and order that form part of the ensemble of goods constituting law's *telos* (not to mention constituting part of the condition of human happiness). The legal enterprise is a fit means for achieving the goods of peace and order (and others such as liberty, privacy, and morality) when that enterprise is governed by the principles of justice, integrity, prescription, and prudence.

As an enterprise committed to practical reason, as a form of *logos* (a rational principle by which we organize our lives), law is most vigorous when it is an active principle constituting the will upon which people act. That is when law-abidingness is not coerced because of fear of arrest, or merely conformed to out of habit, but is rationally chosen by the agent. A police officer makes law more vigorous when he or she persuades someone who has violated some ordinance of the reasonableness of the law in question (perhaps by demonstrating to the violator the harms attendant upon violation or that one could not justly organize a society without such a law) so that this person chooses to conform to it in the future. The officer, thereby, has enforced the law better than by simply issuing a citation or making an arrest without any discussion and without listening to explanations, excuses, or justifications offered by the offender. (Responding to the latter perhaps by showing the folly of the offender's rationalizations, itself, assists in getting the point of the law across.)[5] Of course, excuses and justifications may be fabrications, gullible officers may be taken in or the officer may not distinguish a legally legitimate justification from one that is illegitimate. The officer may lack the requisite knowledge of law or the rhetorical capacity. Officially recognizing the officer's discretion may open the door to corruption and abuse of power. At the very least, discretionary enforcement judgments may make the law's application less certain and incur a utilitarian loss. A persuasive argument may be made that a large measure of discretionary authority is better left to other officials, such as judges. Yet, without a considerable degree of discretionary authority, police cannot fulfill their duty to enforce the law that commits them to doing justice, keeping the peace, maintaining order, and improving the quality of life—an ensemble of goods constituting a *telos* that requires access to a range of means varying widely in formality, especially given the presence of pluralistic orders varying widely in *teloi*, social distances, polycentricity, pluralism, and dynamism.

It must be acknowledged that some if not most people (Aristotle thought it was most) are not responsive to reasoned argument and therefore threats of arrest or actual arrest may be necessary for the law's enforcement—and so the police are authorized to use coercive force.[6] Positivism has tended to focus exclusively on this externalization of the legal (and police) principle.[7] Professional law enforcement, by the same token, has tended to focus on law enforcement as the arrest by the external police that imposes on the offender the law's positive norm. The integrative perspective, however, widens the screen, or rather integrates multiple screens, incorporating analyses of the substance and context of the legal norm enforced and the means by which it may be internalized. To enforce law means to animate law appreciated not merely as an externally imposed structure of posited norms (the perspective of Holmes' bad man) but as a commitment to an enterprise for establishing a just order having distinct formal, social/historical, and teleological dimensions (requiring the internal perspective of the law-abiding citizen). An act of enforcement may involve the making of a formal arrest for violation of some ordinance when that act on balance strengthens law as a formal and social/historical enterprise committed to establishing a just order. An arrest, however, does not always have the effect of "enforcing" some law, but may have the opposite effect. Formal arrest may result in defeating some ordinance when, for example, the violator is engaged in an act of civil disobedience in which the arrest is one step toward what is hoped will be a judicial determination of the law's unconstitutionality or if short of that a demonstration to the broader public of the law's injustice—an appeal that addresses the public conscience and results in the law's eventual repeal. To enforce law in the integrative sense is to take action that contributes to making the law an active internal principle of volition of citizens and public officials including the police and contributes to making the law an enduring material principle regulating the order of society over time in accordance with the requirements of justice. To enforce law is to animate law. When law is fully internalized so is the principle of police. A fully law abiding community, ipso facto, polices itself. The *telos* of police is realized when "the police are the community and the community are the police"—where both police and community are constituted normatively. Pathological "communities" install a "police state." The internalization of their "norms" cannot be consistent with rational desire.

## C

In legal positivism, law's normative structure is defined in terms of its positive formality. A norm is legitimate because it is posited consistent with law's integrity, which requires striking the right balance between formality and discretion in law—a balance that properly allocates discretion according to the division of legal labor among various officials, including the police, preserving the rule of law. In naturalist jurisprudence, law's normative structure is more teleological in its trajectory. A legal norm is legitimated with reference to its justice, where justice constitutes a mean—the right balance between individual and public goods—a balance struck according to norms that properly weigh the force of teleological/consequentialist and deontological justifications in judging disputes where individual claims of right come into conflict with the public pursuit of the general welfare. In sociological/historical jurisprudence, law's normative structure is determined according to its prescription, its capacity to establish an enduring material order that reconciles tensions between the local and universal norms of law generated at any given point in time and over time as law evolves. The degree of prescription appropriate to legal norms depends on the nature of the social order including consideration of: its *telos*, the characteristic social distances involved in social interaction, its degree of polycentricity and plurality, and the degree to which the social order is dynamic or more static. Law's prescription, for example, will vary depending on whether the society is more *gemeinschaft* or *gesselschaft*.

Integrative jurisprudence interprets law's normative structure along these three dimensions of the legal enterprise. To enforce lawfully means to enforce law's norms as derived from a synthesis that strikes the right axial balances throughout law's three dimensions among norms that are in dialectical tension advancing law's justice, its integrity, its prescription, and its prudence. Law's normative structure will interact with social phenomena and this dynamic will yield different balances and imbalances in law's teleological, formal, and social/historical axes. These changes will require corresponding adjustment in law enforcement, explaining why in certain places and at certain times a more professional law enforcement may be appropriate and yet in other places and times a more problem-oriented community police may be appropriate. To enforce the law is not to do the same thing in all cases and all times. (Part of the difficulty plaguing contemporary theorists in defining police is due to this protean nature of the function.) A unified theory of the police function and a unified theory of law takes this relativity into account articulating what is required by the duty to fully enforce the law in the varying contexts to which the police respond.

I shall provide a brief summation on the interaction of principles in law's normative structure. One can infer certain logical relations among the three axial principles so that a shift in the axial balance struck in one of law's dimensions has logical consequences for balances struck in the other two. A shift in law's teleological axis from emphasis on the good of individuality to the good of community (produced let us say by embrace of a more communitarian conception of justice that underwrites law) not only will be reflected in a shift in the form of justificatory reasoning used by officials, from deontological arguments derived from the rights of the individual to consequentialist arguments directed to the general welfare, but also will be reflected in a corresponding shift in law's formal axis from the emphasis on rule bound uniformity in action to allowing official action based on norms of lower formality that invite more discretionary individualized judgments. These more discretionary judgments may be justified by argument from a norm at a higher level of abstraction than the rule itself, such as a broad principle of equity or public policy, or perhaps from a more local norm, such as customary practice—norms that are in any case reconcilable to a conception of the integrity of legal norms. As the good of community requires time to develop and is the product not of discrete acts but the assumption of roles and the development of relationships that endure and the organization of persons around common goals requiring greater dependence on the generation of social capital, such as trust and goodwill, a shortening of what Fuller referred to as "social distances" occurs. The transformation of the nature of social interaction from bipolarity to polycentricity also occurs. (Members of communities are more interdependent and so actions among them have reverberations over time as opposed to transactions among relative strangers where consequences are more discrete and do not result in building relations, whether good or bad, among the transacting parties.) In the area of criminal justice, the increase in the degree of polycentricity in the social order means that offenses constituting crimes are offenses involving not only the immediately harmed victim and the abstract entity of the "state" but also a host of adversely affected persons and associations broadly characterized as the "community." Justice officials will have to adjust their philosophies and practice to provide more informal remedies for these additional injuries—remedies that are mandated by a thicker conception of justice that incorporates, for example, a principle of stewardship. With embrace of a more communitarian good, there will be a corresponding shift in law's social/historical axis toward a greater embrace of continuity in social life enforced by legal norms of increased prescription. This shift will, however, be met with resistance from more dynamic elements in the society that value creativity, individuality, and change, for whom John Stuart Mill's essay *On Liberty* may provide the standard. The tensions generated between libertarian views and communitarian views regarding the new problem oriented/community policing may be explained in these terms. Even Mill, however, who so strongly endorsed creativity and individuality in the essay *On Liberty*, in his treatise *Utilitarianism* recognized that human happiness consists in some balance struck between excitement and repose (between dynamism and stability) and some conformity of the individual will to the requirements of the general welfare.[8] As a society looks, after a period of great change, for more stability, this will be reflected in its stronger emphasis on community, customary norms, and informality in official judgments. A sentencing judge in such a climate may seek more the reconciliation of the offender with the community as that may be more desired than purely formal retributive punishment. He or she would require more discretion when it comes to sentencing to do so. A police officer in this environment may judge that the law in many situations is better enforced by foregoing formal arrest and working toward reconciling offender, victim, and community. To this end, the officer will require discretion to access a host of informal mechanisms of remediation.

What form of law enforcement police adopt depends on factors that the police do not and should not attempt to control. Emile Durkheim saw modern mass society as destructive of the smaller communities that are intermediate between individual and state and he conceived of the emergence of professions as helping to mediate the resulting relations between the state and the individual (*Professional Ethics and Civic Morals* 96). The police may be seen as a profession playing such a mediating role, but to succeed they must help restore intermediating communities. They are no substitute for them. In exercising authority then, police should adopt a principle of subsidiarity, allowing the local communities to generate the more specific norms that are needed to regulate their orders and norms that provide an integral part of the basis on which the police legitimately preserve order, or where conditions frustrate this, to assist communities in their generation, so long as the resulting orders are consistent with law's normative order overall. The preservation of these relatively autonomous intermediary orders, in turn, provides conditions favorable to the preservation of the rule of law itself.

A brief word on the principle of subsidiarity, which John Finnis defines as follows:

> The principle is one of justice. It affirms that the proper function of association is to help the participants in the association help themselves or, more precisely, to constitute themselves through the individual initiatives of choosing commitments (including commitments to friendship and other forms of association) and of realizing these commitments through personal inventiveness and effort in projects (many of which will, of course, be co-operative in execution or even communal in purpose). And since in large organizations the process of decision-making is more remote from the initiative of most of those many members who will carry out the decision, the same principle requires that larger

associations should not assume functions that can be performed efficiently by smaller associations.

What is the source of this principle?...Human good requires not only that one *receive* and *experience* benefits or desirable states, it requires that one do certain things, that one should *act*, with integrity and authenticity; if one can obtain the desirable objects and experiences through one's own action, so much the better. Only in action...does one fully participate in human goods. No one can spend all his time, in all his associations, leading and taking initiatives; but one who is never more than a cog in big wheels turned by others is denied participation in one important aspect of human well-being. (146–7, italics in original)

Hence, individuals should be allowed the opportunity to participate in the good of community by constituting it in their own way, with the police respecting their choices—so long as those choices are consistent with law's norms overall. This liberty is none other than the dignity of self-direction, manifested in the form of communities as associations of self-directing persons and it is, therefore, integrally connected to that basic good served by the rule of law.[9] It is a requirement of integrity in law. The principle of subsidiarity is also conducive to preserving the correspondence of *philia* to the principles of justice, law, and police I examined in chapter 8. The potential for mismatches and miscarriages is greater when justice, law, and police are imposed from on high or by those officials (including legislators) responsible for regulation of the larger impersonal society. When the smaller more communitarian orders are respected in their relative autonomy, they are more likely to find the justice, law, and police natural to them. The principle of subsidiarity may then be considered a corollary of law's historicity, that is, law's relativity to social context over time. It is therefore conducive to law's prescription.

The contemporary social order is an extraordinary dynamic consisting of a plurality of smaller more homogeneous orders regulated by legal norms of lower positive formality within a broader unity that transcends them that is regulated according to more formal positive legal norms. The heterogeneity of the orders constituting contemporary social reality—the variety in terms of ends, social distances, social interconnectedness (polycentricity), and differences in their dynamism or stability—and the corresponding heterogeneity of legal norms regulating that reality—requires a protean police having access to the full spectrum of formal to informal mechanisms: from formal arrest to dispute resolution and mediation, to persuasion, and to order creation where that may access principles of contract and custom. This new police requires transcending the disjunction existing between the professional law enforcement paradigm and problem-oriented/community policing paradigm.

The protean nature of the new police, the complexity of the processes involved, and the sophistication of the judgments required of law enforcement demand that practitioners have practical wisdom, what Aristotle called *phronesis*, united with moral virtue, that is, the qualities of character productive of the firm will to do what is right. That wisdom and character are informed by jurisprudence. In this book, I have attempted to clarify the characteristic virtues, as well as the science and art of the jurisprudence of police. That jurisprudence will have to be translated into an educational curriculum and a regime of professional training. The management curricula offered to police today, in the training institutes and the universities, while helpful in organizing a department efficiently, are not sufficient for their education, as the first principles of police are derived from law where evaluation of means and ends are governed by a synthesis of law's triune norms. The current variety of police ethics courses, as well, is not enough, as what is right in any enforcement decision presupposes an answer to a complex question about what the law determines as right. Furthermore, the smattering of law police are exposed to in many of the training academies must be replaced by a more comprehensive education in law that digs more philosophically into the human goods and reasons that justify the legal enterprise and the role police fulfill in it.

Police require a formal education and professional training that addresses the centrality of jurisprudence to their role as law enforcers or law animators—particularly today, as the underlying communitarian orders and their corresponding customary norms have in many places to which the police are called disintegrated, making the job of order restoration or creation all the more paramount and the question about what legitimates these new orders and the police actions that enforce them all the more pressing. The police may well play the vital role of midwives to the new orders. They do so by fulfilling their duty to enforce law, an end that requires that they fulfill the roles of peacekeepers, maintainers and restorers of order (even quasi-creators of order), and enhancers of the citizens' quality of life. To faithfully do that, however, they must cultivate a jurisprudence that informs the judgments they will have to make.

It is likewise the case that the general unified theory of law that both informs the jurisprudence of police and provides the integrative theory that prescribes the relative roles of other officials in the legal enterprise (legislators, judges, prosecutors and correction officers) has yet to be elaborated in detail. In the meantime, much heat and energy will be expended in the fight over interpreting and applying our law, because so much is at stake. It is the integrative perspective that offers the most promising route out of the fragmentation that plagues so many aspects of contemporary life, especially our legal life.

# Notes

## Preface

1. From Daniel Bell's 1991 Brandeis University Commencement Address, quoted by the *New York Times*.
2. Harold Berman dissects this crisis in *Law and Revolution: The Formation of the Western Legal Tradition*.
3. The phrase "fixing broken windows" is most associated with James Q. Wilson and George Kelling who coauthored a March 1982 *Atlantic Monthly* article of that title. Kelling with Catherine Coles later wrote the book *Fixing Broken Windows* that elaborates the theory. The text contains a foreword by Wilson.
4. A unified theory of law looks to resolve the disproportion between the most general principles of law and the particular actions by legal officials that constitute what some have called the "law in action." It is the material legal order, the experience of law and order on the streets that the police have most familiarity with. A jurisprudence of police is necessary because police have a primary responsibility to ensure that the material order is consistent with law. When a disproportion occurs between what some statute stipulates and what a particular situation may require, as occurs in the Anthony D'Amato hypothetical we shall address in chapter 7, police require a general unified jurisprudence to reconcile the difficulty. For far too long, many police faced with such disproportions have had to rely on common sense alone or, to use an expression I have heard often from police themselves, have had to "fly by the seat of their pants." Disproportion can also occur elsewhere in the administration of justice. An example is when a judicial sentence in some case deviates from legislated sentencing guidelines. I shall argue that integrative jurisprudence, which combines the perspectives of the great schools of jurisprudence (natural law, legal positivism, and the historical/sociological school), offers the best approach to a general unified theory of law and the resolution of such disproportions.

## Introduction

1. The poem "Four Quartets" from which the language is drawn may be found in *Complete Poems and Play 1909–1950*, 144

2. The American Bar Foundation, then the research arm of the American Bar Association, conducted an extensive field operations survey of justice practitioners, including the police, and found considerable discretion in the system. The field work was conducted in three states from 1955 to 1957. The survey is the subject of analysis in *Discretion in Criminal Justice*, eds. Lloyd Ohlin and Frank Remington. See also Samuel Walker, "Origins of the Contemporary Criminal Justice Paradigm," pp. 201–30.

3. See Mark Harison Moore's excellent essay, "Problem Solving and Community Policing" in *Modern Policing*.

4. For a fine analysis of historical jurisprudence, see Harold Berman, "The Origins of Historical Jurisprudence: Coke, Selden, and Hale," *103 Yale Law Review* 1651 (1994).

5. See especially Harold Berman, "Towards an Integrative Jurisprudence" as well as *Law and Revolution*, vols. I and II. Quotations in this book from *Law and Revolution* are all from Volume I unless Volume II is specified.

### i   The Jurisprudence of Police Defined

1. The language from Magna Carta is quoted by Harold Berman in *Law and Revolution: The Formation of the Western Legal Tradition*, p. 294.

2. The Thorne translation of Bracton is quoted by Kmiec and Presser, *The History, Philosophy and Structure of the American Constitution*, p. 32.

3. Ostwald interprets Aristotle this way: "Practical wisdom is itself a complete virtue or excellence, while the excellence of art depends on the goodness or badness of its product," p. 154.

4. Aristotle was quite sensitive to these variations. He and students under his direction wrote well over one hundred treatises each on a constitution in the ancient world. Unfortunately, only one has survived, his *Athenian Constitution*.

5. For a recent conservative exposition of the "living Constitution" where that entails respecting the country's "unwritten constitution"—which includes its collective customs and traditions—that not only checks the activism of judges but also provides the constitution the flexibility necessary for it to endure, see Russell Kirk, *Rights and Duties: Reflections on Our Conservative Constitution*.

6. One might say that the *telos* is more aptly characterized as a "just order." Harold Berman observed that this term contains a fourfold tension. Justice may be in tension with order. Order itself is a concept in which a tension is generated between stability and change (I would add a tension as well between the universal and the particular), and justice is a term in which there is a tension between the

individual good and the general welfare. See Harold Berman, *Law and Revolution*, p. 21. This conception of the *telos*, therefore, requires a complex discretion directed to relieving the tensions produced by the pursuit of these goods.

7. On the European continent, the judiciary is the repository of jurisprudence, which is defined as the decisions of the courts. In the Anglo-American common law tradition, the reference is broader, extending to the philosophy of law. See Surya Prakash Sinha, *Jurisprudence, Legal Philosophy in a Nutshell*, p. 1.

8. The language is from a speech delivered by Burke at Bristol, England, on November 3, 1774, and is quoted in *The Oxford Dictionary of Quotations*, p. 164.

9. See Kenneth C. Davis, *Discretionary Justice*, p. 233 and Lawrence Sherman, "Attacking Crime: Policing and Crime Control," *Modern Policing*, p. 220. Neither, however, elaborates a conception of the jurisprudence of police.

10. Parratt, "How Effective Is a Police Department?" 199 Annals 153 (1938) as qtd. in Joseph Goldstein, "Police Discretion Not to Invoke the Criminal Process: Low Visibility Decisions in the Administration of Justice," pp. 556–7.

11. Warren Burger in his address to local and state administrators graduating from the FBI National Academy, as quoted in Frank J. Remington, *Standards Relating to the Urban Police Function*, p. 2.

12. From the Transcript of Remarks of Warren E. Burger at the FBI National Academy Graduation Ceremony, November 3, 1971.

13. Unfortunately, much of legal education today looks to do the opposite of Hall's instruction and teaches that law's rules are disconnected and dissonant–not arrangeable in any "harmonious order." This, I believe, has contributed to the fragmentation of our jurisprudence.

14. August Vollmer in a similar vein wrote of the police officer:

> No person in the community has more power to create respect for the government than an intelligent and sympathetic police officer. Not only does he protect and defend the people of his district, but he is also parish priest, and legal, medical and social advisor and counselor. To the poor, the ignorant, and the immigrant, he is not merely a government representative: he is the government, or, as expressed in some states, he is the law. (*The Police in Modern Society* 216)

> Oliver Wendell Holmes, Jr. "addressing his law students" similarly urged that they consider the application of their particular case to the legal universe: "Your business as lawyers is to see the relation between your particular fact and the whole frame of the universe" (Holmes qtd. in Berman, *Law and Revolution* vii).

15. Daniel Webster's speech of September 12, 1845, quoted in Edward Tryon, *The New Dictionary of Thoughts*, p. 277.

## 2   A Critique of Positivist Police Science

1. "The Runaway" appeared on the cover of the "Saturday Evening Post," September 20, 1958. It is in the Norman Rockwell Museum, Norman Rockwell Art Collection Trust. The painting is from a photograph of a scene staged at a Howard Johnson's in Pittsfield, MA. Rockwell's illustrations were often based on photographs of scenes that he staged. Ron Schick, the author of *Norman Rockwell Behind the Camera* writes, "In the five decades since 'The Runaway's' publication, Clemens [the Massachusetts state trooper photographed for the illustration] has seen it 'become synonymous with law enforcement,'" "emblematic of the mission to protect and serve." Clemens reports, "Wherever you go, in state police agencies or law enforcement agencies, you'll find a picture of 'The Runaway' hanging somewhere," p. 186, brackets mine.

2. Kant characterized imperatives of skill this way: "Here there is no question at all whether the end is reasonable and good, but there is only a question as to what must be done to attain it. The prescriptions needed by a doctor in order to make his patient perfectly healthy and by a poisoner in order to make sure of killing his victim are of equal value so far as each serves to bring about its purpose perfectly." *Grounding For The Metaphysic of Morals*, tr. James W. Ellington, p. 25.

3. Nevertheless, police need to know how crime is committed both to detect and prevent crime. This is particularly so where the crime involved demands a high degree of technical expertise; computer crimes leap to mind.

4. For an explication of Aristotle's concept of the pros hen see John Finnis, *Natural Law and Natural Rights*, p. 9ff.

5. Although Bittner does not explicitly endorse "rule skepticism" (*Functions of Police in Modern Society* 4), his position suggests another more acute form of the incongruity thesis, one that could be tied to the internal legal skepticism associated with the Critical Legal Studies movement in the law schools. One might assert that law does not bind officials to any coherent set of moral obligations because law inescapably reflects the contradictions and conflicts of class or some other prejudicing principle. Official decisions are based on extra-legal considerations by default. Police work, therefore, is inevitably antinomic. This more radical form of the incongruity thesis can be seen in the Marxist approaches of Robinson, Scaglion, and Olivero in their book *Police in Contradiction: The Evolution of the Police Function in Society* (1994). However, the antinomic thesis requires clear and convincing support. We should not assume that law's norms cannot be rendered coherent.

6. The text is from *Aquinas, Treatise on Law*, Question 90, Richard Regan tr., Hackett Publishing, p. 6.

7. See generally this very useful compendium of law enforcement codes: *Professional Law Enforcement Codes—A Documentary Collection*, Eds. Kleinig and Zhang.

8. For the Preamble's language, see the earlier quotation in chapter 1. Article 29 of the United Nations Universal Declaration of Human Rights provides that the rights of the individual are subject to duties owed the community, the equal rights of others, and "the just requirements of morality, public order and the general welfare in a democratic society." In full Article 29 states:

1. Everyone has duties to the community in which alone the free and full development of his personality is possible.

2. In the exercise of his rights and freedoms, everyone shall be subject only to such limitations as are determined by law solely for the purpose of securing due recognition and respect for the rights and freedoms of others and of meeting the just requirements of morality, public order, and the general welfare in a democratic society.

3. These rights and freedoms may in no case be exercised contrary to the purposes and principles of the United Nations.

   Law's *telos* synthesizes rights and duties as the flourishing of the human person entails securing both individual and social goods.

9. History instructs us to be skeptical about appeals to "discretionary justice." In Nazi Germany "discretionary justice" was "an instrument of repression and even a pretext for barbarism and brutality" as Harold Berman observed. See *Law and Revolution*, pp. 40–1. In the former Soviet Union, the Gulag was administered with a "discretionary justice." Alexander Solzhenitsyn wrote in *The Gulag Archipelago* "the Prosecutor General—informs us that the All-Russian Executive Committee . . . 'pardons and *punishes* at its own discretion *without any limitation whatever*.' For example, a six month sentence was changed to ten years . . . All problems *can be decided quickly*" (qtd. in Delattre 21, italics in original). Even good intentions are not trustworthy, but liable to be deflected by passion and poor judgment. Both Aristotle (see, e.g., *Rhetoric I*, 1354a31–34 and *Politics*, Book I, 8, Book III, 86, 97, Warrington, ed.) and Aquinas (*Treatise on Law*, Question 95, First Article) held that it is better to have law rule than men.

### 3  A Critique of Normative Police Theory

1. In *Handled with Discretion* Kleinig does talk of subsumption. In the "Response" to Joan MacGregor's "From the State of Nature to Mayberry," he asserts that the IACP Police Code of Conduct "expands the discretionary authority of police in certain respects by **subsuming** the specific task of law enforcement under the more general social ends" (68, emphasis mine). I shall later explain why I think he is wrong in resolving the subsumption question this way.

2. On the connection between family disorder and crime, see Travis Hirschi, "The Family."

3. For Aquinas, it is of the "essence of law" to be directed toward the "common good." This involves direction toward the "last end" of human life, which is "happiness." Drawing on Aristotle, Aquinas states that human happiness is found in a "perfect community." See *Aquinas, Treatise on Law*, Question 90, Second Article, p. 3.

4. See Kelling and Coles treatment of the subject in *Fixing Broken Windows*, p. 51ff.

5. This section draws heavily on Harold Berman's explication in *Law and Revolution: The Formation of the Western Legal Tradition*.

6. The language is from Hall, *Treatise Called Glanville* (qtd. in Berman, *Law and Revolution*, p. 457). Berman writes that the *Treatise on the Laws and Customs of the Kingdom of England* while attributed to Glanville was "very likely" written by his nephew Hubert Walter. This work is widely regarded as the first systematic treatise on the English common law.

7. From the Thorne translation of Bracton (qtd. in Kmiec, Presser, eds., *The History, Philosophy and Structure of the American Constitution*, p. 39, brackets in text). St. John of Salisbury developed one of the earliest arguments justifying a right and even a duty to depose a tyrant. See his *Polycraticus*. For an insightful discussion of John of Salisbury's *Polycraticus*, see Harold Berman, *Law and Revolution*, pp. 276–88. The right and duty to throw off a tyrant's rule is, of course, invoked in the American Declaration of Independence.

8. See Harold Berman's analysis of the development of western legal science in *Law and Revolution*, particularly Chapter 3, "The Origin of Western Legal Science in the European Universities."

9. In her senate confirmation hearings in 2010, Supreme Court Associate Justice Elena Kagan (in testimony widely thought to be a response to Chief Justice Roberts, who at his confirmation hearings held that the judge serves as an "umpire") said that the role of umpire suggested that of a "robot." The judge instead, she held, exercises "judgment." I argue below that the umpire's role in sports is hardly "robotic." In any event, the Kagan and Roberts testimony indicate the continuing relevance of the analogy of law to the rules of a game and of certain legal officials to umpires.

10. I might add that it is in terms of historical contexts that the conflicts arising between natural law and legal positivism may be resolved. Harold Berman puts it this way: "[Positivism and Natural Law] cannot possibly be reconciled, except in the context of the ongoing history of a given legal order. That, in fact, is how they are often reconciled by American Courts, which in deciding cases will turn a positivist eye to the applicable legal rules, a naturalist eye to the equities of the particular case in light of the moral principles underlying the rules and a historicist eye (they do have three eyes!) to custom

and precedent, having in mind not only the precedents of the past but also the significance of their decisions as precedents for the future. A conscientious judge cannot solely be a positivist or solely a naturalist or solely a historicist. The three 'schools' are three dimensions of his judicial role" ("Law and Logos," 153, brackets mine). The same is true for the police officer as he takes action to secure observance of law, making account for the differences in the judicial and law enforcement roles. The term "historical" is to be preferred to "historicist," which Berman used in the above quoted text, as it conveys law's historicity rather than "historicism." The historical axis provides for the realization of law's universal in the particular historical situation. Historicism rejects the proposition that there is a universal.

## 4 THE RISE AND LIMITS OF THE FORMAL POSITIVE POLICE

1. The work usually consulted to start with is his classic text, *The Concept of Law*.
2. The Second Amendment to the US Constitution's "right to bear arms," as it entails a right to possess firearms in the home, may be considered in connection with this historical duty of the citizen who was required to be armed in order to police. On recent construction of the Second Amendment in light of the historical right of self-protection in the home, see *District of Columbia v. Heller*, 554 U.S. 570 (2008) and *McDonald v. City of Chicago*, 561 U.S. 3025 (2010).
3. See Stephen Light's *Understanding Criminal Justice*, pp. 96–9. For detailed coverage, see William A. Morris, *The Frankpledge System*.
4. See generally Lawrence Freidman's: *A History of American Law*. It is perhaps the best single-volume treatment of its subject.
5. Reith includes in "moral force" a mix of elements not necessarily moral: "communal loyalty, patriotism, enhanced religious consciousness, fear, and faith" (*The Blind Eye of History* 18).
6. See *Nicomachean Ethics*. Aristotle also holds that courage pertains, although less so, to the proper regulation of confidence. He characterizes overconfidence as producing recklessness.
7. Douglas MacArthur understood the importance of a "musical" or liberal education for soldiers. When he was Superintendent of West Point he introduced poetry reading and writing into the curriculum for cadets. Dare we not require a liberal arts curriculum for our police? In addition to reading the great texts on justice in the philosophical tradition, police should be exposed to great literature in the humanities bearing on law and justice: Shakespeare's *Merchant of Venice*, Dostoevski's *Crime and Punishment*, Hugo's *Les Miserables*, Melville's *Billy Budd*, Robert Bolt's *A Man For All Seasons*, to name only a few that readily come to mind.

8. Roger Lane has contended that the problem was not increased crime but increased intolerance of crime. See "Urban Police and Crime in 19th Century America," p. 32. It is likely to have involved both.

9. The police power has been variously defined by the US Supreme Court as

> The people, in their sovereign capacity, have established their agencies for the preservation of the public health and the public morals. (1880).

> We hold that the police power of a State embraces regulations designed to promote the public convenience or the general prosperity, as well as regulations designed to promote the public health, the public morals or the public safety (1906).

> The liberty safeguarded [by the Constitution] is liberty in a social organization which requires the protection of law against the evils which menace the health, safety, morals and welfare of the people (1937).

> Public safety, public health, *morality*, peace and quiet, law and order—these are some of the more conspicuous examples of the traditional application of the police power to municipal affairs (1954).

The quotations are compiled by David Lowenthal in *No Liberty for License*, pp. 95–6 (brackets and italics in original), where he offers an important analysis of what he calls the "forgotten logic" of the First Amendment. First Amendment liberties, he insists, are not to be confused with license.

10. For more background on the history of English policing, see J. R. Critchley, *A History of the Police in England and Wales, 1000–1966*.

11. See Robert Bellah, *Habits of the Heart*. In the United States, the trend in the latter half of the twentieth century has been to exclude the biblical tradition from public education, driven by a new jurisprudence of the First Amendment prohibition against the establishment of religion. The tradition of civic republicanism would be weakened by, inter alia, moral relativism spurred by the new individualism. Schools of education would instruct that public school students should receive an education dedicated to values clarification rather than to the formation of moral character—a triumph of formal as opposed to substantive rationality in education.

12. Consider how in the twentieth century this would be exacerbated with the flight to the suburbs. Now a person would be both a stranger at home and at work, not spending enough time in either place. In contemporary suburbs, it is not unusual for next-door neighbors not to know one another. The anonymity of life in the city would spread out to what was formerly country. The new police would be required in the new suburbs.

13. The twentieth century produced a highly mobile form of capital, intellectual capital that could travel at the speed of light in cyberspace. This

would exacerbate the individualism as more workers were no longer needed to be in physical proximity to work together. They could work increasingly alone in cyberspace. Conference calls and chat rooms could replace boardrooms and socializing could be virtual. Indeed, reality itself could be virtual. It could be a construct. Moreover, in multiple ways, the new technologies magnify exponentially the individual's capacity to affect others. Never before could an individual inflict so much harm on so many, as in cyber-terrorism.

14. This helps explain what seems to have been increased intolerance of crime and vice.

15. Police today attempt to achieve panopticon effects by the strategic placement of surveillance devices in public places. Fear of 9/11-type terrorism has made their use more prevalent. However, knowing that crime is committed is not enough, one must have the will to oppose it. The panopticon itself does not ensure that officials will abide by law, that criminals will not be found on both sides of the camera. Corrupt officials may extort bribes from criminals rather than arrest and prosecute them. Furthermore, often people know about official corruption or criminal behavior, but because of a lack of courage or moral conviction, resignation, a widespread culture of corruption, or some other factors, do nothing about it. Ethical character and the internalization of moral norms remain necessary conditions of law abidingness defined as an internal principle regulating the behavior of people.

16. On the contradictions produced by the new capitalist society, see Daniel Bell's penetrating text, *The Cultural Contradictions of Capitalism*.

17. The epidemic of immoderate behavior related to the unleashing of desire (particularly in the areas of food, drink, and sex) has done damage not only to the public order and morality but also to the public health, as it has produced illnesses associated with drug addiction, contributed to the rise in sexually transmitted diseases such as AIDS, and increased obesity levels, which have produced an alarming rise in Type II diabetes. It is becoming increasingly clear that the public morality and public health are connected—but so are the other ends (the general prosperity and the public safety) traditionally pursued by exercise of the police power. The damage to the public health has resulted in a steep rise in health-care costs, putting great strain on the purse. Irrational and immoderate behavior (in the home, on Main Street, on Wall Street, and in the halls of government) apparently contributed to the recent economic collapse, which seems to have resulted from buying that grossly exceeded financial means, lending practices predicated on a gross disregard of risk, investment decisions driven by greed, and governments run on dangerous levels of debt, that also neglected their supervisory duties particularly with respect to the financial sector. The collapse, in turn, is having a direct impact on police. The fiscal crisis in Camden, New Jersey, for example, the most crime ridden city in the United States, led that city in January 2011,

to lay off half of the police force. Under such circumstances, I cannot be sanguine about the safety of the citizens of that beleaguered city. In 2013 as this book goes to press, it was reported that the Camden Police Department will soon join forces with the county police to augment its ranks by approximately two hundred officers. This makes Camden's future look less bleak.

18. Lobban observes that Peel did not reject common law entirely but that his reforms were a synthesis of positivism and the older communitarian law. Colquhoun, I should note, also sought to defend not only individual rights to life and property but public morality (a social good) as well. Recall that by police he said he meant, "the correct administration of whatever related to the Morals of a People." His was hardly a libertarian perspective on police.

19. It might be observed, however, that the friendship referred to could be construed as a formal equality of friendship rather than that friendship characterized by an affective bond, which is exclusive or discriminating and therefore implies inequality.

20. This term is from Atiyah and Summers in *Form and Substance in Anglo-American Law*. For their definition, see Chapter 7, note 17.

21. Recall Vollmer's reference to the police officer as "parish priest." See chapter 1, note 14. Norman Rockwell's depiction of the avuncular officer having an ice cream soda with the boy running away from home evokes the image of a police officer in Thornton Wilder's *Our Town*.

22. I should note that Socrates does not even offer his Republic as a politically practicable regime. See Book IX where Glaucon states: "I don't suppose it exists anywhere on earth" and Socrates replies: "But in heaven perhaps a pattern is laid up for the man who wants to see and found a city within himself on the basis of what he sees. It doesn't make any difference whether it is or will be somewhere. For he would mind the things of this city alone, and of no other," pp. 274–5. Instead, his Republic is a heuristic guide offered to the individual seeking the happiness that may be derived from a well-ordered soul.

23. Durkheim saw professions as playing an intermediate role in the new relations of individual and state (*Professional Ethics and Civic Morals*).

24. Consistent with the point made in the text are recent studies that question the appropriateness of mandatory arrest in domestic cases. See, e.g., Raymond Parnas, "Criminal Justice Responses to Domestic Violence" in *Discretion in Criminal Justice*.

25. Socrates does refer to the guardians as "preservers of the city's freedom" (Plato, *Republic*, 73).

26. This is consistent with contemporary analysis. Harvard's Mark Moore wrote in 1993: "Most current analyses of conditions in cities indicate a significant breakdown in the important mechanisms of informal social control including responsibilities to family and community.

The collapse of these intermediate institutions allows disorder, crime, and fear to flourish" ("Problem-Solving and Community Policing," *Modern Policing*, 143).

### 5 THE AMERICAN POLICE EXPERIENCE AND THE LIMITS OF THE MANAGERIAL PERSPECTIVE

1. The following texts are helpful in acquainting oneself with American police history: Kappeller, *The Police and Society*, Samuel Walker, *The Police in America*, and for America's largest department, Lardner and Repetto, *NYPD*.
2. Wilbur Miller provides an excellent comparative analysis in *Cops and Bobbies*.
3. See Patrick V. Murphy, Preface in Edwin Delattre, *Character and Cops*. Also see Kathleen McGuire and Ann L. Pastore, *Bureau of Justice Statistics Sourcebook of Criminal Justice Statistics 1997* (Washington, DC: Bureau of Justice Statistics, 1998). As of that counting in 1997, there were the following numbers of agencies at these levels: local 13,578; state, 49; sheriff 3,083; and special police 1316. Total: 18,769.
4. He is reputed to have said, "There's a lot of law at the end of a night-stick," quoted in Elizabeth Frost-Knappman and David S. Shrager, *A Concise Encyclopedia of Legal Quotations*, p. 204.
5. Moore acknowledges at least that the concept "organizational strategy" requires modification for "public sector executives" that addresses the "level and nature of crime" and a set of "collectively valued purposes...that justify public investment in their activities" ("Problem-Solving and Community Policing" (106)). However, he underestimates what this requires.
6. For a general treatise on economic analysis, see Richard Posner, *The Economic Analysis of Law*.

### 6 THE NEW POLICE AND IMPLICATIONS FOR A CONCEPTION OF LAW

1. See William Bratton with Peter Knobler, *Turnaround: How America's Top Cop Reversed the Crime Epidemic*. New York City remains one of the safest big cities in the country. Bratton's "turnaround" does not appear to be a short-term fluke.
2. There are a number of contending theses of varying plausibility. Some credit the crime reductions to increasing incarceration rates since the 1980s when federal, state, and local governments enacted more severe prison terms for major and minor crimes, keeping more criminals off the streets for longer periods of time. However, one should not discount the improved economic conditions. These have allowed the NYPD, for example, to substantially increase its deployment of

officers and that has helped with crime control. The NYPD today is considerably larger than the force in the tough days of the early 1970s when the city's fiscal crisis left the department anemic and unable to respond to crime in the streets and parks. In support of the thesis that application of broken windows theory has produced crime reduction is a 2008 Dutch study headed by Kees Keiser, a graduate student in behavioral science at the University of Groningen, The Netherlands. *The Week*, July 16, 2010, in "How to keep law and order" reported that Keiser "tested the broken windows theory in a half-dozen kinds of public places, and found that it had a major effect on people's behavior in every one. If a sidewalk is kept clean, for example, only 33 percent of people will toss an unwanted flier onto the ground; if there's lots of trash and litter, 69 percent will choose to add to it. Just 13 percent of passers-by will steal money from an envelope left sticking out of a mailbox, but 27 percent will steal if the box is covered in graffiti. 'It is quite shocking that the mere presence of litter resulted in a doubling of the number of people stealing,' Keiser tells the *Los Angeles Times*." The reduction in violent crime may be partly attributable to the aging of the population. Reduction in traditional crimes, thefts as in robberies and burglaries, may be partly explained by the shift of crime to cyberspace. Identity thefts are on the rise. I might mention some other less conventional hypotheses. Some researchers, such as the economist Rick Nevin, attributed increased violence in the 1980s to the toxic effects of lead poisoning. The phasing out of lead paint and leaded gasoline reduced toxic exposure and it was claimed reduced violent behavior. See, for example, the *Washington Post* article by Shankar Vedantam, "Research Links Lead Exposure, Criminal Activity" of July 8, 2010. Steven Levitt, the self-styled "rogue economist" and coauthor of *Freakonomics*, went so far as to contend that increased abortions reduced the numbers of children born into violence prone households, who would have gone on to commit crimes. However, the recent economic downturn, high unemployment, budget cuts to police, lay-offs of officers, and early release of prisoners to cut costs may well threaten to reverse the crime reductions.

3. George Kelling, in a highly influential discussion, argues that an offense constituting a crime has different meaning depending on variables such as the place in which it occurs, the time, the previous behavior and reputation of the offender, the condition of the victim, and aggregation—the numbers of individuals involved. See *"Broken Windows" and Police Discretion*, pp. 32–6. Kelling's list, however, should be seen as only partial—pointing toward a more nuanced holistic account of offenses that (1) identifies additional variables affecting crime and (2) interprets formally codified acts in terms of their experiential context, their developmental dimension, and in terms of the law's rational purposes. Police are challenged to take such variables into account in responding to crime.

4. On how legal labels may "mask important distinctions" that police need to grasp if the problems underlying offenses are to be addressed, see Herman Goldstein, *Problem-oriented Policing*, p. 38ff.

5. For the relationship of the conduct requirement to liberty, see Herbert Packer, *The Limits of the Criminal Sanction*, p. 73ff.

### 7 INTEGRATIVE JURISPRUDENCE: LAW AND LAW ENFORCEMENT'S THREE DIMENSIONS

1. For more on this three-dimensional account of law, see Thomas V. Svogun, "Law's Virtue: The Formal Structure of an Integrative Jurisprudence," and for Harold Berman's approach, see also "Towards an Integrative Jurisprudence".

2. For a discussion on negative and positive precepts of justice, see Mortimer J. Adler, *Six Great Ideas*, particularly the chapter on justice.

3. Deontological argument typically reasons from a priori duties, not from a good to be realized or achieved by action. "Deontological" comes from the Greek *deon* (meaning duty) and *logos* (meaning account of, but also, the rational principle by which order is brought into our lives). Deontologically, the right thing to do is determined apart from the good that may follow from action taken in accordance with the right. One fulfills a duty, come what may. A right also may be considered deontologically—as an end in itself to be respected despite the consequences of action taken in accordance with the right. Hence, Kant's injunction that justice should be done even if the whole world were to be destroyed is on its face strictly deontological. An absolute right of the rational agent never to be treated as a means but rather only as an end in himself (Kant's principle of humanity) can also be considered deontological. Yet, rights in our jurisprudence are usually subject to limitation. The US Supreme Court, for example, has allowed that fundamental rights may be limited when a countervailing state interest is sufficiently strong. Such rights may be considered "deontological" only in a partial sense, that is, as ends-in-themselves up to that point where a countervailing good overrides them—where argument that may be consequentialist prevails. Consequentialist argument, of which utilitarianism is a version, reasons that the right thing to do is that which promotes a desirable consequence or good. (In utilitarianism, which is a hedonism, it is something pleasant or something that mitigates pain.) A right or duty is argued for based on the consequences of acknowledging it. "Deontological" may be further contrasted with the term "teleological," which is derived from the Greek *telos* (meaning end) and *logos*. Teleological theories define the right in terms of what furthers the good or set of goods that constitute the end to which a nature is directed. A teleological theory may be distinguished from a simply consequentialist one,

in that the former presupposes that the good advanced is a principle immanent in the nature of the phenomenon under review—a nature that inclines toward its own completion or perfection. Argument is from that nature rather than simply forward looking to consequences of action. Teleological theories speak of natural rights and duties. In this book, I refer to the teleological dimension of law and teleological formality. This dimension of law's ends, as a binding formality, will include "deontological" duties, rights, principles, and other norms (though they might be taken as ends-in-themselves only in the above partial sense) as well as rights, duties, principles, and other norms that are derived from argument that is teleological (naturalist) as defined above. Arguments may be consequentialist in form and still be part of law's *telos* when the consequences desired may be considered goods to which the legal enterprise, given its nature, is committed.

4. On Jane Jacobs and the "small change of life," see her *The Death and Life of Great American Cities*." The phrase is quoted and discussed in *Fixing Broken Windows*, p. 14ff. For empirical support of "Broken Windows" theory, see Wesley Skogan's research published in *Disorder and Decline: Crime and the Spiral of Decay in American Neighborhoods*." Also see Kelling and Coles' account of New York City's successes under Bratton in reducing serious crime by cracking down on misdemeanor subway crimes such as turnstile jumping in *Fixing Broken Windows*. Consider as well the Dutch study cited in chapter 6, note 2. Socrates' assertion seems to reflect an early version of broken windows thinking: "'It's plain therefore,' I said, 'that in a city where you see beggars, somewhere in the neighborhood thieves, cutpurses, temple robbers, and craftsmen of all such evils are hidden'" (Plato, *Republic* 230).

5. For a discussion on liberty as a limited good regulated by justice, see Mortimer Adler, *Six Great Ideas*.

6. On occasion, caught behind a long line of traffic stopped by a school bus in Rhode Island, I have thought Bentham's characterization of precedent especially *apropos* of this kind of high formality: "acting without reason, to the declared exclusion of reason, and thereby in opposition to reason" (qtd. in Atiyah and Summers 24). The monitors seem more like automatons than human beings as they go about their ritual. It is a good example of a mechanical jurisprudence.

7. See Atiyah and Summers, pp. 88–93. When I have asked American police officers to define law, more than a few have defined it as "a set of guidelines."

8. On the twelfth century jurists' transformation of the concept of rules, see Harold Berman, *Law and Revolution*, pp. 138–40.

9. *Riggs v. Palmer*, New York Court of Appeals, 1889, in Feinberg and Gross, eds. "*Philosophy of Law*," Fifth Edition, pp. 151–6.

10. For a discussion on discretion as it varies throughout the justice system read Lloyd E. Ohlin and Frank J. Remington, editors, *Discretion*

*in Criminal Justice*. On the connection between formal conceptions of the rule of law and police discretion, it is useful to study Ronald Allen's debate with Kenneth Culp Davis. See Ronald J. Allen, "The Police and Substantive Rulemaking: Reconciling Principle and Expediency"; Kenneth Culp Davis, "Police Rulemaking on Selective Enforcement: A Reply"; and Ronald J. Allen, "The Police and Substantive Rulemaking: A Brief Rejoinder."

11. Anthony D'Amato, "On the Connection Between Law and Justice." While D'Amato intends to prove the thesis that justice is integral to law, he does not develop the conceptual framework necessary for that proof. In my view, that would require showing how rational interpretation is as much a part of law (here, law's teleology and the formality that it generates) as the positive formality of law. Moreover, what justice in law is, as such, D'Amato does not explain.

12. The full text of the traffic law is as follows: "Section 205. Streets shall be clearly marked for the purpose of traffic regulation.
   (a) If a roadway is marked by a broken white line which traverses its length, motorists may cross the broken line if it is safe to do so and only after first signaling their intention to do so.
   (b) If a roadway is marked by a solid white line which traverses its length, motorists may not cross the line except: in an emergency, and only if it is safe to do so.
   (c) If a roadway is marked by double white lines (parallel lines) which traverse its length, motorists may not cross the lines.
Section 206. The penalty for violating any provision of section 205 shall be fifty dollars. The defendant shall be charged with a moving vehicle traffic violation." (c) is applicable to the instant case. As in Feinberg and Gross, Fifth Ed., *Philosophy of Law*, p. 22.

13. On Rutherford see *Riggs v. Palmer*, in Feinberg and Gross, Fifth Ed., 152. Closely associated with this permissive interpretation of mandatory language is "equitable construction," which construes language in light of equity to avoid injustice. It has a respectable and ancient pedigree. Approved by Rutherford, Bacon, and Blackstone, it had been endorsed by Aristotle, and has been applied by courts. For Aristotle, see his discussion of equity in Book V, ch. 10 of the *Nicomachean Ethics*. Thomas Aquinas, drawing on the authority of Justinian, quoted the Pandect. Justin: "By no reason of law, or favor of equity, is it allowable for us to interpret harshly, and render burdensome, those useful measures which have been enacted for the welfare of man." For Aquinas, law as an ordinance of reason promulgated for the common good may not be rendered in a way that makes it irrational and unjust. See *Summa Theologica of St. Thomas Aquinas*, Question 96, Sixth Article, p. 61, and for his definition of law, Question 91, First, Second, Third, and Fourth Articles. Judge Earl and Judge Gray, writing in *Riggs v. Palmer* for the majority and the dissent, respectively, present a clear division in jurisprudence. The

majority overcame the positive formality of the rules of wills in favor of the principle that "no man should profit from his wrongdoing" stating "all laws, as well as all contracts, may be controlled in their operation and effect by general, fundamental maxims of the common law" and "These maxims are dictated by public policy, have their foundation in universal law administered in all civilized countries, and have nowhere been superseded by statutes" (Feinberg and Gross, Fifth Ed., 153). Judge Grey for the dissent rejected the majority's approach as outmoded, citing as it did from English authorities, Roman law, the Code of Napoleon, etc., and asserted that in "modern jurisprudence," specifically the positive law of New York (which he argued gave effect to the liberty of the individual through the "freedom of testamentary disposition") the Court was "bound by the rigid rules of law." He added: "The capacity and the power of the individual to dispose of his property after his death, and the mode by which that power can be exercised, are matters of which the legislature has assumed complete control." Judge Gray concluded that in the absence of legislation, "the courts are not empowered to institute...a system of remedial justice" (154–5). Therefore, in the probate of wills, they are largely restricted to formally positivist rather than teleological reasoning. For the dissent, liberal values, particularly freedom of testamentary disposition, supported such a highly formal jurisprudence in which the court's discretion to do justice, however, was thwarted. Nevertheless, this argument did not prevail on the court, which sought instead to do substantive justice. How, we might ask, could freedom of testamentary disposition be consistent with granting an inheritance to a person who murdered the testator in order to prevent his revocation of the will? That freedom is presumably better respected when the murderer is denied his inheritance. Lastly, it should be observed that *Black's Law Dictionary* in the Fourth Edition offered this definition of the word *shall*: "As used in statutes...this word is generally imperative or mandatory," adding "But it may be construed as merely permissive or directory, (as equivalent to 'may,') to carry out the legislative intention..." And so the statutory words "shall not cross the double solid lines" could mean "may cross." Words in law are not to be taken at face value alone! I would like to credit Ralph Costantino, one of my former graduate students, for bringing the Black's definition to my attention. The recent Eighth edition, however, does not contain the language just quoted but does indicate that *shall* can mean *may*, stating: "When a negative word such as *not* or *no* precedes *shall*, the word *shall* often means *may*. What is being negated is a permission not a requirement" (italics in the original).

14. In engineering, it is a truism that too rigid a structure will cause a suspension bridge to collapse, so will too loose a structure. The bridge must have just the right amount of flexibility (and tension), neither too much nor too little, if it is to have structural integrity. So, it is with

integrity in law. Too rigid a normative structure produces injustice, such as inequity. An example is Shylock's "jurisprudence" in Shakespeare's Merchant of Venice—his insistence that the Court enforce his bond and order that he be granted a pound of Antonio's flesh. Too loose a normative structure produces injustice by granting a discretion that enables capricious and arbitrary action by officials. The right balance must be struck and this will depend on factors particular to the cases and the legal systems involved.

15. Not all executives can be expected to respond so virtuously. *The Week*, 13 September 2009 reported that Cpl. Joshua Rowell of the Stockton, Utah, police department was suspended for ticketing the mayor's son for driving without a license. The new police officer did not realize who he had cited until he handed the ticket to the town clerk. She reportedly told him, "Hey, you know you just gave the mayor's son a ticket?" To which Officer Rowell reportedly responded, "Oh, crap." He should have been able to respond, "The mayor would have wanted me to do my legal duty." Perhaps the people should, among other things, consider recalling the Stockton mayor, who has violated his duty to faithfully execute the laws, if indeed he had the officer punished for holding his son to the law.

16. The practical effect of postulating a right as fundamental under the US Constitution, in the Supreme Court's jurisprudence, is to shift the axial balance toward the formal pole so that only compelling state interests outweigh it. This is often the result of regarding rights as quasi-"deontological." Rights are postulated as "givens," although only up to a certain point close to the formal pole. They are not practically regarded as "absolutes"—at least no majority of the Court has held that constitutional rights are absolutes. Some rights, such as gender equality and First Amendment liberty pertaining to some "expressive conduct," may be said to enjoy less protection. They are less formal than the right to racial equality as they may be overridden based on "important" or "substantial" governmental interests as opposed to "compelling" interests. See *United States v. O'Brien*, 391 U.S. 367 (1968). The issue as to gender is complicated by the Supreme Court's recent adoption of an "exceedingly persuasive justification" test, which seems to approach strict scrutiny. See *United States v. Virginia*, 518 U.S. 515 (1996), where the Court held that the Virginia Military Institute's male-only admissions policy violated the equal protection clause of the Fourteenth Amendment.

17. Atiyah and Summers differentiate types of formality in an illuminating discussion. In their book, they distinguish validity formality, mandatory formality, content formality, and interpretive formality, among others. In this part, I use their term "interpretive formality." It refers to "the degree of formality involved in the interpretive process. Interpretive methods may be more or less formal...An interpretation is highly formal if it merely focuses on literal meanings, or

on the narrow confines of normative conduct or other phenomena interpreted. Interpretation may be less formal and more substantive." When interpretation involves searching for "substantive purposes and reasons behind words" Summers and Atiyah refer to this as a case of "low interpretive formality." See P. S. Atiyah and R. S. Summers, *Form and Substance in Anglo-American Law: A Comparative Study of Legal Reasoning, Legal Theory, and Legal Institutions,"* Introduction and p. 15. In this book, I also use their term "mandatory formality" on which they say, "a formal reason typically has the attribute to some degree of overriding, or excluding from consideration, or diminishing the weight of, at least some contrary substantive reasons. This is what we call mandatory formality" (16).

18. For a Supreme Court case holding a maintenance of order ordinance unconstitutional as vague and delegating too much discretion to police officers, see *Chicago v. Morales,* 527 U.S. 41 (1999).

19. See P. S. Atiyah and R. S. Summers, *Form and Substance in Anglo-American Law: A Comparative Study of Legal Reasoning, Legal Theory, and Legal Institutions."* For their analysis of the nature of formal and substantive reasoning, see especially, pp. 5–11.

20. For Sir Carlton Kemp Allen's classic discussion on customary law, read his *Law in the Making,* especially pp. 129–51.

21. Lon L. Fuller states the condition that the custom must have existed "from time immemorial" is directed to a very special question, that is, "When should custom be regarded as overriding provisions of general law. This obviously can be something quite different from asking when custom should control an issue not previously regulated by law at all" (*The Principles of Social Order* 229). It is also different from the case where custom is used to give concrete meaning to the term "order" for the purposes of enforcing a "disorderly conduct" ordinance. It remains to be seen, therefore, how the respective criteria for evaluating custom may be adapted to the various situations in contemporary societies where there is a need for customary norms. Custom may fill gaps in law or be introduced into areas where other legal standards allow room for interpretive judgments without being frank exceptions to the general law of the land or norms "overriding" law. The common law criteria are a point of reference in developing tests that may be used to legitimate norms constituting the customary dimension to law and that determine the weight these norms may be given in law enforcement judgments. The tests should be derived from law's triune normative structure.

22. Carl Friedrich's characterization of the medieval restriction on the legislative power may be critiqued in light of the text's analysis. He asserts:

> In the context of the modern state unrestricted legislated power is central. Yet it was precisely such unrestricted legislated power which the medieval natural law denied to the prince...Really

crucial was the notion that all law was basically legal custom and that legislation had only the function of clarifying and elucidating such customary law. And since the executive in the sense of modern administration did not play an important role either— a central bureaucracy such as that characteristic of the modern state was only faintly beginning in the thirteenth century—the main task of the prince, aside from war and foreign relations, was the effecting of justice through his being the highest judge and meting out the punishments connected with the enforcement of law. It is only within this framework of a primarily judicial government that the legal philosophy of medieval and natural law can be comprehended." (43–4)

The medieval king did play a large role in enacting law, that is, in legislation. That legislative authority, however, was based in the king's adjudicative authority—his duty to adjudicate and do justice—as in the analysis of Azo. See note 33. In his royal legislation, the king was bound to "do justice." The custom from which he was also bound to draw was itself subject to the constraints of a natural law, as indicated in the text. Legislation did not merely clarify or elucidate custom. Hence, the "restriction" on legislation in the medieval legal mind was to be found in the constraints of custom and natural law, both together. That said, the medieval restriction on the legislative power so necessary for understanding the medieval philosophy of law is also helpful in indicating how positive law itself and the legislative power in the modern period still require restriction. The point to be made is that legislatures in their legislation must take into account law's historical as well as its teleological rationality. The formality generated by either kind of rationality restricts what it is that the legislative power should enact, if it is to produce legislation having full normative authority. The legislative power should not be construed as "unrestricted."

23. It might be observed that current community policing is to some extent a return to this quasi-judicial role as suggested by Mark Moore. Through "the experience of negotiating solutions to problems among several interested parties, the police will learn to rely on legal principle. That, in turn, may encourage them to become 'street corner judges' as well as 'street corner politicians' (Muir 1977). They might also rediscover why it was once considered plausible that they should be part of the judicial branch of government rather than the executive and might thereby discover a commitment to legal values that has so far eluded them" (145–6). Informal methods, such as negotiation, require that police acquire knowledge of legal principles, but also knowledge of law's teleology and historicity, to guide the discretion that they inevitably engage—a discretion at odds with the conception of the formal rule bound professional associated with the reform model of policing. Of course, rediscovering such a role (enlarging the police function and

police discretion) implicates the separation of powers and needs to be addressed in these terms. Relaxing formality or recentering the formal axis to advance, e.g., the end of public safety by way of a more quasi-judicial or quasi-legislative police raises questions regarding preserving rule of law values such as liberty and equality, which are at the basis of rule of law formality.

24. For an explication of Aquinas on determination, see John Finnis, *Natural Law and Natural Rights*, p. 284ff.

25. For John Finnis's interesting discussion of determinations in the instance of legislating rules of the road, see *Natural Law and Natural Rights*, p. 285. On the authoritative force of custom for legislative determinations, see pp. 287–8.

26. The focus will be on what custom establishes "park" to mean. In an interesting passage Aquinas in his *Treatise on Law* refers to custom as law's "interpreter." See his "Answer" to Question 97, Article III.

27. The analysis may be complicated by disabilities laws prohibiting discrimination against handicapped persons that may require overriding other considerations about order by necessitating special accommodation for motorized wheelchairs on sidewalks and in malls.

28. In Providence, Rhode Island the police have had to balance the general community's demand for peace and quiet against a minority's expectation that its traditional celebration be respected—in this case, the Dominican Republic minority's custom of celebrating its native country's independence day in a parade of automobiles with flags flying, horns blaring, and substantial disruption to traffic and the general peace.

29. George Kelling describes these rules of the street:

> These informal rules covered such behaviors as panhandling, lying down or congregating on sidewalks and in parks, drinking in public areas, and drug use. They did not merely prohibit specific acts, such as soliciting for prostitution, but often defined the conditions and manner under which activities could be carried out: for example, panhandling was permissible, but not from people standing still or waiting at a bus stop; sitting on the stoops of stores was accepted, but not lying down; drinking alcohol in public could be done only if the bottle was in a brown paper bag, and only off main thoroughfares. Not surprisingly, such rules varied by neighborhood. (*Fixing Broken Windows* 17–18)

These rules no doubt reflect some accommodation of written regulations to local conditions and vice versa. Police enforce law when such accommodations move local conditions efficiently toward realization of law's *telos*, in keeping with the requirements of law's formalities, and keeping in mind what local conditions make feasible and that local norms themselves form an integral part of the law's *telos* that they enforce.

30. Jeffrey Reiman's argument against police discretion in his article "Is Police Discretion Justified in a Free Society?" seems to presuppose

such a highly formalistic conception of the separation of powers and law enforcement—though one should attend to the particular qualifications he places on his thesis. The discretionary judgment not to make an arrest, in the event that an act has been committed that formally constitutes an offense, requires a complex judgment that weighs its implication for law's formality, teleology, and historicity. Joseph Goldstein's article: "Police Discretion Not to Invoke the Criminal Process: Low Visibility Decisions in the Administration of Justice" is an excellent study of multiple factors that bear on these decisions.

31. See Kmiec and Presser, eds., *The History, Philosophy and Structure of the American Constitution*, reprinting excerpts of Federalist 47, pp. 180–2. Capitals are in the Kmiec text.

32. See Lon Fuller, *The Anatomy of Law*, p. 56. The derivation of the law-making power from the adjudicatory power extends deep in the Western legal tradition. Harold Berman observes that implicit in the theory of jurisdiction and *imperium* of Azo, the great Romanist of the twelfth and thirteenth centuries, was the view "that the ruler's right and power to legislate . . . is viewed as an aspect of his right and power to adjudicate"—that is, to exercise judgment and to do justice. See *Law and Revolution*, pp. 289–94. It is a logical step to the notion that the king—or the sovereign whether Parliament or the people—rule by and under law, that is, to the doctrine of the rule of law; and to the view that the law of the state is bound to a higher law.

33. Discretion here can be controversial. The decision of the Cambridge police officer to arrest Harvard Professor Henry Louis Gates, Jr., for "disorderly conduct" in 2009 became the subject of a national debate in which even President Obama became embroiled.

34. Some display more sophistication than others. Edward Conlon in *Blue Blood* provided this anecdote of David Durk, an NYPD colleague of Serpico:

> In a chance encounter, he upbraided some hecklers at a speech in the park, and his eloquent explanation of the First Amendment was overheard by Jay Kriegel, a young volunteer to John Lindsay's inner circle of advisors. Kriegel stopped to talk to Durk, and in a conversation it emerged that he, too, was an Amherst graduate, and a friendship was struck. Durk, while still a rookie, wrote much of a Lindsay policy paper on crime and policing, and opened up a critical line of access to City Hall. (263–4)

And, I might add, the possibility of a more integrative law enforcement practice. Not only should police be in close touch with mayoral officials, but also they should act when appropriate in consultation with prosecutorial, legislative, and judicial authorities (not to mention the community itself). This anecdote also suggests the value of bringing more college-educated people into policing. For literature pertaining to this issue, see PACE website at www.police-association.org.

35. Deference to local judgments has some basis in constitutional jurisprudence. For example, Justice Powell citing *Federalist* No. 17 by Hamilton in his dissenting opinion in *Garcia v. San Antonio*, 469 U.S.528 (1985) stated: "The Framers recognized that the most effective democracy occurs at local levels of government, where people with firsthand knowledge of local problems have more ready access to public officials responsible for dealing with them." Justice Breyer in his dissent in *District of Columbia v. Heller*, 554 U.S. 570 (2008) cited this language from Powell in support of his argument that the Court owed deference to local legislatures "with particular knowledge of local problems and insight into appropriate local solutions." He also cited the plurality decision in *Los Angeles v. Alameda Books*, 535 U.S.425 (2002), "[W]e must acknowledge that the Los Angeles City Council is in a better position than the judiciary to gather and evaluate data on local problems." Breyer continued: "Different localities may seek to solve similar problems in different ways, and a 'city must be allowed a reasonable opportunity to experiment with solutions to admittedly serious problems.'" Citing *Renton v. Playtime Theatres, Inc.*, 475 U.S. 41 (1986). Breyer concluded: "We owe that democratic process some substantial weight in the constitutional calculus" (qtd. in Kmiec et al., *Combined 2008 Supplement* 300–1). *Heller* involved the question whether the District's ban on handguns violated the Second Amendment "right of the people to bear arms." In a 5 to 4 decision, the Court held that it did. An argument can be made that the police are in a particularly favorable position to know the local conditions (perhaps better than that of local legislators) and that this knowledge of ultimate particular facts justifies a qualified deference to their judgments. Some deference to local judgments would also seem to be required by the principle of subsidiarity discussed in chapter 9.

36. Aristotle's comparative analysis of *phronesis*, intellect, sympathetic understanding, and equity in the *Nicomachean Ethics* is especially illuminating of faculties that may be engaged by the discretionary judgments involved in law enforcement. See *Nicomachean Ethics*, Book Six.

37. See Ostwald on *phronesis* and *sophia* in the glossary, *Nicomachean Ethics*, pp. 312–13.

38. The speech by the "laws" to Socrates in Plato's *Crito*, by which Socrates is persuaded that he is bound by the legal judgment against him to submit to the Athenian verdict, is an example of law as rhetoric. Law is also *logos* in the additional sense that it is the rational principle by which order is brought into our lives. Recognizing that police work requires more, rather than less, communication between police and the public is at odds with some past police policy. An example is the New Jersey State Police Policy (1924), which in pertinent part stated: "Particular attention is invited to the fact that the basis of great majority [sic] of [public] complaints refers to what Troopers said and how

they said it, and the one thing that probably has caused most complaints and most trouble, is talking too much" (Kleinig and Zhang
69). The professional law enforcement model encouraged less rather
than more talk.

## 8 The Relativity of Justice, Law, and Police to the Social Bond

1. While police officers may deal with maintenance of order issues more
   informally than expected (and than consistent with strict liberal theory) formal due process seems more the exception than the rule even
   after arrest. The vast majority of criminal cases are resolved before
   trial through plea-bargaining where formal due process is relaxed. On
   what might be called a hypotrophy of formal due process in the history of criminal trials, see Lawrence Friedman, *A History of American
   Law*, p. 434ff. After conviction, discretionary judgments continue
   to play a substantial role. This indicates that the ends sought by the
   criminal justice system are more integrative. They include not just
   retributive considerations achieved by a more formal jurisprudence
   but also other considerations such as deterrence, rehabilitation, and
   restorative justice that demand a less formal jurisprudence. This will
   be further discussed infra. To a significant degree reliance on less
   formal means is also necessary because formal due process is too
   cumbersome and too expensive to be used given the large volume
   of cases inundating the system. However, the volume of cases itself
   is an index of deficiency in law as a material principle ordering society. That deficiency points to the need, inter alia, to reinvigorate the
   customary dimension of law and that requires access to less formal
   mechanisms.
2. My analysis draws on Lon Fuller's trenchant work in this area. On the
   significance of social distance to law discussed infra see, for example,
   *The Principles of Social Order*, pp. 237–46. For a discussion of the
   significance of bipolarity and polycentricity, see pp. 111–21. I should
   note that my focus on five factors should not be taken to exclude others that may be identified.
3. See also Aristotle's discussion in *Politics*, Book II, where he refers to
   homicides, assaults, and other crimes as "most unholy acts when per-
   petrated against one's parents or near relations, though not to the same
   degree where there is no kinship." *Aristotle's Politics and Athenian
   Constitution*, edited and translated by John Warrington, p. 32.
4. A similar discrimination seems to occur in hate crime legislation
   where crimes committed against the groups statutorily identified as
   objects of hatred, such as violence motivated on account of the race
   of the victim, are punished more severely than when they are committed against members of the general public. The Supreme Court
   in *Wisconsin v. Mitchell* has emphasized, however, that it is the greater

injury inflicted and greater danger posed by hate crimes that justifies increased penalties for these offenses. It is not justified by attributing greater value to the well-being of the individuals protected (a violation of the equal protection of the law) or by the offensiveness of the "hater's" opinions (a violation of the First Amendment.) On the latter see *Wisconsin v. Mitchell*, 508 U.S.476 (1993).

5. The didactic Broadway Danny Rose quoting his father in the Woody Allen movie of the same title.

6. While primitive man may have developed strong bonds of friendship based on mutual other-regardingness, he did not have access to the richer form of friendship available to the citizens of the *polis* who have access to the intellectual, cultural, and even philosophical goods that the *polis* furnishes.

7. Nor for Edmund Burke, a society. He admonished social contract theorists: "Society is indeed a contract...[B]ut the state ought not to be considered as nothing better than a partnership agreement in a trade of pepper and coffee, calico, or tobacco...to be dissolved by the fancy of the parties...It is a partnership in all science, a partnership in all art; a partnership in every virtue and in all perfection. As the ends of such a partnership cannot be obtained in many generations, it becomes a partnership not only between those who are living, but between those who are living, those who are dead, and those who are to be born." From Burke's *Reflections on the Revolution in France* (1790), as quoted in Harold Berman, *Law and Revolution II: The Impact of the Protestant Reformations on the Western Legal Tradition*, p. 387, n. 18.

8. Fuller's elaboration of the nature and genesis of customary law can be found in *The Principles of Social Order*, pp. 212–24.

9. The times have also produced the curiosity of cyber-social networks such as Facebook, which seems to satisfy some desire for a kind of virtual intimacy with others, if not a certain narcissism, while preserving the perhaps only illusory "safety" of the social distance provided by computers. Cyber-*philia* also has facilitated "flash mobs"—where socially networked individuals agree to meet at a prescribed time and place to commit acts of vandalism, violence, etc.

10. Aristotle states: "it makes no difference whether a good man has defrauded a bad man or a bad man a good one, nor whether it is a good man or a bad man that has committed adultery; the law looks only to the distinctive character of the injury, and treats the parties as equals." (*Nicomachean Ethics*, Ostwald tr. 120–1). Of course, the operative term is "injury." Communitarians define that in terms of damage to relationships that are ongoing, liberal individualists in terms of discrete acts committed in the past.

11. This would appear to be the appropriate disposition as (1) Aristotle states that "the gravity of an unjust act increases in proportion as the person to whom it is done is a close friend" indicating that justice

in punishment involves the principle of proportionate rather than arithmetical equality, as in distributive justice and (2) elsewhere in the *Nicomachean Ethics* Aristotle treats the infliction of pains, of which punishment is a form, as directed to transforming the character of offenders. See Book X, Chapter 9 where he states: "the pains inflicted ought to be of the sort that are most opposed to the pleasures people like," "as a corrupt person who strives for pleasures is disciplined by pain like a beast of burden" (Ostwald tr., 197). Punishment then does not follow primitive retribution: "The truth is that reciprocity suits neither distributive nor rectificatory justice." (*Nicomachean Ethics*, Irwin tr. 74). On reciprocity, Aristotle cites Rhadymanthy's principle, "If he suffered what he did, upright justice would be done" (74). I use reciprocity here as an example of retributivism, recognizing that other less primitive forms of retributivism may well reach different conclusions. Aristotle then states: "For in many cases reciprocity conflicts [with rectificatory justice]. If, for instance, a ruling official [exercising his office] wounded someone else, he must not be wounded in retaliation, but if someone wounded a ruling official, he must not only be wounded but also receive corrective treatment. Moreover, the voluntary or involuntary character of the action makes a great difference" (74, brackets in text). An eye for an eye, therefore, also appears to conflict with distributive justice. As corrective treatment addresses what the character of the agent deserves, I believe that it entails a form of distributive justice that justly distributes the burden of punishment.

12. Anthropological evidence may be adduced to support this. Malinowski had observed that where exchanges occurred between an island and coastal village, a principle of reciprocity (a deontological principle) governed the interaction, whereas Gluckman found that among the Barotse when exchanges were intra-tribe (where the tribe was like an extended family) the ordering principle was one of reasonableness, with conflict management after the style of mediation being the preferred ordering mechanism rather than more formal adjudication. Evidence referenced by Fuller, *Principles of Social Order*, pp. 242–3.

13. Aristotle differentiates three teleological kinds: the good of the friend, utility, and pleasure. Finnis dilated on the variety of *philia* found in political community:

> political community exists partially (and sometimes primarily) as a kind of business arrangement between self-interested associates (the kind of mutual insurance association or "social contract" derided by Aristotle and all the classics for its meagerness as a form [or account] of community; partially (and sometimes primarily) as a form of play, in which the participants enjoy the give-and-take, the dissension, bargaining, and compromise, for its own sake as a vastly complex and absorbing performance; partially (and sometimes primarily) as an expression of disinterested

benevolence, reinforced by recognition of what one owes to the community in which one has been brought up and in which one finds and founds one's family and one's life plan, and further reinforced by a determination not to be a "free rider" who arbitrarily seeks to retain the benefits without accepting the burdens of communal interdependence; and characteristically by some admixture of all these rationales. (149)

14. On *gemeinschaft* and *gesselschaft* society see the classic text by Ferdinand Tonnies, *Community and Society*, translated by Charles Loomis (1957).

15. See Lon L. Fuller in *Anatomy of Law*, p. 77ff. The United States District Court in *Graham v. Graham*, 33 Fed.Supp 936, 938 (E.D. Mich., 1940) stated that regulation of marriage by explicit contract opens "an endless field for controversy and bickering and would destroy the element of flexibility needed in making adjustments to new conditions." (*Principles of Social Organization* 238). But intimacy in family life is, as we have seen, a matter of degree. Fuller remarked: "it is probable that most of the world's inhabitants would be shocked to learn that it is not uncommon for an American farmer and his adult sons to operate the family farm under a written agreement not distinguishable from one that might be entered into by businessmen wholly unrelated to one another" (*Anatomy of the Law* 78). The centrifugal pressures of the surrounding society (including the legal culture) stretch the American family structure as compared to familial structures in other parts of the world, so that relations may seem more arms-length and appropriate for regulation by explicit contract. This may give to the American family structure a more egalitarian quality (as father and sons are equally bound by the contracts entered into) but at some point the fabric of the family, as a communitarian order, may be torn. One might ask, why the father and sons did not have sufficient trust in one another? For an instance of cross-cultural conflict between American individualism and Vietnamese communitarianism in the context of norms applying to the family, see the often poignant documentary film, *Daughter from Danang*, which examined the conflict that arose concerning the responsibility owed by offspring to family when a young Vietnamese woman reared in the United States returned to Vietnam to meet her biological family.

## 9 Summation and Closing Reflections

1. For the approach taken in Bryant Park, see Kelling and Coles, *Fixing Broken Windows*, p. 111ff. I witnessed the transformation. On my first day as a law student intern in a mid-town law firm in the late 1970s, I decided to take a brown bag lunch to a bench in the park. Within seconds, however, I was accosted by a drug dealer. I fled the park never to return on lunch break. I recently revisited the park, with wife

and family, and enjoyed an extended stay in this beautifully r⌐
space—no drug dealers in sight.

2. In response to tensions generated between local resident⌐
University of Dayton students regarding parties, noise levels,
Dayton Police Chief Igleberger used a hybrid approach combining ⌐
use of contract, mediation, negotiation, and custom formation. Th⌐
custom formation was in play, however, did not seem to be appre-
ciated. See Igleberger's "Directive Order" and Kelling's analysis in
George Kelling, "*Broken Windows*" *and Police Discretion*, pp. 28–30.
I shall evaluate Igleburger's approach in a subsequent volume.

3. For an interesting analysis of the dynamics of the behavior of parks
and their surrounding neighborhoods, see Jane Jacobs, *The Life and
Death of Great Cities*, p. 89ff. The police should assist in developing
uses that contribute to the life and vibrancy of parks and their surrounding communities. For Jacobs what would be required is "to use
parks and squares and public buildings as part of [the] street fabric,
use them to intensify and knit together the fabric's complexity and
multiple uses. They should not be used to island off different uses
from each other, or to island off sub-district neighborhoods" (129).

4. To compensate for the difficulty that the legal theory associated with
professional law enforcement has in accounting for relativity and discretion in law enforcement judgments, current community police
theory has substituted "community standards" for law as the subject
of what the police are to enforce in their communities. This substi-
tution is necessitated because current theory conceives of law and
law enforcement in positivist terms, lacking the broader integrative
jurisprudence that provides the appropriate standards. The standards,
however, that govern police maintenance of order must be deriv-
able from law's triune normative structure, if they are to enjoy full
legal legitimacy. Not all community standards will be, for example,
reconcilable to the Bill of Rights. Only when legitimated through
law may the community standards be regarded as fully authoritative
and the police exercise of discretion in enforcing them consistent
with the duty of police to enforce law. Community standards must be
consistent with law's more general norms—although they may be so
while still accommodating relativity in the local orders. The standards
must satisfy the criteria identified for a custom to be a binding legal
norm.

5. Where the law itself is unreasonable and/or unenforceable, taking
into account the long run, it is incumbent on the police to make that
case to the legislature.

6. For Aristotle's view, see *Nicomachean Ethics*, Ostwald tr., p. 295ff.

7. Consider, for example, Austin's definition of law as the threat backed
general command of the sovereign, reflecting what H. L. A. Hart
called the "external point of view" and the centrality of that perspective in the Austinian cosmos. See H. L. A. Hart, *The Concept of Law*.

8. The principle of utility, Mill insisted, enjoined not the individual's happiness but the greatest happiness overall. According to Mill, this may well require that in certain circumstances the individual sacrifice his individual happiness in service of the general welfare. See *Utilitarianism*, pp. 11–12. One thing to avoid is the pursuit of extremes in either direction of the teleological axis (whether embracing too much individualism or too much communitarianism) as that is likely to produce an equally extreme reaction in the opposite direction. Socrates articulated this principle of natural law in *The Republic*, Book VIII:

> And, really, anything that is done to excess is likely to provoke a correspondingly great change in the opposite direction—in seasons, in plants, in bodies, and, in particular, not least in regimes. (242)

A significant danger today lies in the increasing polarization of society. Moderating principles in justice, law, and police should be sought to help avert this.

9. In a highly compressed account, Finnis identifies eight features constituting the rule of law:

> A legal system exemplifies the Rule of Law to the extent...that (i) its rules are prospective, not retroactive, and (ii) are not in any other way impossible to comply with; that (iii) its rules are promulgated, (iv) clear, and (v) coherent with one another; that (vi) its rules are sufficiently stable to allow people to be guided by their knowledge of the content of the rules; that (vii) the making of decrees and orders applicable to relatively limited situations is guided by rules that are promulgated, clear, stable, and relatively general, and that (viii) those people that have authority to make, administer, and apply the rules in an official capacity (a) are accountable for their compliance with rules applicable to their performance and (b) do actually administer the law consistently and in accordance with its tenor. (270–1)

Finnis observes: "The fundamental point of the desiderata is to secure to the subjects of authority the dignity of self-direction and freedom from certain forms of manipulation" (273).

By "desiderata" he refers to the above eight features.

# BIBLIOGRAPHY

Adler, Mortimer Jerome. *Six Great Ideas: Truth, Goodness, Beauty, Liberty, Equality, Justice: Ideas We Judge By Ideas We Act On.* New York City, NY: Simon and Schuster, 1997. Print.

Allen, Sir Carlton Kemp. *Law in the Making.* 7th ed. Oxford, England: Clarendon Press. 1964. Print.

Allen, Ronald J. "The Police and Substantive Rulemaking: A Brief Rejoinder." *125 University of Pennsylvania Law Review* (1977). Print.

———. "The Police and Substantive Rulemaking: Reconciling Principle and Expediency." *125 University of Pennsylvania Law Review* 62 (1977). Print.

Aquinas, St. Thomas. *Treatise on Law.* Trans. Richard Regan. Indianapolis, IN: Hackett, 2000. Print.

Aristotle. *Aristotle's Politics and Athenian Constitution.* Trans. John Warrington. London: J. M. Dent and Sons, 1959. Print.

———. *Nicomachean Ethics.* Trans. Martin Ostwald. Upper Saddle River, NJ: Prentice Hall, 1962. Print.

———. *Nicomachean Ethics.* Trans. Terence Irwin. 2nd ed. Indianapolis, IN: Hackett, 1999. Print.

———. *The Politics.* Trans. Carnes Lord. Chicago, IL: U of Chicago P, 1985. Print.

Atiyah, Patrick S., and Robert S. Summers. *Form and Substance in Anglo-American Law: A Comparative Study of Legal Reasoning, Legal Theory, and Legal Institutions.* Oxford, England: Clarendon, 1991. Print.

Austin, John. "A Positivist Conception of Law." *Philosophy of Law.* Eds. Joel Feinberg and Jules Coleman. 8th ed. Belmont, CA: Thomson Wadsworth, 2008. 55–68. Print.

Bell, Daniel. "Commencement Address." Brandeis University Commencement 1991. *New York Times* 27 May 1991. Print.

———. *The Cultural Contradictions of Capitalism.* New York: Basic, 1978. Print.

Bellah, Robert Neelly. *Habits of the Heart: Individualism and Commitment in American Life: Updated Edition with a New Introduction.* Berkeley, CA: U of California P, 1996. Print.

Bentham, Jeremy. "Anarchical Fallacies." *The Works of Jeremy Bentham.* New York City, NY: Russell & Russell, Vol. 2. 1962. Print.

———. "Of Laws in General." *Philosophy of Law.* Eds. Joel Feinberg and Jules Coleman. 8th ed. Belmont, CA Thomson Wadsworth, 2008. 36–7. Print.

————. *The Panopticon Writings*. Ed. Miran Bozovic. London, England: Verso, 1995. Print.

Berman, Harold Joseph. "Law and Logos." *44 DePaul Law Review* 143 (1994). Print.

————. *Law and Revolution: The Formation of the Western Legal Tradition*. Cambridge, MA: Harvard UP, 1999. Print.

————. *Law and Revolution II: The Impact of the Protestant Reformations on the Western Legal Tradition*. Cambridge, MA: Harvard UP, 2003. Print.

————. "The Origins of Historical Jurisprudence: Coke, Selden and Hale." *103 Yale Law Journal* 1651 (1994). Print.

————. "Towards an Integrative Jurisprudence." *76 University of California Law Review* 779 (1998). Print.

Bittner, Egon. *Aspects of Police Work*. Boston, MA: Northeastern UP, 1990. Print.

————. *The Functions of the Police in Modern Society: A Review of Background Factors, Current Practices, and Possible Role Models*. Cambridge, MA: Oelgeschlager, Gunn & Hain, 1980. Print.

Black, Henry Campbell. *Black's Law Dictionary*. Revised 4th ed. St. Paul, MN: West, 1968. Print.

————. *Black's Law Dictionary*. Revised 8th ed. St. Paul, MN: West, 2004. Print.

Blackstone, William. *Commentaries on the Laws of England*. Chicago, IL: U of Chicago P, 1979. Print.

Bolt, Robert. *A Man for All Seasons: A Play in Two Acts*. New York City, NY: Vintage, 1990. Print.

Bratton, William J., and Peter Knobler. *Turnaround: How America's Top Cop Reversed the Crime Epidemic*. New York City, NY: Random House, 1998. Print.

Brinkley, David. *Washington Goes to War*. New York City, NY: Ballantine, 1988. Print.

*Broadway Danny Rose*. Dir. Woody Allen. Perf. Woody Allen, Mia Farrow, Nick Apollo Forte. MGM, 1984. Film.

Burger, Warren E. "Transcript of Remarks of Warren E. Burger." FBI National Academy Graduation Ceremony. Quantico, VA. 3 Nov. 1971. Address.

Clear, Todd R., and Karp, David Allen. *The Community Justice Ideal: Preventing Crime and Achieving Justice*. Boulder, CO: Westview, 1999. Print.

Colquhoun, Patrick. *A Treatise on the Police of the Metropolis*. Montclair, NJ: Patterson Smith, 1969. Print.

*The Compact Edition of the Oxford English Dictionary*. Oxford, England, Oxford UP. 1971. Print.

Conlon, Edward. *Blue Blood*. New York City, NY: Riverhead, 2004. Print.

*Corpus Juris Secundum*. Mack, William, Ed. Brooklyn, NY: American Law Book Company, 1936, 1998. Print.

Cotterrell, Roger. *The Politics of Jurisprudence: A Critical Introduction to Legal Philosophy*. London, England: Butterworths, 1989. Print.

Critchley, J. R. *A History of the Police in England and Wales, 1000–1966.* London, England: Constable, 1967. Print.

D'Amato, Anthony. "On the Connection between Law and Justice." *Philosophy of Law.* Eds. Joel Feinberg and Hyman Gross. 5th ed. Belmont, CA: Wadsworth, 1995. 19–30. Print.

*Daughter from Danang.* Dir. Gail Dolgin and Vicente Dolgin. Perf. Heidi Bub, Mai Thi Kim, Tran Tuong Nhu. Interfaze Educational Productions, 2002. Film.

Davis, Kenneth Culp. *Discretionary Justice: a Preliminary Inquiry.* Baton Rouge, LA: Louisiana State UP, 1969. Print.

———. *Police Discretion.* St. Paul, MN: West, 1975. Print.

———. "Police Rulemaking on Selective Enforcement: A Reply." *125 University of Pennsylvania Law Review* 1167 (1977). Print.

Davis, Michael. "Police, Discretion, and Professions." *Handled with Discretion: Ethical Issues in Police Decision Making.* Ed. John Kleinig. Lanham, MD: Roman and Littlefield, 1966. Print.

Delattre, Edwin J. *Character and Cops: Ethics in Policing.* Washington, DC: AEI, 2002. Print.

Dostoevski, Fyodor, and Gideon, George. *Crime and Punishment.* New York City, NY: W. W. Norton and Company, 1975. Print.

Durkheim, Emile. *The Division of Labor in Society.* New York City, NY: Free Press, 1984. Print.

———. *Professional Ethics and Civic Morals.* Westport, CT: Greenwood, 1983. Print.

Dworkin, Ronald M. *Law's Empire.* Cambridge, MA: Harvard UP, 1986. Print.

———. "The Model of Rules." *Philosophy of Law.* Eds. Joel Feinberg and Hyman Gross. 5th ed. Albany: Wadsworth, 1995. 134–51. Print.

Ehrlich, Eugen. *Fundamental Principles of the Sociology of Law.* New York City, NY: Arno, 1975. Print.

Eliot, T. S. *Complete Poems and Plays 1909–1950.* New York City, NY: Harcourt Brace and World, 1971. Print.

Feinberg, Joel, and Hyman Gross, Eds. 5th ed. *Philosophy of Law.* Belmont, CA: Wadsworth, 1995. Print.

Feinberg, Joel, and Jules Coleman, Eds. 8th ed. *Philosophy of Law.* Belmont, CA: Wadsworth, 2008. Print.

Fielding, Nigel. *Community Policing.* Oxford, England: Clarendon, 1995. Print.

Finnis, John. *Natural Law and Natural Rights.* Oxford, England: Clarendon, 1982. Print.

Friedman, Lawrence Meir. *A History of American Law.* New York City, NY: Simon & Schuster, 2005. Print.

Friedrich, Carl J. *The Philosophy of Law in Historical Perspective.* Chicago, IL: U of Chicago P, 1963. Print.

Frost-Knappman, Elizabeth, and David S. Shrager. *A Concise Encyclopedia of Legal Quotations.* NY: Barnes & Noble, 2003. Print.

Fuller, Lon L. *Anatomy of the Law*. New York City, NY: F. A. Praeger, 1968. Print.

———. *The Morality of Law*. New Haven, CT: Yale Univ., 2010. Print.

———. "Positivism and Fidelity to Law—A Reply to Professor Hart." *71 Harvard Law Review* 630 (1958). Print.

———. *The Principles of Social Order: Selected Essays of Lon L. Fuller*. Ed. Kenneth I. Winston. Durham, NC: Duke UP, 1981. Print.

George, Robert P. *Making Men Moral: Civil Liberties and Public Morality*. Oxford, England: Clarendon, 2001. Print.

Gibbon, Edward. *The Decline and Fall of the Roman Empire*. Ed. Dero A. Saunders. London, England: Penguin, 1985. Print.

Glanville, Ranulf De., and G. D. G. Hall. *The Treatise on the Laws and Customs of the Realm of England, Commonly Called Glanville*. Ed. G. D. G. Hall. London, England: Nelson, 1965. Print.

Goldstein, Herman. *Problem-oriented Policing*. Philadelphia, PA: Temple UP, 1990. Print.

Goldstein, Joseph. "Police Discretion Not to Invoke the Criminal Process: Low Visibility in the Administration of Justice." *69 Yale Law Journal* 543 (1960). Print.

Hale, J. R. *The Civilization of Europe in the Renaissance*. New York City, NY: Atheneum, 1994. Print.

Hamilton, Alexander, John Jay, and James Madison. *The Federalist*. New York City, NY: The Modern Library, n.d. Print.

Hanawalt, Barbara A. *Crime and Conflict in English Communities*. Cambridge, MA: Harvard UP, 1979. Print.

Hart, H. L. A. *The Concept of Law*. Oxford, England: Clarendon Press, 1961. Print.

———. "Positivism and the Separation of Law and Morals." *71 Harvard Law Review* 593 (1958). Print.

Hawthorne, Nathaniel. *The Scarlet Letter*. New York: Bantam, 1986. Print.

Hirschi, Travis. "The Family." *Crime*. Eds. James Q. Wilson and Joan Petersilia. San Francisco, CA: ICS, 1995. 121–40. Print.

"How to Keep Law and Order." *The Week* 16 July 2010. Print.

Hugo, Victor. *Les Miserables: A Novel*. n.p. For the Members of the Limited Editions Club, 1938. Print.

Inkster, Norman. "The Essence of Community Policing." *Police Chief* (1992): 59:28–31. Print.

Jacobs, Jane. *The Death and Life of Great American Cities*. New York City, NY: Vintage, 1992. Print.

"John of Salisbury, Policraticus, Books 1, 2, 3." *Constitution Society Home Page*. Web. 28 Nov. 2010. <http://www.constitution.org/salisbury/poli crat123.htm>.

Kant, Immanuel. *Grounding for the Metaphysics of Morals: With a Supposed Right to Lie Because of Philanthropic Concerns*. Trans. James W. Ellington. Indianapolis, IN: Hackett, 1993. Print.

Kappeler, Victor E., Ed. *The Police and Society: Touchstone Readings*. Prospect Heights, IL: Waveland, 1999. Print.

Kelling, George L. *"Broken Windows" and Police Discretion*. Washington, DC: National Institute of Justice, 1999. Print.

Kelling, George L., and Catherine M. Coles. *Fixing Broken Windows: Restoring Order and Reducing Crime in Our Communities*. New York City, NY: Simon & Schuster, 1997. Print.

Kelling, George L., and Mark H. Moore. "The Evolving Strategy of Policing." Ed. Victor E. Kappeler. *The Police and Society*. 2nd ed. Prospect Heights, IL: Waveland, 1999. Print.

Kirk, Russell, and Mitchell S. Muncy. *Rights and Duties: Reflections on Our Conservative Constitution*. Dallas: Spence, 1997. Print.

Kleinig, John, and Yurong Zhang. *Professional Law Enforcement Codes: A Documentary Collection*. Westport, CT: Greenwood, 1993. Print.

Kleinig, John. *The Ethics of Policing*. Cambridge, England: Cambridge UP, 1996. Print.

——, Ed. *Handled with Discretion: Ethical Issues in Police Decision Making*. Lanham, MD: Roman and Littlefield, 1996. Print.

Klockers, Carl B. *The Idea of Police*. Beverly Hills, CA: Sage Publications, 1985. Print.

Kmiec, Douglas W., and Stephen B. Presser. *2008 Supplement to the Second Edition of The American Constitutional Order: History Cases And Philosophy; The History, Philosophy, And Structure of the American Constitution; Individual Rights And the American Constitution*. Newark, NJ: Lexis Nexis, 2008. Print.

——, Eds. *The History, Philosophy and Structure of the American Constitution*. Cincinnati, OH: Anderson, 1998. Print.

Lane, Roger. "Urban Police and Crime in 19th Century America." *Modern Policing*. Eds. Micheal Tonry and Norval Morris. Chicago, IL: U of Chicago P, 1992. Print.

LaFave, Wayne R. "Police Rule Making and the Fourth Amendment: The Role of the Courts." *Discretion in Criminal Justice*. Eds. Lloyd E. Ohlin and Frank J. Remington. 1st ed. Albany, NY: State U of New York P, 1993. Print.

Lardner, James, and Thomas Reppetto. *NYPD: A City and Its Police*. New York, NY: Henry Holt and Company, 2000. Print.

Levitt, Steven D., and Dubner, Stephen J. *Freakonomics: A Rogue Economist Explores the Hidden Side of Everything*. Revised and Expanded Edition. New York City, NY: William Morrow: An Imprint of Harper Collins Publishers, 2006. Print.

Light, Stephen C. *Understanding Criminal Justice*. Belmont, CA: Wadsworth Publishing Company, 1999. Print.

Lobban, Michael. *The Common Law and English Jurisprudence: 1760–1850*. Oxford, England: Clarendon, 1991. Print.

Locke, John. *Two Treatises of Government: And a Letter Concerning Toleration*. New Haven, CT: Yale UP, 2003. Print.

Lowenthal, David. *No Liberty for License: The Forgotten Logic of the First Amendment.* Dallas, TX: Spence, 1997. Print.

MacGregor, Joan. "From the State of Nature to Mayberry: The Nature of Police Discretion." *Handled with Discretion: Ethical Issues in Police Decision Making.* Ed. John Kleinig. Lanham, MD: Roman and Littlefield, 1966. Print.

Maine, Henry Sumner. *Ancient Law.* Berkeley, CA: Stanford UP, 2009. Print.

Manning, Peter K. "Economic Rhetoric and Policing Reform." *The Police and Society.* Ed. Victor E. Kappeler. 2nd ed. Prospect Heights, IL: Waveland, 1999. 446–62. Print.

———. *Police Work: The Social Organization of Policing.* Prospect Heights, IL: Waveland, 1997. Print.

Mansfield, Harvey Claflin. *America's Constitutional Soul.* Baltimore, MD: Johns Hopkins UP, 1991. Print.

McCullough, David G. *John Adams.* New York City, NY: Simon & Schuster, 2001. Print.

McGuire, Kathleen, and Ann Pastore. *Bureau of Justice Statistics Sourcebook of Criminal Justice Statistics 1997.* Washington, DC: Bureau of Justice Statistics, 1998. Print.

Melville, Herman. *Billy Budd, and Other Tales.* New York City, NY: New American Library, 1979. Print.

Mill, John Stuart. *On Liberty.* Ed. Gertrude Himmelfarb. London, England: Penguin, 2003. Print.

———. *Utilitarianism.* Ed. George Sher. Indianapolis, IN: Hackett, 2001. Print.

Miller, Wilbur R. *Cops and Bobbies: Police Authority in New York and London, 1830–1870.* Columbus, OH: Ohio State UP, 1999. Print.

Monkkonen, Eric H. "History of Urban Police." *Modern Policing.* Eds. Michael Tonry and Norval Morris. Vol. 15. Chicago, IL: U of Chicago P, 1992. 547–80. Print.

Moore, Mark Harrison. "Problem-solving and Community Policing." *Modern Policing.* Eds. Michael Tonry and Norval Morris. Vol. 15. Chicago, IL: U of Chicago P, 1992. 99–158. Print.

Morris, Charles R. "Cross Purposes." *Boston College Magazine.* Spring, 1998. Print.

Morris, William A. *The Frankpledge System.* New York City, NY: Longmans, Green, 1910. Print.

Muir, William. *Police: Streetcorner Politicians.* Chicago, IL: U of Chicago P, 1977. Print.

Ohlin, Lloyd E., and Frank J. Remington, Eds. *Discretion in Criminal Justice: The Tension between Individualization and Uniformity.* Albany, NY: State U of New York P, 1993. Print.

*Oxford Dictionary of Quotations.* Ed. Elizabeth Knowles. 5th ed. Oxford, England, Oxford UP, 1999. Print.

Parnas, Raymond I. "Criminal Justice Responses to Domestic Violence." *Discretion in Criminal Justice.* Eds. Lloyd E. Ohlin and Frank J. Remington. 1st ed. Albany, NY: State U of New York P, 1993. 175–210. Print.

Parratt, "How Effective Is A Police Department." 199 *Annals* 153 (1938). Print.

Plato. *The Republic of Plato*. Trans. Allan David Bloom. New York City, NY: Basic Books, 1991. Print.

———. *The Trial & Death of Socrates: Plato's Euthyphro, Apology, Crito, and Death Scene from Phaedo*. Trans. G. M. A. Grube. Indianapolis, IN: Hackett, 1975. Print.

Posner, Richard. *Economic Analysis of Law*. Austin, TX: Wolters Kluwer for Aspen, 2007. Print.

Potts, Lee W. *Responsible Police Administration: Issues and Approaches*. University, AL: U of Alabama P, 1983. Print.

Rawls, John. *A Theory of Justice*. Cambridge, MA: Belknap of Harvard UP, 2000. Print.

Reiman, Jeffrey. "Is Police Discretion Justified in a Free Society?" *Handled with Discretion: Ethical Issues in Police Decision Making*. Ed. John Kleinig. Lanham, MD: Rowman and Littlefield, 1996. Print.

Reith, Charles. *The Blind Eye of History: A Study of the Origins of the Present Police Era*. Montclair, NJ: Patterson Smith, 1975. Print.

———. *A New Study of Police History*. Edinburgh, Scotland: Oliver and Boyd, 1956. Print.

Remington, Frank J., *Standards Relating to the Urban Police Function*. American Bar Association Advisory Committee on the Police Function, 1972. Print.

Report on Stockton Police Chief. *The Week* 13 Nov. 2009. Print.

Robinson, Cyril, Richard Scaglion, and J. M. Olivero. *Police in Contradiction: The Evolution of the Police Function in Society*. Westport, CT: Praeger, 1994. Print.

Schick, Ron. *Norman Rockwell: Behind the Camera*. New York City, NY: Little, Brown and Company, 2009. Print.

Shakespeare, William. *The Merchant of Venice*. New York City, NY: W. W. Norton and Company, 2006. Print.

Sherman, Lawrence W. "Attacking Crime: Policing and Crime Control." *Modern Policing*. Eds. Michael Tonry and Norval Morris. Vol. 15. Chicago, IL: U of Chicago P, 1992. 159–30. Print.

Sinha, S. Prakash. *Jurisprudence, Legal Philosophy, in a Nutshell*. St. Paul, MN: West, 1993. Print.

Skogan, Wesley G. *Disorder and Decline: Crime and the Spiral of Decay in American Neighborhoods*. Berkeley, CA: U of California P, 2001. Print.

Skolnick, Jerome H. *The Police and the Urban Ghetto*. Chicago, IL: American Bar Foundation, 1968. Print.

Svogun, Thomas V. "Law's Virtue: The Formal Structure of an Integrative Jurisprudence." *The Catholic Social Science Review* 2: 87–116 (1997). Print.

*Three Days of the Condor*. Dir. Sydney Pollack. Perf. Robert Redford, Faye Dunaway, Max Von Sydow. Paramount, 1975. Film.

Tocqueville, Alexis De. *Democracy in America*. Eds. Harvey Claflin Mansfield and Delba Winthrop. Chicago, IL: U of Chicago P, 2002. Print.

Tonnies, Ferdinand, and Charles Loomis. *Community and Society.* 1957. Print.

Tonry, Michael H., and Norval Morris, Eds. *Modern Policing.* Chicago, IL: U of Chicago P, 1992. Print.

Tryon, Edward. *The New Dictionary of Thoughts, a Cyclopedia of Quotations from the Best Authors of the World.* New York City, NY: Standard Book Company, 1957. Print.

*Ultimate Visual Encyclopedia.* New York City, NY: Covent Garden, 2001. Print.

*Universal Declaration of Human Rights.* G.A.res.217A (III), U.N. Doc. A/810 at 71 (1948). Print.

Vedantam, Shankar. "Research Links Lead Exposure, Criminal Activity." *Washington Post* 8 July 2007. Print.

Vollmer, August. *The Police and Modern Society.* Montclair, NJ: Patterson Smith, 1971. Print.

Walker, Samuel, "Origins of the Contemporary Criminal Justice Paradigm." *Justice Quarterly* 9: 47–76 (1992). Print.

———. *The Police in America: an Introduction.* Boston, MA: McGraw Hill College, 1999. Print.

Weber, Max. "Politics as a Vocation." *From Max Weber: Essays in Sociology.* Eds. and trs. H. H. Gerth and Mills C. Wright. New York City, NY: Oxford UP, 1973. Print.

Wilder, Thornton. *Our Town: A Play in Three Acts.* New York City, NY: Perrenial, 2003. Print.

Wilson, James Q. *Varieties of Police Behavior: The Management of Law and Order in Eight Communities.* Cambridge, MA: Harvard UP, 1968. Print.

Wilson, James Q., and George Kelling. "Fixing Broken Windows." *Atlantic Monthly* 249, No.3: 29–38 (1982). Print.

Wilson, James Q., and Joan Petersilia, Eds. *Crime.* San Francisco, CA: ICS, Institute for Contemporary Studies, 1995. Print.

## CASES CITED

*Brandenburg v. Ohio,* 395 U.S. 444 (1966)

*District of Columbia v. Heller,* 554 U.S. 570 (2008)

*Garcia v. San Antonio,* 469 U.S. 528 (1985)

*Graham v. Graham,* 33 Fed. Supp. 936 (E.D. Mich., 1940)

*Los Angeles v. Alameda Books,* 535 U.S. 425 (2002)

*McDonald v. City of Chicago,* 561 U.S. 3025 (2010)

*Michigan v. Summers,* 452 U.S. 692 (1967)

*Motor Vehicle Manufacturer's Association v. State Farm Mutual Insurance Co.,* 463 U.S. 29 (1983)

*Perry Education Association v. Perry Local Educator's Association,* 460 U.S. 37 (1983)

*R. v. Waddington,* 1 East 143 (1800)

*Renton v. Playtime Theatres, Inc.,* 475 U.S. 41 (1986)

*Riggs v. Palmer*, 115 N.Y. 506 (1889)
*Roth v. United States*, 354 U.S. 476 (1957)
*Tinker v. Des Moines Independent School District*, 393 U.S. 503 (1969)
*Wisconsin v. Mitchell*, 508 U.S. 476 (1993)
*Young v. New York City Transit Authority*, 729 F.Supp. 341 (S.D.N.Y., rev'd and vacated), 903 F.2d 146 (2d Cir., 1990)
*Youngberg v. Romero*, 457 U.S. 307 (1982)

## Statutes Cited

*Racketeer Influenced and Corrupt Organizations Act*, 18 U.S.C. sections 1961–68 (1976)

# INDEX